A Special Issue of
Cognitive Neuropsychology

Computational Modelling

Edited by

Gary S. Dell
University of Illinois, Urbana, IL, USA

and

Alfonso Caramazza
Harvard University, Cambridge, MA, USA

LONDON AND NEW YORK

First published 2009 by Psychology Press

Published 2018 by Routledge
2 Park Square, Milton Park, Abingdon, Oxon, OX14 4RN
52 Vanderbilt Avenue, New York, NY 10017

First issued in paperback 2018

Routledge is an imprint of the Taylor & Francis Group, an informa business

Copyright © 2009 by Taylor & Francis.

All rights reserved. No part of this book may be reprinted or reproduced or utilised in any form or by any electronic, mechanical, or other means, now known or hereafter invented, including photocopying and recording, or in any information storage or retrieval system, without permission in writing from the publishers.

Notice:
Product or corporate names may be trademarks or registered trademarks, and are used only for identification and explanation without intent to infringe.

British Library Cataloguing in Publication Data
A catalogue record for this book is available from the British Library

This book is also a special issue of the journal *Cognitive Neuropsychology* and forms Issues 2 of Volume 25 (2008).

This publication has been produced with paper manufactured to strict environmental standards and with pulp derived from sustainable forests.

Cover by Hybert Design, Waltham St Lawrence, Berkshire, UK
Typeset by Techset Composition Limited, Salisbury, Wiltshire, UK

ISBN 13: 978-1-138-87780-1 (pbk)
ISBN 13: 978-1-84169-855-7 (hbk)

COGNITIVE NEUROPSYCHOLOGY

Volume 25 • Issue 2 • March 2008

Contents

Gary S. Dell and Alfonso Caramazza *Introduction to special issue on computational modelling in cognitive neuropsychology*	131
Katia Dilkina, James L. McClelland, and David C. Plaut *A single-system account of semantic and lexical deficits in five semantic dementia patients*	136
Lyndsey Nickels, Britta Biedermann, Max Coltheart, Steve Saunders, and Jeremy J. Tree *Computational modelling of phonological dyslexia: How does the DRC model fare?*	165
Simone Cutini, Andrea Di Ferdinando, Demis Basso, Patrizia Silvia Bisiacchi, and Marco Zorzi *Visuospatial planning in the travelling salesperson problem: A connectionist account of normal and impaired performance*	194
Ariel M. Goldberg and Brenda Rapp *Is compound chaining the serial-order mechanism of spelling? A simple recurrent network investigation*	218
Mark Knobel, Matthew Finkbeiner, and Alfonso Caramazza *The many places of frequency: Evidence for a novel locus of the lexical frequency effect in word production*	256
Matthew Goldrick *Does like attract like? Exploring the relationship between errors and representational structure in connectionist networks*	287
Subject index	314

Introduction to special issue on computational modelling in cognitive neuropsychology

Gary S. Dell
University of Illinois, Urbana-Champaign, IL, USA

Alfonso Caramazza
Harvard University, Cambridge, MA, USA, and Center for Mind/Brain Sciences-CIMeC, University of Trento, Rovereto (TN), Italy

Recently, *Cognitive Neuropsychology* altered the statement of the journal's aims that appears in every issue, the new material expressing an interest in publishing "computational modelling research that is informed by consideration of neuropsychological phenomena". The journal's interest in computational models, however, is anything but recent. When *Cognitive Neuropsychology* was in its first decade, it devoted an entire issue to a single article reporting a model of impaired reading by Plaut and Shallice (1993). This now classic treatment of dyslexic errors from a connectionist perspective—it is currently the third most cited article in the journal—and later examples of what Coltheart (2006) calls "computational cognitive neuropsychology" have influenced the interpretation of neuropsychological data for some time now. This special issue thus comes at a time when a variety of computational models and modelling frameworks have had their say on neuropsychological data.

What is a computational model? It is a model expressed as a computational implementation, the implementation being necessary to understand the model's implications for data and for theory. What, then, is a model? The term "model" has been used in the context of accounts of impaired cognition since the inception of the field. For example, the Wernicke–Lichtheim model of aphasia (e.g., Lichtheim, 1885) was a diagram containing nodes representing mental content (e.g., auditory lexical images) and directional arrows indicating the flow of processing among the nodes during various tasks (e.g., speech comprehension). Lesions could be associated with nodes or arrows, and, because each of these components was identified with both a cognitive function and a brain region, the model generated accounts of aphasic symptoms—how they clustered and how they were associated with brain areas. For example, the poor comprehension and repetition associated with Wernicke's aphasia was attributed to a lesion to the auditory-image node. The diagram revealed that this node is a necessary part of the path for the tasks of both comprehension and repetition. Thus, the model, in the form of Lichtheim's diagram, made concrete the links between the theory and potential patterns of data.

Modern computational models are, of course, much more than diagrams. But they have much the same function. The model's computer program specifies a cognitive architecture, including processing levels or subsystems, and a variety of operations and parameters. This program is analogous to the diagram. Running the program simulates the cognitive processes involved in the performance of some task, just as following the arrows does in a diagram. Of course, the program is necessary because the complexity of most computational models precludes working things out by hand. Various aspects of the program can be altered, simulating lesions, and the consequences of the lesions on task performance can be determined when the altered program is run. Finally, the lesioned model's performance can then be compared to that of impaired individuals, thus providing a test of the theoretical principles behind the model. Five of the six articles in this issue test specific models of some cognitive domain by using exactly this method, and the sixth, Goldrick's analysis of how errors reflect representational structure in models (Goldrick, 2008), applies this logic at a more general level.

The first explicitly computational models of cognition treated the mind as a digital computer program (e.g., Newell & Simon, 1972). The models' processing operations were discrete and were carried out in strict serial order. There was a principled separation between representations, which were ordered strings of symbols, and the processing rules that transformed these strings into other representations. The major alternative to this digital-computer framework is the *connectionist* approach, in which processing is carried out by a network of simple processing units that operate in parallel by sending continuous quantities (activation) to one another through weighted connections. All of the models presented here are connectionist or have connectionist properties. In fact, the words "computational" and "connectionist" are often, but incorrectly, treated as synonyms because connectionism pervades modern cognitive theories to such an extent that the major models based on these theories all employ at least some connectionist features. For example, although the dual-route cascade (DRC) model of reading presented in the article by Nickels, Biedermann, Coltheart, Saunders, and Tree (2008) was derived from the classic dual-route model that has often been contrasted with connectionist reading models, it uses spreading activation through weighted connections to do its computations. Other canonical connectionist notions are fully on display in other papers: learning as adaptive weight change (Cutini, Di Ferdinando, Basso, Bisiacchi, & Zorzi, 2008; Dilkina, McClelland, & Plaut, 2008; Goldberg & Rapp, 2008), nonlinear activation functions (e.g., Cutini et al., 2008; Dilkina et al., 2008; Goldberg & Rapp, 2008; Nickels et al., 2008), and an interactive or recurrent flow of activation (Dilkina et al., 2008; Goldberg & Rapp, 2008; Knobel, Finkbeiner, & Caramazza, 2008). An important distinction within the connectionist framework is whether the model's representations (how patterns of activation correspond to particular cognitive elements) are *localist* (e.g., there is an abstract network unit for the lexical item CAT) or *distributed* (e.g., the lexical representation of CAT is a pattern of activation across many units). Both localist (e.g., Knobel et al., 2008; Nickels et al., 2008) and distributed (e.g., Dilkina et al., 2008; Goldberg & Rapp, 2008) models are explored here, and the function of these representational formats for cognitive neuropsychology is revealed (see, particularly, Goldrick's, 2008, paper).

The common connectionist ancestry of the papers in this issue, though, should not obscure the striking differences among them in how the models were used. In three of the papers, the model was the theoretical centrepiece, and the neuropsychological data that were examined supported, for the most part, the theories that the models implemented. In the remaining three papers, however, the models served other diverse theoretical purposes. Let us begin with the models that were supported by the data. Dilkina et al.'s (2008) analysis of lexical and semantic deficits from a single-system perspective, Cutini et al.'s (2008) study of performance on the travelling salesperson problem, and Nickels et al.'s (2008) application of the DRC model to phonological dyslexia all included successful simulations of the performance of brain-injured subjects (and also normal individuals experiencing transcranial magnetic stimulation in Cutini et al.'s study). That is, in these cases, the model worked; it fitted the data to the satisfaction of the authors.

But how can we tell whether or not a model works? There has been considerable discussion among those who apply models to patient data about how model evaluation should take place (see Ruml, Caramazza, Capasso, & Miceli, 2005; and Schwartz, Dell, Martin, Gahl, & Sobel,

2006, for recent commentary), and the first group of papers highlight a number of issues on this topic. First, should the model be matched to individual cases or to mean data from a group of cases that are assumed to be similar? When models were initially applied to impaired cognition, simulated lesions were informally compared both to data from individual cases (e.g., Patterson, Seidenberg, & McClelland, 1989) and to data from patient-group means (e.g., Haarmann & Kolk, 1991). Currently, computational cognitive neuropsychology, as illustrated by most of the papers here (e.g., Dilkina et al., 2008; Nickels et al., 2008), emphasizes matching to individual cases. There are several reasons for this choice, but a compelling one is simply that it is possible—even likely, if care is not taken in defining the group—that in a group of brain-damaged individuals mean performance may not be typical of many or even any of the individuals. Thus, one may be modelling a performance pattern that was not the product of a single brain. Second, the papers also exhibit a time-honoured feature of model-based hypothesis testing: the explicit comparison among competing models or model versions. For example, Cutini et al. (2008) implemented two different accounts of flexibility in the application of heuristics for the travelling salesperson problem, and the comparison between these and the data allowed for a valuable conclusion about the incremental nature of the planning process. Dilkina et al. and Nickels et al. explored the effect of variation in parameters and possible lesions in their models, effectively comparing different model versions as potential accounts of the data. A third issue in model evaluation concerns the role of inferential statistics when comparing models and data. Nickels et al. explicitly recommended (and did) such testing to determine whether one can reject the null hypothesis that the human data and the simulation's output are the same. Failure to reject the hypothesis of difference does indeed provide evidence of a good correspondence between the model and the data, provided that the data are extensive and precise. The alternative perspective argues that such null hypotheses are never in fact true and that model evaluation should focus on the *degree* of fit (How full is this glass?), rather than on whether there are statistically significant deviations (Is this glass not full?). If we grant, however, that our simulations will never be perfect matches to our neuropsychological data, how are we then to decide that a simulation study has successfully supported a particular model (Ruml & Caramazza, 2000)? There is no simple answer to this question. One evaluation method that has been increasingly used in computational cognitive neuropsychology focuses on predictions—specifying or parameterizing a model based on data from some conditions or tasks and then using that model to predict performance in other conditions or tasks (e.g., Dell, Martin, & Schwartz, 2007). Dilkina et al.'s analysis of the relation between picture naming and word reading illustrates the method. First, for each patient a general extent-of-lesion parameter value was selected so that the model mimicked the patient's overall naming performance. Then, with that parameter set, the model's ability to predict the patient's reading performance for item groups varying in frequency and regularity was assessed.

The second group of papers (Goldberg & Rapp, 2008; Goldrick, 2008; Knobel et al., 2008) is a bit out of the ordinary in that the analysis offered did not explicitly support any particular model, but instead centred on a theoretical question whose answer required a computational treatment. Goldberg and Rapp started with the question of whether serially ordered behaviour—specifically in spelling—is carried out by compound chaining and answered the question in the negative. In a compound-chaining theory, the production of each item in a sequence is cued by representations of previously retrieved items. Goldberg and Rapp specifically evaluated a model of spelling that implemented compound chaining, a simple recurrent network or SRN (Elman, 1990). Not only does the SRN model clearly employ compound chaining, but SRNs are also a key component of large-scale psycholinguistic theories of production and comprehension (e.g., Chang, Dell, & Bock, 2006). Thus, their failure to account for the spelling errors made by the two patients in the study is noteworthy.

Knobel et al. (2008) asked the question: Where is the effect of frequency in word retrieval during production? Experimental psycholinguistic studies that measure response times to retrieve picture names have led to conflicting results on the question of the locus of frequency effects, and so Knobel et al. took a different approach. They examined the production errors made by an individual with aphasia, E.C., and particularly how different *kinds* of errors were influenced by frequency. Then they used a model of word retrieval to systematically determine the implications of possible frequency loci on error patterns. For example, if frequency impacts, say, the mapping from semantic to lexical representations, what kinds of errors should and should not be affected by frequency? Knobel et al.'s comparisons between the simulated and actual influences of frequency in E.C. and other patients allowed them to conclude that frequency impacts both the interface between lexical and phonological representations and the processes that generate semantic errors. More generally, the results suggested that the effects of frequency are distributed throughout the lexical system, a conclusion that comports well with theories in which linguistic representations and the mappings among them are products of the incremental learning by which connectionist models acquire their networks (e.g., Dilkina et al.'s, 2008, analysis of how learning creates frequency and regularity effects).

Goldrick's (2008) paper stands apart from the others because no particular theoretical claim is tested. Instead, the analysis constitutes perhaps the first example of what can be called "metacomputational cognitive neuropsychology", a formal examination of the validity of the assumptions behind the use of models and other theoretical constructs in the field. The assumption in this case is that errors reflect the sharing of representational components: If cognitive item X's representation overlaps more (shares representational elements) with that of Y than it does with that of Z, then errors in which X is the target of a retrieval effort should more often create Y than Z. So, if the representation of the phoneme /t/ overlaps with /d/ more than with /g/, then /t/s should be replaced by /d/s more than by /g/s. This assumption, which is entirely taken for granted in error-based studies of cognitive processing, was shown by Goldrick to be valid for most, but surprisingly not all, representational schemes.

Goldrick's (2008) analysis raises the thorny question of the ties between neuropsychological data, computational models, and the brain. The Wernicke–Lichtheim model was not just a model of what clusters of aphasic symptoms we should expect and what we should not expect. It also made claims about where damage in the brain should be found for each symptom cluster. These kinds of claims are, for the most part, de-emphasized in the papers in this issue. Just as "computational" does not mean "connectionist", "connectionist" does not mean "neural". The models describe cognitive rather than neural architectures, and they explain patient performance data through hypothesized lesions to the architectures. This is not to say that neural data are irrelevant to computational cognitive neuropsychology. For example, in Cutini et al.'s (2008) nested incremental modelling approach, properties of some model components were motivated by neural data (e.g., properties of simple cells in V1). Moreover, the top-down controller in their model was implicitly identified with frontal brain regions, because the lesion to this model component was matched to data obtained from individuals with frontal damage. Similarly, Dilkina et al. (2008) suggested that their patient differences may be explicable in terms of region-specific atrophy in temporal areas. Thus, their modelling study could be profitably augmented with assessments of lesion locations. In general, the theoretical claims that are advanced in the papers in this issue can be tested by a variety of data sources, behavioural or neural.

A final point: Models are simpler than the cognitive processes they represent. This truism clearly applies to the box-and-arrow models that are commonly used to illustrate cognitive architectures. But it also applies to the computational models that are designed to open up the boxes and reveal the transformations behind the arrows. The models presented here are circumscribed in their domain (e.g., errors in spelling single words; performance on simple picture naming or reading tests), stingy in their processing assumptions (e.g., mathematically simple spreading activation rules), and limited in the number of parameters that can be varied. This simplicity is a virtue. The properties of simple models can be systematically explored, and such models can easily be compared to others that implement alternative theories. In this way, a limited, well-crafted model promotes the understanding of cognitive mechanisms and reveals the ramifications of these mechanisms for data.

REFERENCES

Chang, F., Dell, G. S., & Bock, K. (2006). Becoming syntactic. *Psychological Review, 113,* 234–272.

Coltheart, M. (2006). Acquired dyslexias and the computational modeling of reading. *Cognitive Neuropsychology, 23,* 96–109.

Cutini, S., Di Ferdinando, A., Basso, D., Bisiacchi, S. P., & Zorzi, M. (2008). Visuospatial planning in the travelling salesperson problem: A connectionist account of normal and impaired performance. *Cognitive Neuropsychology, 25,* 194–217.

Dell, G. S., Martin, N., & Schwartz, M. F. (2007). A case-series test of the interactive two-step model of lexical access: Predicting word repetition from picture naming. *Journal of Memory and Language, 56,* 490–520.

Dilkina, K., McClelland, J. L., & Plaut, D. C. (2008). A single-system account of semantic and lexical deficits in five semantic dementia patients. *Cognitive Neuropsychology, 25,* 136–164.

Elman, J. L. (1990). Finding structure in time. *Cognitive Science, 14,* 179–211.

Goldberg, A. M., & Rapp, B. (2008). Is compound chaining the serial order mechanism of spelling? A simple recurrent network investigation. *Cognitive Neuropsychology, 25,* 218–255.

Goldrick, M. (2008). Does like attract like? Exploring the relationship between errors and representational structure in connectionist networks. *Cognitive Neuropsychology, 25,* 287–313.

Haarmann, H. J., & Kolk, H. H. J. (1991). A computer model of the temporal course of agrammatic sentence understanding: The effects of variation in severity and sentence complexity. *Cognitive Science, 15,* 49–87.

Knobel, M., Finkbeiner, M., & Caramazza, A. (2008). The many places of frequency: Evidence for a novel locus of the lexical frequency effect in word production. *Cognitive Neuropsychology, 25,* 256–286.

Lichtheim, L. (1885). On aphasia. *Brain, 7,* 433–484.

Newell, A., & Simon, H. A. (1972). *Human problem solving.* Englewood Cliffs, NJ: Prentice Hall.

Nickels, L., Biedermann, B., Coltheart, M., Saunders, S., & Tree, J. J. (2008). Computational modelling of phonological dyslexia: How does the DRC model fare? *Cognitive Neuropsychology, 25,* 165–193.

Patterson, K., Seidenberg, M. S., & McClelland, J. L. (1989). Connections and disconnections: Acquired dyslexia in a computational model of reading. In R. G. M. Morris (Ed.), *Parallel distributed processing: Implications for psychology and neuroscience* (pp. 131–181). Oxford, UK: Oxford University Press.

Plaut, D. C., & Shallice, T. (1993). Deep dyslexia: A case study of connectionist neuropsychology. *Cognitive Neuropsychology, 10,* 377–500.

Ruml, W., & Caramazza, A. (2000). An evaluation of a computational model of lexical access: Comment on Dell et al. (1997). *Psychological Review, 107,* 609–634.

Ruml, W., Caramazza, A., Capasso, R., & Miceli, G. (2005). Interactivity and continuity in normal and aphasic language production. *Cognitive Neuropsychology, 22,* 131–168.

Schwartz, M. F., Dell, G. S., Martin, N., Gahl, S., & Sobel, P. (2006). A case-series test of the interactive two-step model of lexical access: Evidence from picture naming. *Journal of Memory and Language, 54,* 228–264.

A single-system account of semantic and lexical deficits in five semantic dementia patients

Katia Dilkina
Carnegie Mellon University, Pittsburgh, PA, USA, and Stanford University, Stanford, CA, USA

James L. McClelland
Stanford University, Stanford, CA, USA

David C. Plaut
Carnegie Mellon University, Pittsburgh, PA, USA

In semantic dementia (SD), there is a correlation between performance on semantic tasks such as picture naming and lexical tasks such as reading aloud. However, there have been a few case reports of patients with spared reading despite profound semantic impairment. These reports have sparked an ongoing debate about how the brain processes conceptual versus lexical knowledge. One possibility is that there are two functionally distinct systems in the brain—one for semantic and one for lexical processing. Alternatively, there may be a single system involved in both. We present a computational investigation of the role of individual differences in explaining the relationship between naming and reading performance in five SD patients, among whom there are cases of both association and dissociation of deficits. We used a connectionist model where information from different modalities feeds into a single integrative layer. Our simulations successfully produced the overall relationship between reading and naming seen in SD and provided multiple fits for both association and dissociation data, suggesting that a single, cross-modal, integrative system is sufficient for both semantic and lexical tasks and that individual differences among patients are essential in accounting for variability in performance.

Keywords: Semantic processing; Lexical processing; Semantic dementia; Connectionist modelling.

Is lexical knowledge separate from other kinds of knowledge (sensory-motor, encyclopaedic, etc.)? Is it represented or processed differently in the brain? Ultimately, these kinds of questions come down to the topic of a "mental lexicon"—a theoretical construct that includes detailed orthographic, phonological, and morpho-syntactic knowledge about words. Essentially, a mental lexicon stores and organizes a person's vocabulary. While lexical knowledge can be viewed as knowledge of words, semantic or conceptual knowledge is the knowledge of things, which are in turn

---

Correspondence should be addressed to Katia Dilkina, Jordan Hall (Bldg 420), Stanford, CA, 94305–2130, USA (E-mail: knd@andrew.cmu.edu).

Supported by National Institute of Mental Health (NIMH) Interdisciplinary Behavioral Science Center Grant MH 64445 (JLM, Program Director). We thank Tim Rogers and Matt Lambon Ralph for their helpful discussions and comments on earlier versions of this paper.

named or described with words. For example, one's knowledge of the word "dog", how to spell and pronounce it, and how to make its plural, is lexical knowledge, while knowing what dogs look and sound like, how they behave, and how to interact with them is semantic knowledge. The core of the issue is whether lexical knowledge and semantic knowledge are represented separately in the brain.

A relevant set of data that speaks to this question comes from semantic dementia patients. Semantic dementia (SD) is a selective impairment of conceptual knowledge (Hodges, Patterson, Oxbury, & Funnell, 1992; Snowden, Goulding, & Neary, 1989) due to progressive atrophy of the anterior inferior and lateral aspects of the temporal cortex (Galton et al., 2001; Mummery et al., 2000). The atrophy typically starts from the pole and progresses posteriorly. It is usually bilateral but often asymmetric. Tasks that present difficulty to SD patients span input and response modalities: They include object and picture naming (e.g., Hodges, Graham, & Patterson, 1995), smell naming (Luzzi et al., 2007), object recognition from touch (Coccia, Bartolini, Luzzi, Provinciali, & Lambon Ralph, 2004), smell-to-picture matching (Luzzi et al., 2007), word-to-picture matching, category matching, delayed copying (e.g., Lambon Ralph & Howard, 2000), matching environmental sounds to pictures (Bozeat, Lambon Ralph, Patterson, Garrard, & Hodges, 2000), and nonverbal tests of semantic association such as the picture versions of the Pyramids and Palm Trees (PPT) test (Howard & Patterson, 1992) and the Camel and Cactus test (Bozeat et al., 2000). Impaired performance on these and similar tasks and findings of association and item consistency across tasks (Bozeat et al., 2000; Luzzi et al., 2007) indicate a cross-modal semantic deficit (see also Garrard & Carroll, 2006).

Not only do SD patients consistently score very poorly, but the majority of overt errors they make are classifiable as "semantic" (Hodges et al., 1995; Rogers et al., 2004a). For example, in naming, calling a tiger "a lion" is a semantic error (which can be contrasted with a phonological error, for example, "a timer", or an unrelated error, e.g., "a piano"). Semantic errors often involve choosing an item from the same category as the target or an item closely associated with the target (e.g., bed instead of hammock), even in the absence of visual similarity between the target and the foil (e.g., pliers vs. hammer). Remarkably, despite the semantic deficit, other cognitive abilities such as memory for recent episodes, nonverbal reasoning, visuo-spatial abilities, working memory, phonology, and syntax are largely spared (Patterson & Hodges, 2000; Snowden, Neary, & Mann, 1996).

Notably, SD patients are also impaired on a number of tasks that are traditionally considered lexical in that they tap knowledge about words other than the word's meaning. These include word reading (Funnell, 1996; Patterson & Hodges, 1992), word spelling (Graham, Patterson, & Hodges, 2000), verb past-tense inflection (Cortese, Balota, Sergent-Marshall, Buckner, & Gold, 2006; Patterson, Lambon Ralph, Hodges, & McClelland, 2001), and lexical decision (Rogers, Lambon Ralph, Hodges, & Patterson, 2004b). The deficit is most prominent for atypical low-frequency items. The patients show surface dyslexia and surface dysgraphia—inability to read and spell irregular (especially low-frequency) words. Most errors are legitimate alternative rendering of components (LARC) errors (Patterson, Suzuki, Wydell, & Sasanuma, 1995), a large subset of which are regularizations (Funnell, 1996; Patterson & Hodges, 1992; Woollams, Lambon Ralph, Plaut, & Patterson, 2007). A similar pattern is also seen in verb past-tense inflection (Patterson et al., 2001).

In the vast majority of patients, there is an association between semantic deficits and impairment on lexical tasks such as word reading. A recent paper by Patterson et al. (2006) reported an investigation of the relationship between semantic proficiency and each of four lexical tasks and two nonverbal tasks. A total of 14 semantic dementia patients were tested using the same testing battery. A strong positive correlation was found between the patients' composite semantic score and their performance on atypical items in each of the tasks. Such findings have motivated the idea that impairment on all of these tasks arises as a consequence of damage to a single integrated system that mediates both semantic and lexical processing.

This association seen in the patient data has been accounted for in a number of connectionist models (e.g., Plaut, McClelland, Seidenberg, & Patterson, 1996; Rogers et al., 2004a; Seidenberg & McClelland, 1989) with an overall architecture as depicted in Figure 1. Within this theory, damage to the integrative layer called "semantics" leads to disruption of naming and verbal definition, since the integrative layer mediates between the visual input and the phonological output. Damage to the integrative layer also leads to difficulties in reading. This is true even though the model provides a "direct route" from orthography and phonology. As discussed in Plaut et al. (1996), when reading is learned in a system with the architecture shown in Figure 1, a division of labour develops, such that the direct pathway becomes particularly effective at pronouncing items that are high in either frequency or spelling–sound consistency, including pronounceable nonwords, since it is sensitive to the systematicity in the mapping between spelling and sound. The pathway mediated by the integrative layer, on the other hand, must learn the largely arbitrary mappings between spelling and various types of semantic information (including, for example, what a DOG looks like) and so is less sensitive to this systematicity. It therefore comes to play an especially important role in reading exceptional items, particularly those of low frequency. Although all words draw on both pathways, and items of high frequency tend to be robustly encoded in both pathways, regular items of low frequency can still be processed by the direct pathway. Exceptions will often be regularized by this pathway acting alone, so that the input from the integrative layer is crucial for reading such items. As the integrative layer is damaged more and more, the system becomes impaired on reading irregular (especially low-frequency) items, because they are the items that most strongly rely on semantic support. Thus, this framework is able to account for the observed association between impairment on tasks such as naming and PPT and deficits such as surface dyslexia and dysgraphia.

It must be noted, however, that in addition to the growing collection of reports of patients with associations between semantic and lexical processing, there have been a few case studies of individual patients showing dissociation—patients W.L.P. (Schwartz, Saffran, & Marin, 1980), E.M. (Blazely, Coltheart, & Casey, 2005), and D.R.N. (Cipolotti & Warrington, 1995) showed little or no impairment on reading despite their profound semantic deficits. E.M. showed impairment on picture naming (34% correct), name comprehension (65% correct), and word–picture matching (written: 63% correct; spoken: 62% correct), and very little impairment on word reading (98% correct) and lexical decision (97% correct). Similarly, D.R.N. performed remarkably well on reading (98% overall performance averaged over four independent tests). In addition to reading, she was only tested on naming and verbal definition, and showed severe impairment on both tasks (25% correct on naming and 52% overall performance on verbal definition averaged over four tests). Finally, when patient W.L.P. was first tested, despite her very poor performance on word–picture matching (15% correct) and category sorting (60% correct averaged over three categories), she did exceptionally well (98% correct) on reading a list of high-frequency words, half of which had atypical spelling-to-sound correspondence. Case reports of SD patients without surface dyslexia have been rare. We are aware of only 6 such patients, while there have been an overwhelming number of individuals who do

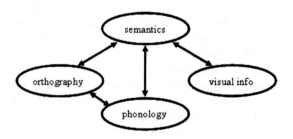

Figure 1. *Generic parallel distributed processing (PDP) model of semantic and lexical processing.*

show a reading disability, 48 such cases reported by Woollams et al. (2007) alone. Furthermore, when such individuals have been followed longitudinally, a surface dyslexia pattern eventually ensues. For example, in the case of W.L.P., only six months after the testing session described above, her reading performance on the same set of items dropped to 85% and, four months after that, to 77%.

A recent study documenting the reading performance of seven SD patients found that even when reading may appear intact in terms of accuracy, the reading latencies of the patients are much larger than those of age-, education-, and occupation- matched controls, suggesting that whatever mechanism may underlie reading, it has been compromised in these individuals (McKay, Castles, Davis, & Savage, 2007). Just like the rest of the patients in this group, patient R.R., whose reading accuracy was within the normal range, also showed significantly slower reaction times than controls. In addition, the longer latencies were associated with items that showed impairment in the semantic tasks, supporting the notion that the reading mechanism is not divorced from the semantic system (McKay et al., 2007).

Despite these findings and the rarity of SD patients with spared reading, such cases have been used as support for the argument that the semantic and the lexical deficits—though often co-occurring—are in fact distinct deficits and are caused by neurological damage to two functionally distinct (even if anatomically neighbouring) systems (e.g., Coltheart, 2004).

The present study includes a set of computational simulations investigating the possibility that it is unnecessary to postulate separate lexical and semantic systems. We adopt a single-system perspective in which information of different types (e.g., what an object looks like, what it is called, how one interacts with it) and from different modalities (visual, auditory, etc.) is integrated. We suggest that the cases of association and the cases of dissociation may lie on a continuum of performance that is shaped by individual differences existing prior to brain damage—including both biological differences based on genetic factors and differences in experience—and individual differences in the severity and spatial distribution of the progressive brain damage within the semantic system. In this approach, the different SD patients are seen as coming from a single distribution and falling at different points within that distribution rather than as individual cases somehow fundamentally different from each other. A similar approach has been taken by Dell and colleagues (Dell, Martin, & Schwartz, 2007; Schwartz, Dell, Martin, Gahl, & Sobel, 2006) to account for the picture-naming profiles of a large group of aphasic patients. Variability in the patient performance and error patterns was modelled in their interactive two-step model of lexical access by lesioning semantic and/or phonological connections. The model was then used to successfully predict how the same set of patients perform on word repetition.

The aim of the current project was to shed more light on the reasons why performance on naming and reading may be partially but not perfectly correlated across SD patients. Within a single integrative system, the robustness of performance on the different tasks may depend on a number of factors, so that the observed differences in performance in SD patients might arise from any (or a combination of) individual differences.

The idea that premorbid individual differences may play an important role in accounting for SD patients' performance on lexical tasks has been already suggested by Plaut (1997), where a parallel distributed processing (PDP) model was used to show how the competence of the direct pathway (i.e., the pathway between orthography and phonology, which does not rely on semantics and is therefore crucial for nonword reading) could vary drastically depending on its learning properties and the strength of the semantic contribution to phonology. Differences in the division of labour between the direct and the semantic pathways of reading could account for the variability in the data—since semantic damage does not affect the direct pathway.

The importance of individual differences in explaining the reading performance of semantic dementia patients has recently been supported by an extensive report documenting 100 observations of reading data from 51 patients (Woollams et al., 2007). Similarly to Patterson et al. (2006), the authors found a strong correlation between the patients' semantic impairment and their reading deficit. The very occasional cases showing semantic deterioration but relatively preserved reading ability as well as the opposite pattern of unusually impaired reading could be accounted for by positing individual differences in premorbid reliance on semantics during reading. This was demonstrated in simulations of a connectionist network using the architecture and stimuli of Plaut et al. (1996), following the methods used in Plaut (1997). Also, longitudinally, all cases with initially spared reading inevitably showed the expected reading deficit as the semantic impairment worsened. Their longitudinal profiles paralleled the longitudinal profile of the group mean, showing that individual differences were relatively stable over time.

In the current study, we further explore the individual differences hypothesis and extend this work to address several important issues. Firstly, the Plaut et al. model provided only an in-principle argument about the role of semantics. It did not implement semantics, but instead, provided an input to the network's phonological layer with characteristics presumed to mimic those that would actually be generated by semantics. Here we implemented semantics in the form of an integrative layer of hidden units mediating orthographic, phonological, visual, and motor/action information. Second, the Plaut et al. model only simulated reading while the architecture of the present model allows us to simulate both reading and naming. Finally, the Plaut et al. (1996) and Plaut (1997) simulations involved manipulating weight decay and semantic strength in the network; it is not clear how these parameters are grounded in actual characteristics of the population. In contrast, the model we describe here allows us to explore network parameters that are explicitly related to potentially measurable individual difference variables.

Specifically, the parallel distributed processing model presented here implemented and manipulated three individual differences: (a) differences in reading experience (i.e., training regime in the network); (b) differences in the neural pathway mapping orthography to phonology (i.e., direct pathway size in the network); and/or (c) differences in the spatial distribution of the atrophy (i.e., lesion distribution bias in the network). We now discuss the motivation for each of these three manipulations.

Motivation for the reading experience manipulation

Nationwide annual surveys show that there is large variability in all age groups in the amount that people read and in their literacy skills. According to a 2002 survey of the reading habits of Americans above 25 years old, only 47.3% of the population reported reading any literary piece in the past year (Rooney et al., 2006, p. 143). The results from the 2003 National Assessment of Adult Literacy (NAAL) survey indicated that about a third (31.6%) of Americans above 16 years old read books every day, and another third (37.9%) do so less than once a week, or never (Rooney et al., 2006, p. 154).

Given this wide range of reading experience, it is interesting to consider the two SD patients reported by Blazely et al. (2005). One of these patients, E.M., was a secretary who had completed high school and a secretarial course, while the other, P.C., was an air conditioning salesman who had not even completed high school. Based on their education and occupations, and in the context of the findings reported above, it seems plausible that these two individuals had significantly different amounts of reading and/or spelling experience in their lives, which probably resulted in different premorbid competence levels of their reading systems. Not surprisingly, it is patient E.M. who showed spared reading abilities after being diagnosed with SD.

Our implementation of the varying amounts of reading experience focused on the ratio between orthographic and visual input. One can think of it as the ratio of how much time an individual spends reading versus watching TV. Naturally, such a statistic would correlate with other demographics such as years of education and occupation. An alternative would be to look at a network with more training versus less training on reading. We chose to focus on the ratio variable because of its correspondence to stable differences in the relative amount of time spent in activities such as reading and writing. Evaluating the impact of absolute rather than relative reading experience is left to future work.

Motivation for the reading pathway capacity manipulation

Just as reading proficiency heavily depends on how much time one spends reading, it also depends on the neural substrate used for reading. The capacity of that neural substrate may be shaped or altered by experience, but it is also biologically constrained, and there are individual differences along both of these dimensions. For example, developmental dyslexia is a condition characterized by underdeveloped reading skills (compared to age-matched controls) despite normal intelligence. Behaviourally, this can be seen in significantly slower and more error-prone word and pseudoword reading in dyslexic children. Functional neuroimaging studies have found that the posterior areas associated with orthographic processing and the integration of orthographic and phonological codes (i.e., occipito-temporal and temporo-parietal regions) consistently show decreased activation compared to those of nondyslexics in a range of lexical tasks (Pugh et al., 2001). This is the case in adult dyslexics even when they perform like the control subjects behaviourally (Brunswick, McCrory, Price, Frith, & Frith, 1999; McCrory, Mechelli, Frith, & Price, 2005). Thus, in early adulthood, even when the reading skills of dyslexics have improved sufficiently so that in nonspeeded reading conditions they achieve high levels of accuracy, the underlying neurobiological differences are still there and can be observed using functional neuroimaging (McCrory et al., 2005).

While the data on dyslexia reviewed above treat reading ability (and the underlying neurophysiological differences) dichotomously, is seems likely that these traits vary continuously, so that there are differences in the relevant pathways even within the population of individuals categorized as nondyslexics.

Motivation for the lesion distribution manipulation

Our final manipulation is motivated by the fact that no two patients have the exact same lesion. Even though it is well documented that in semantic dementia the atrophy starts from the temporal poles, affects predominantly the anterolateral temporal cortex, and progresses towards the posterior of the temporal lobes (Galton et al., 2001; Mummery et al., 2000, Whitwell, Anderson, Scahill, Rossor, & Fox, 2004), the rate of progression, the specific subregions affected, and the relative tissue loss in each of these regions may vary. So far, unfortunately, there has not been a detailed investigation of individual differences in the temporal lobe atrophy and its progression, and how that relates to performance on clinical tests.

One study looking at hemispheric differences in the lesion distribution in SD patients and how this relates to task impairment found that, even though in most SD cases the temporal atrophy is bilateral but more pronounced on the left, there is substantial variability (Lambon Ralph, McClelland, Patterson, Galton, & Hodges, 2001). There are cases where the atrophy is more pronounced in the right hemisphere. Importantly, it was also found that the degree and orientation of the asymmetry was correlated with the patients' relative performance on naming and word–picture matching.

A possible relationship between processing of words versus pictures and laterality has also been suggested by another study, which looked at SD patients' knowledge of famous people (Snowden, Thompson, & Neary, 2004). The laterality of the temporal lobe lesion was correlated with performance with names versus faces. Patients with predominantly right atrophy performed better with names while those with predominantly left atrophy performed better with faces. The authors interpreted their findings as supporting the view that the anterior temporal lobes (ATL) are crucial for semantic processing, which involves the integration of information across different modalities, with the left ATL being particularly important for verbal processing and the right for visual (Snowden et al., 2004).

In addition, there have been a few reports about common regions of brain damage in groups of SD patients (Chan et al., 2001; Galton et al., 2001; Mummery et al., 2000; Rosen et al., 2002; Studholme et al., 2004). While findings agree on the anatomical regions most severely affected in SD, there is great variability in the full set of implicated regions reported by the different studies. If there are differences in the damaged brain regions reported for groups of SD patients, then there must be substantial differences between individuals taken from the different groups. Of course, this kind of reasoning applies also to reports of performance on clinical tests and the correlations between affected brain areas and performance.

While there is clearly variability in lesion distribution, there is very little information in any of these reports on the relation between lesion distribution and performance on reading and naming. Indeed, few of the studies use more than one task, and the two that do (Galton et al., 2001; Lambon Ralph et al., 2001) do not include reading. Clearly, this is an issue that requires further investigation. For now, it seems fair to conclude that there is a great deal of variability among the patients with respect to the distribution of their lesions. The third manipulation in the neural network model presented here explores the effects of such variability on naming and reading performance.

Using the three manipulations outlined above, we examined whether the model can fit the naming and reading data from five SD patients reported in the literature. The five patients selected for these simulations were chosen for two reasons: (a) to include patients who were all tested with the same materials, and (b) to include one of the three patients discussed above who does not show the usually observed association between semantic and lexical deficits—patient E.M. Three of the patients were reported in Graham, Hodges, and Patterson (1994) and were tested on a set of materials first used in that paper; the other two patients, including E.M., were tested on exactly the same materials by Blazeley et al. (2005). To anticipate, the results show that the data from all of the patients can be captured, and in all cases, the data are consistent with several different simulations involving one or more of the three manipulations. As suggested earlier, these findings have implications for the long-standing tradition in cognitive neuropsychology to view each case separately and to focus on individual reports of association and dissociation of symptoms. The results from our investigation support an approach whereby each patient is seen as a member of a population within which there is variability largely due to individual differences (and not simply noise).

Method

Patient data

The five patients included in the current investigations were the three patients initially reported in Graham et al. (1994), J.L., F.M., and G.C., and the two patients reported by Blazely et al. (2005), E.M. and P.C., who were tested with the same materials. The set includes 106 pictureable nouns, half of which have regular spelling-to-sound correspondences and the other half irregular. The two halves were matched for syllable length and frequency and formed three frequency bands. The advantage of using this set is that the patients can be tested on all tasks with the same materials, which allows for a detailed analysis of the error patterns across tasks.

Figure 2 shows the patient data broken down by frequency for naming and by frequency and regularity for reading. The original materials included three frequency bands but the simulation materials had only two bands (high frequency, HF, vs. low frequency, LF). Therefore, for the purposes of the simulation, low- and medium-frequency items were combined in the results reported here.

Network

Network architecture. The architecture of the neural network is shown on Figure 3. It includes four input/output layers: orthography, phonology, vision, and action. There is full bidirectional connectivity between the input/output (also called *visible*) layers and the integrative hidden layer and full recurrence within the hidden layer. In addition, there is a fully recurrent direct-pathway hidden layer between orthography and phonology. Also, there are five task units that can be turned on or off to regulate which of the layers participate in a given task. This is implemented by having a very strong negative bias on all other units in the network, so that in the absence on input from the task units, the other units are virtually insensitive to inputs and do not participate in processing or learning. Activating a task unit raises the resting level of units in the participating layers up to −3.00, a value that then allows further excitatory input to bring the units into play during processing.

The inclusion of task units like those used here originates with Cohen, Dunbar, and McClelland (1990) and has subsequently been used in other networks (e.g., Plaut, 2002) where production of one of several alternative responses to a particular

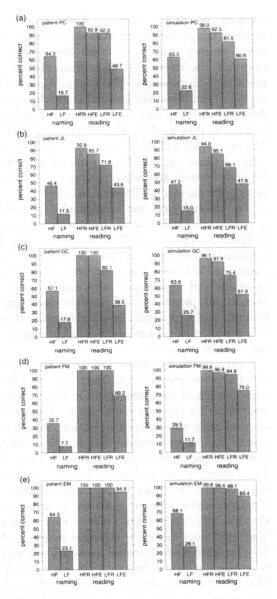

Figure 2. *Patient data along with representative successful simulations for each of the five patients: (a) P.C.: simulation fit with training O:V = 1:1 (O:V = orthographic-to-visual ratio), direct pathway of 20 units, and unbiased lesion; (b) J.L.: simulation fit with training O:V = 1:1, direct pathway of 20 units, and unbiased lesion; (c) G.C.: simulation fit with training O:V = 1:1, direct pathway of 20 units, and 75% orthographically biased lesion; (d) F.M.: simulation fit with training O:V = 2:1, direct pathway of 30 units, and 100% visually biased lesion; (e) E.M.: simulation fit with training O:V = 2:1, direct pathway of 20 units, and 100% visually biased lesion.*

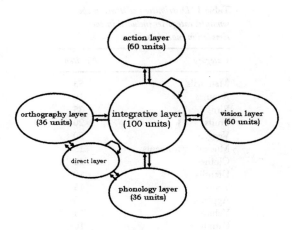

Figure 3. *Network architecture.*

input and/or responding based on one of several different available inputs is required. In our case, the use of task units also allows different strategies for performing a single task. For example, word reading could in principle be carried out by the direct pathway alone or by way of the integrative layer alone, or it could be carried out with both participating. The presence of task units during training encourages the network to develop the ability to do each task with only those parts of the network that are presently allowed to participate, instead of requiring the engagement of the entire network independent of the task.

Simulation materials. The same patterns were used for both training and testing. They consisted of 240 items from 12 categories (see Table 1). The visual patterns corresponded to visual representations of the object, and each of the 240 items had a unique visual representation. The action patterns, on the other hand, corresponded to representations of how one interacts with these objects, and each item did not necessarily have a unique action pattern. For example, we do more or less the same things with many types of fruit; peaches and nectarines are not really treated very differently. Both the visual and the action representations were 60-item long binary patterns that were generated randomly from a set of 12 category prototype patterns. Each prototype specifies the probability of occurrence of each of several binary values, so that items within categories are drawn essentially from the same probability distribution. These prototypes and the algorithm of pattern generation are shown in Appendix A. They were created using a procedure similar to that used in Rogers et al. (2004a). The prototypes and their similarity to each other were adjusted by hand to approximate the pattern of within- and between-category similarity of the patterns used by Rogers et al. (2004a).

The phonological and orthographic patterns were not real English words in general but were designed to approximate English spelling–sound consistency. They had a CVCC (where C is consonant, and V is vowel) structure with 12 possible onset and coda consonants (with matching graphemes and phonemes), 12 possible vowel graphemes, and 8 possible vowel phonemes. The only irregularities between spelling and pronunciation were in the vowels.

There were four groups of two vowel phonemes and three vowel graphemes as shown in Table 2 (60 items in each of these four groups). Every group comprised five types of items. Each of the five occupied cells was further divided into high-frequency and low-frequency items. The exact number of each type of item is shown in Table 3. These numbers are based on about 50,000 spoken word lemmas from the Celex English Lemma Database, where a lemma is defined as including all of the inflected forms of a word—for example, "dog" and "dogs" belong to the same lemma, and their frequencies of occurrence are added together to produce the lemma frequency (Burnage, 1990). The analysis of the corpus proceeded as follows: For each of the 20 grapheme–phoneme

Table 1. *Distribution of items in the semantic categories included in the simulation materials*

Category	No. items
Mammals	55
Reptiles	10
Birds	35
Fruits	20
Veggies	20
Musical instruments	15
Clothes	25
Utensils	10
Tools	15
Appliances	10
Vehicles	15
Furniture	10

Table 2. *Vowel phoneme–grapheme combinations*

	Grapheme		
Phoneme	1	2	3
1	regular	irregular	
2	irregular	regular	regular, rare

Table 3. *Number of high-frequency and low-frequency items in each of the four groups of vowel phoneme–grapheme combinations*

	Grapheme					
	1		2		3	
Phoneme	HF	LF	HF	LF	HF	LF
1	4	33	1	1		
2	1	1	2	12	1	4

Note: HF = high frequency. LF = low frequency.

correspondences (four groups of five types of items), the number of monosyllabic monomorphemic lemmas that matched that type of item was found. Frequency was also taken into account. High-frequency words were defined as having frequency of more than 70, while low-frequency words were defined as having frequency of less than 30 (Kucera & Francis, 1967). The relevant numbers were added to produce 10 sums—two (HF and LF) for each of the five types of items. These were then normalized to add up to 60— and these are the numbers presented in Table 3.

The phonological and orthographic prototypes and the method of pattern generation are presented in Appendix B. Once all the patterns were generated, the two groups—visual and action patterns on one hand and phonological and orthographic patterns on the other—were randomly matched to produce 240 items each with four patterns— visual, action, phonological, and orthographic.

Network training. Training consisted of a series of pattern presentations. In each presentation, the network was given either a visual or an orthographic pattern as input and was trained to produce either just the phonological or all four patterns as output. Processing in the network was regulated by a set of five task units. The five task units were used as summarized in Table 4. If no task unit is turned on, even in the presence of input, nothing happens in the network because all layers have a strong negative bias keeping the units' activations at 0. When a task unit is turned on, it sends positive activation to the layers it is connected to, effectively eliminating the negative bias of those layers and encouraging them to participate in the task at hand. Table 4 lists all the task units and the layers they are connected to. Task units are not uncommon in connectionist networks. They were included in order to encourage the network to make full use of all the pathways. For simplicity, we hard-coded the connection weights between the task units and the layers; other models have used training to learn task weights (e.g., Plaut, 2002).

The relative occurrence of visual versus orthographic input was one of the manipulations and is explained further in the experimental design section. However, for each of these two kinds of input, the relative occurrence of the requested output (phonology vs. all four output patterns) had the constant ratio of 1:1. Furthermore, when the network was trained to read (i.e., given the orthographic input to produce the phonological output), a third of the time only the direct pathway was used, while the rest of the time both the direct pathway and the integrative layer participated.[1]

A frequency manipulation was applied to both visual and orthographic training so that high-frequency items were seen 8 times more often than low-frequency items. Also, the different training tasks were not blocked. The network was trained on all items and tasks in an interleaved manner, and the order of the items was random. Back-propagation was used to update weights between units after every example. The presentation of each example lasted for seven simulated unit time intervals, each divided into a number of ticks; in each tick, net inputs to units were adjusted according to:

$$\Delta n_i = \frac{1}{(\text{number of ticks})} \sum_j (a_j w_{ij} - n_i),$$

---

[1] Because the majority of the learning involves semantic connections, those connections quickly grow in size and thus become responsible for the error in subsequent learning. The direct pathway needed to be trained by itself in order for any learning to occur for its connections.

Table 4. *Training details*

Input	Output	Relative occurrence	Task unit/task	Participating layers
Visual	Phonology	1/2	Name	Visual, phonological, integrative
	All	1/2	Think (from vis input)	All but direct pathway
Orthography	Phonology	1/3	Read for meaning	Orthographic, phonological, integrative, direct pathway
		1/6	Read	Orthographic, phonological, direct pathway
	All	1/2	Think (from orth input)	All

Note: vis = visual. orth = orthographic.

where j indexes the units connected to the current unit i, a_i and n_i are, respectively, the activation and the net input to unit i, and w_{ij} is the value of the connection weight to unit i from unit j. After each unit's net input is updated, the activation is also updated, based on the logistic function:

$$a_i = \frac{1}{1 + e^{-n_i}}.$$

The number of ticks determines how closely the network approximates the assumed underlying continuous evolution of activations. We used 4 ticks per interval, which provides a reasonably smooth evolution of the activations of the units in the network (see Plaut et al., 1996).

The seven time intervals were subdivided as follows. During the first three intervals, the visual or orthographic input pattern corresponding to the item being processed was clamped onto the appropriate layer. For the remaining four intervals, the input was removed, and the network was allowed to adjust the activation of all units in all layers, including the one previously clamped. During the final two intervals, the activations of units are compared to their corresponding targets (which were patterns over the phonological layer only or over all four visible layers, as described earlier). The relevant task unit was clamped on for the entire duration of the example presentation.

The network was trained using standard gradient descent with no momentum. The learning rate was set to 0.001 and the weight decay to 0.000001. Training continued for 2,500 sweeps through the training set.

Network testing. During testing, the network was again presented with either the orthographic or the visual pattern of each item. The phonological response was determined by selecting the most active units at each of the onset, vowel, and coda positions. Responses were either correct or incorrect depending on whether the network was able to exactly produce the actual phonological pattern. For both tasks, all layers were encouraged to participate during testing (by using the *think from orthographic input* task unit). At the end of training, performance on both reading and naming was perfect.

The network was tested following damage by selectively removing units in the integrative hidden layer as well as connections between that layer and the four visible layers. The damage to connections could be unbiased, visually biased, or orthographically biased, and the degree of bias could be 50%, 75%, or 100%. In all cases, when $x\%$ of integrative units were removed, $x\%$ of incoming and $x\%$ of outgoing integrative connections were also removed, where x is an average over the four sets of bidirectional pathways between the visible and the integrative layer. In the unbiased lesion, $x\%$ of connections were removed between the integrative layer and each of the visible layers. In the 50% biased lesion, 50% of the damage was in the direction of the bias. That is, $2x\%$ of the connections in the direction of the bias (visual or orthographic) were removed. The remaining damage was equally distributed among the remaining three pathways, so that $0.67x\%$ of the connections were damaged in each of those three pathways. In the 75% biased lesion,

$3x\%$ of the connections in the direction of the bias were removed, and $0.33x\%$ of the connections were removed in the other three pathways. Finally, in the 100% biased lesion, $4x\%$ of the connections were removed in the directions of the bias, and all other connections were unaffected. Ten levels of damage were examined (1–10%). To ensure appropriate sampling, the model was tested 20 times for each combination of lesion extent and distribution (using 20 different random number generator seeds).

Experimental design
The current project measured the relationship between naming and reading performance of the network. Reading was investigated as a function of the severity of the naming deficit and the values of three parameters: (a) training regime, (b) direct pathway size, and (c) lesion distribution. In order to map out the form of this relationship, the network was tested at 10 levels of lesioning, as mentioned above. A baseline was chosen for each parameter: The baseline training regime included visual and orthographic input in the ratio 1:1; the baseline direct pathway was 20 units, and the baseline lesion distribution was unbiased. The baseline level simply represents a point of comparison, chosen to be neutral and/or intermediate between the other values of the parameters explored. Each parameter was then manipulated individually, so as to promote either better or worse reading performance than that at baseline.

The training regime had an orthographic-to-visual input ratio (V:O) of 1:1 (baseline), 1:2, or 2:1. Having more experience with the orthographic labels than baseline (i.e., the V:O = 2:1 condition) supported better reading than baseline, while having less experience with the labels than baseline (i.e., the V:O = 1:2 condition) supported worse reading than baseline. The direct pathway size was 10, 20 (baseline), or 30 units. Having a larger or a smaller direct pathway fostered respectively better or worse reading than baseline. Finally, the lesion distribution was unbiased (baseline), visually biased, or orthographically biased. As explained earlier, the bias of the lesion had three degrees: 50%, 75%, or 100%. The 100% visually biased and the 100% orthographically biased lesions were the most extreme manipulations of this parameter. Visually biased lesions supported better reading than the baseline unbiased lesion, while orthographically biased lesions were worse at reading than baseline.

In summary, this was a $3 \times 3 \times 7$ full factorial design. All combinations of the three parameters were allowed.

Results and discussion

Fitting the patient data
In order to evaluate the ability of the model to fit the five patients' data discussed earlier, the following steps were taken. For each combination of values of the three network parameters, we first selected an appropriate lesion extent to best match each patient's overall naming performance. We then assessed the network's performance on both naming and reading at that lesion level in relation to the patient's data. The criterion for a successful fit was that for each task and item type (HF vs. LF for naming, and high-frequency regular, HFR, vs. high-frequency exception, HFE, vs. low-frequency regular, LFR, vs. low-frequency exception, LFE, for reading) the patient's data fitted within the 95% confidence interval of the network.

That is, we treated the network's proportion correct on each item type in each task as if it represented the underlying probability of correct performance in that condition for the patient.[2] We then calculated whether the observed patient proportion correct fell within the 95% confidence

---

[2] Note that the network values were based on 240 items each tested 20 times; while there may be some uncertainty in these values due to the fact that they are based on a random sampling process, the number of samples is such that the variability is small enough to have a negligible effect in these analyses.

interval of that value—that is:

$$net \pm 2\sqrt{\frac{net(1-net)}{n}},$$

where *net* is the network's proportion correct, and *n* is the actual number of items on which the patients' performance had been tested. Finally, we used a chi-square test with four degrees of freedom to confirm that the reading performance of each simulation was indeed a good fit for the patient data. The three network manipulations of training regime, direct pathway size, and lesion bias were applied individually and in combination for each of the patients.

With the neutral baseline parameters (training regime of O:V = 1:1, direct pathway of 20 units, and an unbiased lesion), successful fits were found for two of the patients: P.C. ($\chi^2 = 5.494$, $p = .240$) and J.L. ($\chi^2 = .531$, $p = .970$). There were many more fits for both of these patients when the three network parameters were manipulated, individually or in combination. None of the other three patients was successfully modelled by the baseline simulation. However, all of them—including patient E.M., who was the dissociation case reported by Blazely et al. (2005)—also had multiple fits when the parameter values were varied. Appendix C includes a full list of the successful fits for all five patients. Figure 2 shows the performance predicted by one of the best fitting simulations for each patient, along with the patients' actual data. The simulations shown for P.C. and J.L. are networks with baseline parameters, the simulation for G.C. is a network with baseline training, a direct pathway of 20 units, and 75% orthographically biased lesion (fit: $\chi^2 = 5.930$, $p = .204$), the one for F.M. has a training regime O:V = 2:1, a direct pathway of 30 units, and 100% visually biased lesion (fit: $\chi^2 = 2.646$, $p = .619$), and finally, the one for E.M. has training O:V = 2:1, a direct pathway of 20 units, and 100% visually-biased lesion (fit: $\chi^2 = 2.141$, $p = .710$).

As can be seen in Appendix C, patient J.L. had the greatest number of successful fits. Many different combinations of the three parameters produced a pattern similar to J.L.'s data. Generally, most fits were from networks with a direct pathway of 20, a baseline training of 1:1, or training O:V = 2:1, and an unbiased or slightly biased lesion (in either direction). This pattern confirms that the baseline simulation was indeed most suitable for fitting J.L.'s data. A similar trend is seen for P.C.'s fits—they tend to involve a baseline training regime and direct pathway size and an unbiased or slightly biased lesion. Patient G.C.'s fits also involve baseline training and direct pathway, but predominantly lesions with orthographic bias.

Turning to the two more extreme cases, F.M. and E.M., there was a clear preference for a training of O:V = 2:1, a larger direct pathway, and a visually biased lesion. Interestingly, there were more fits for E.M. than for F.M., and the fitting tendencies for all three parameters were more marked for F.M. than E.M. This observation belies the idea that patient E.M. has any "special" status as a dissociation case. We were able to fit all five patients with multiple simulations manipulating the same three network parameters. If the four patients who exhibited surface dyslexia come from a single distribution then E.M. falls within that distribution as well and is no more of an outlier than patient F.M.

It may be, in fact, that it is patient F.M., rather than patient E.M., who is the outlier in this series. Unlike the other patients in this set, F.M. showed an extreme deficit in naming relative to her performance on other tests of semantic knowledge including word–picture matching. An explanation for this (consistent with the earlier analysis of this patient by Lambon Ralph et al., 2001) is that in the case of F.M. there is a special problem in the connections from semantics to phonology. Further consideration of this possibility is beyond the scope of the present simulations and is left for future research.

Our simulation involved three individual differences variables. Are all three necessary to account for the individual patient data? We now consider each of the three individual differences variables in turn. Considering first the lesion distribution variable, it appears that this factor alone is enough to allow an account for the data of all five of the patients. That is, for each patient, there is at least one simulation that falls within the 95% confidence interval of the data while the other two individual differences variables (direct pathway size and training regime) remain at baseline levels. Also of considerable interest is the fact that four of the five patients can be fitted by manipulating only the training regime variable: J.L., P.C., G.C., and E.M. all can be fitted with baseline values of the direct pathway and lesion distribution variables. It is thus possible to account for the data from patient E.M. by assuming only an experience manipulation (although in this case the fit is not as good as others involving a combination of training regime and other variables). Varying the direct pathway size by itself allowed the model to account only for the three patients J.L., P.C., and G.C., although it is possible that a more extreme direct pathway manipulation would have allowed a fit to E.M. and F.M.

Relationship between reading and naming

A multiple regression was performed to look at the relative contribution of each of the three individual difference parameters to the relationship between naming performance and reading of irregular items. For each combination of the three parameters, a set of naming and reading data was obtained at the 10 lesion levels. The analysis included one outcome—the logit of the reading performance on all irregular items—and four predictors: training regime, direct pathway size, lesion bias, and the logit of the naming performance.[3] The training regime was quantified by coding the baseline (O:V = 1:1) as 0, less orthographic training (O:V = 1:2) as −1, and more orthographic training as 1. Similarly, the lesion bias was coded as 0 for unbiased lesions, −100, −66.7, and −33.3 for orthographically biased lesions (most extreme to least extreme), and 100, 66.7, and 33.3 for visually biased lesions. This coding preserved the linear relationship among the different biases as implemented in the network where the bias levels are 100%, 75%, and 50%, and the unbiased lesion is in fact 25% in each direction.

Not surprisingly, naming impairment and reading impairment were found to be highly correlated, $R^2 = .946$, $t(58) = 4.76$, $p < .0005$. More importantly, each of three manipulations were significant predictors of the reading deficit after controlling for naming impairment as well as the variance accounted for by the other manipulations: training regime manipulation, $R^2 = .609$, $t(58) = 11.10$, $p < .0005$; direct pathway size manipulation, $R^2 = .140$, $t(58) = 15.48$, $p < .0005$; lesion bias manipulation, $R^2 = .940$, $t(58) = 7.72$, $p < .0005$. The lesion bias was found to account for the greatest amount of unshared variance.

Figure 4 illustrates the spread produced by the three manipulations in the relationship between naming impairment and reading of irregular items. While lesion bias resulted in the largest spread compared to the other manipulations when naming was relatively low (<30% correct; which is where the majority of the data points are), it is the training regime manipulation that produced the largest spread at higher levels of performance and also produced a relatively high spread at lower levels of performance. Finally, the direct pathway manipulation consistently resulted in the lowest spread at all levels of performance. For example, at naming 20% correct, the difference in reading performance between the two extremes of the direct pathway size was 23%, the difference between the two extremes of the training regime was 29%, and the difference between the two extremes of the lesion bias was 31%; on the other hand, at naming 50% correct, this difference was 9% for the direct pathway manipulation, 10% for the lesion bias manipulation, and 18% for the training regime manipulation. Our model, therefore, has an interesting implication: While overall the distribution of the

---

[3] $logit(x) = log[x/(1 - x)]$. The raw probability correct was replaced by the respective log odds of success in order to avoid effects of logistic compression in the performance.

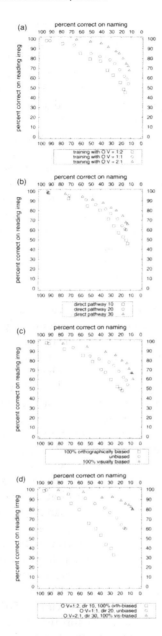

Figure 4. *The effect of the three manipulations on the relationship between naming deficit and impairment on irregular-word reading in the damaged model: (a) effect of training regime (with a direct pathway of 20 and unbiased lesion); (b) effect of direct pathway size (with training of O:V = 1:1 and unbiased lesion; O:V = orthographic-to-visual ratio); (c) effect of lesion bias (with training of O:V = 1:1 and direct pathway of 20 units); (d) cumulative effect of the three factors (only the most extreme cases shown).*

lesion has the most profound impact on how well naming and reading performance correlate in a given patient, it is perhaps individual differences in premorbid reading experience that can explain variability in the correlation between naming and reading performance early in the course of the disease.

Characterization of network behaviour

Thus far we have analysed our networks by showing how they exhibit sensitivity to particular factors and examining goodness of fit to individual patients. Here we consider how the network's behaviour might be captured by a reduced mathematical description, for the purposes of summarizing in a succinct way how its performance is affected by different variables. This characterization relies on the idea that the underlying strength of the network's tendency to accurately perform a particular task may reflect a variety of factors in a simple, perhaps additive way, while the relationship between this strength variable and overt performance has a sigmoidal or logistic shape. With such a function, performance reaches a ceiling level as strength increases such that further strengthening will have little effect, and similarly, below a certain level performance is at floor so that further weakening will have little effect. We pursued this idea by asking how well we can capture the effects of our manipulations of the network's performance in a logistic regression, where lesion extent, direct pathway size, training regime, lesion bias, frequency, and regularity are all factors that should contribute to the strength of the tendency to read an item correctly. The idea is based in part on an analysis previously presented in Plaut et al. (1996), indicating how frequency and regularity both contribute in an additive way to the strength of the connections subserving a particular grapheme–phoneme correspondence in a highly simplified version of their model of single-word reading.

Here, we performed a separate logistic regression of the reading data for each level of each of the three network parameters—that is, direct pathway size, training regime, and lesion bias (while the other two parameters were held constant at baseline), as well as for the two most extreme cases of combining the three manipulations. Four factors were entered as predictors in these analyses—the lesion extent, the frequency and regularity of the items, and an interaction term coding for the frequency-by-regularity relationship.

One of the most important findings was that the frequency-by-regularity interaction was not significant in any but one of the nine logistic regressions (for the 100% orthographically biased lesion $p = .033$; all other $p > .05$), while lesion extent, frequency, and regularity were all highly significant (all $p < .0005$). The occurrence of only one significant frequency-by-regularity interaction term out of nine logistic regression tests suggests that the frequency-by-regularity interaction found in an analysis of variance (ANOVA) run on the raw performance data, $F(1, 171) = 298.78$, $p < .0005$; see Figure 5) and seen in the patient data (e.g., Patterson et al., 2006) is simply a consequence of the compression of performance near the high end of the logistic function. Using the coefficients given by the logistic regression analyses, we plotted the relationship between lesion extent and reading performance. On the same graphs we also plotted the actual data from the network. Three of these graphs, showing the baseline case and the two most extreme cases of combining the three manipulations, can be seen in Figure 6. The logistic functions generally provided excellent fits to the data. One slight exception is that the network performance in the case of the largest

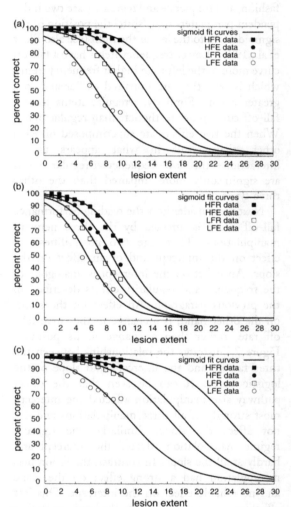

Figure 6. *Logistic regression of the reading data: Effects of frequency and regularity: (a) in the baseline simulation: direct pathway of 20, training regime O:V = 1:1 (O:V = orthographic-to-visual ratio), and unbiased lesion; (b) in simulation with direct pathway of 10, training regime O:V = 1:2, and 100% orthographically-biased lesion; (c) in simulation with direct pathway of 30, training regime O:V = 2:1, and 100% visually biased lesion.*

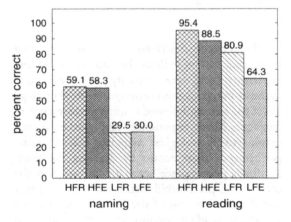

Figure 5. *Frequency by regularity by task three-way interaction in the network. HFR = high-frequency regular. HFE = high-frequency exception. LFR = low-frequency regular. LFE = low-frequency exception.*

lesions seems to be consistently better than the prediction of the logistic function, which suggests that the effect of lesioning may be levelling off, reflecting the residual functional capabilities of the direct pathway.

These figures illustrate that reading performance falls off with lesion extent in a sigmoid-like fashion, and frequency and regularity are two independent parameters that "shift" the position of the sigmoid curve to the left or the right (see also Plaut et al., 1996). Lower frequency items have a fall-off curve more to the left than higher frequency items, which is why they are impaired earlier and to a greater extent. Similarly, irregular items have a fall-off curve more to the left than regular items. When the two effects are superimposed on each other, they result in what appears as an interaction—the low-frequency irregular items are significantly more impaired than the other three types of item.

Next we consider how the reading performance fall-off curve is affected by the three network manipulations. There are two possibilities—an effect on the intercept and/or an effect on the slope. An effect on the intercept is analogous to the frequency and regularity effects described in the previous paragraph. An effect on the slope, on the other hand, is a change in the curve fall-off rate, rather than a change in its position. Figure 7 illustrates the relationships between the three factors and the intercept and slope of the logistic curve. It can be seen that the direct pathway size manipulation affected the intercept most strongly of all three manipulations and did not affect the slope. Similarly, the training regime manipulation affected the intercept and hardly at all the slope. In contrast, the lesion bias manipulation had a strong effect on the slope and no reliable effect on the intercept. This last effect was not surprising given the implementation of the bias manipulation—for any one lesion extent, as we go from an orthographically biased lesion through unbiased to visually biased, the amount of severed links which contribute to reading decreases, which is equivalent to larger versus smaller lesion with respect to reading performance.

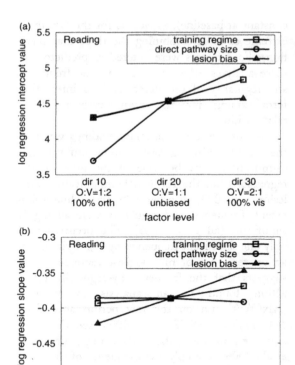

Figure 7. *Logistic regression of the reading data: Effects of the three network manipulations on the intercept and the slope of the logistic function: (a) effects on the intercept; (b) effects on the slope. O:V = orthographic-to-visual ratio.*

The effects described above suggest that premorbid factors such as the amount of reading experience and the capacity of the neural pathway mapping from orthography to phonology affect the susceptibility of reading performance to damage. More experience and better orthographic-to-phonological mapping make reading performance more robust by delaying the point at which performance starts to fall off. On the other hand, postmorbid factors such as the extent and distribution bias of the lesion affect the rate at which reading performance falls off with damage. A lesion oriented away from the orthographic input layer and more towards the visual object input has less effect on reading, as evidenced by the decreased rate at which performance falls off.

It is worth noting that one reason why training only slightly affected the rate of decrease in reading ability may be the fact that there was no retraining after initial lesioning. In contrast, semantic dementia is a progressive disease, and the patients have a chance to try to maintain their skill even as their condition worsens. Using a feed-forward connectionist network, Welbourne and Lambon Ralph (2005) showed that continued training while a network underwent a progressive loss of connections led to considerable preservation of reading ability. Reading habits and occupation, therefore, may relate not only to the initial susceptibility of reading performance to damage, as we have seen here, but also to the rate at which this performance falls off.

Turning to the other task, naming, we performed a similar set of analyses. Initially, we included the same four predictors as those for reading: lesion extent, frequency, regularity, and frequency by regularity. However, regularity and the frequency-by-regularity interaction were not significant in all but one of the nine logistic regressions (for the network combining training O:V = 1:2 with direct pathway of 10, and 100% orthographically biased lesion $p < .05$; all other $p > .08$), while lesion extent and frequency were highly significant (all $p < .0005$). These findings confirmed the results of the ANOVA run on the raw performance data, which also indicated that frequency but not regularity affected naming performance (see Figure 5). This was expected since the regularity of the spelling-to-sound correspondence of a word is irrelevant for naming, where a spoken word is produced in response to a picture. Parallel to the network's performance, the patient naming data lack an effect of regularity and show a pronounced frequency effect. We therefore reran the analyses including only lesion extent and frequency as predictors. These analyses again confirmed the highly significant effect of lesion extent and frequency on naming (all $p < .0005$). Furthermore, they allowed us to explore how the naming performance fall-off curve was affected by the three network

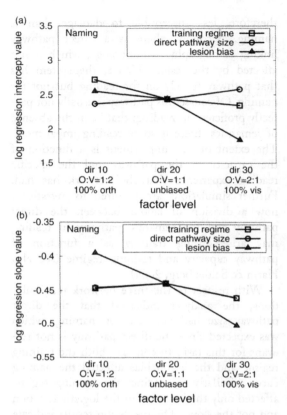

Figure 8. Logistic regression of the naming data: Effects of the three network manipulations on the intercept and the slope of the logistic function: (a) effects on the intercept; (b) effects on the slope. O:V = orthographic-to-visual ratio.

manipulations. The results are presented in Figure 8.

The slope of the naming fall-off curve was consistently steeper than that of the reading fall-off curve while the intercept was consistently smaller, indicating that naming was more sensitive to semantic lesions than was reading. There are at least two explanations for this. First, while reading involves a *systematic* mapping between graphemes and phonemes, naming involves an *arbitrary* mapping between the visual characteristics of an object and its name. This is true even though word reading is acquired later and with greater effort than naming; ultimately, reading is an "easier" task in that it involves a highly systematic mapping from one modality to another and is, therefore, less susceptible to damage than is naming. Secondly, there is a direct pathway linking orthography to phonology, which is not affected by the lesion. Hence, the system has that pathway to rely on for reading but not for naming. Of course this pathway is usually not perfectly proficient in reading; that is, in the absence of semantics, there is some reading impairment. The extent of this impairment is a function of the capacity of the pathway and the specific reading experience that the network has had. Further simulations are required to investigate how a division of labour between the direct pathway and the semantic pathway in reading may arise during training as a function of pathway capacity and training regime (see also Harm & Seidenberg, 2004).

With respect to the three network manipulations, the analyses indicated that the direct pathway size had no effect on naming, which was expected since the direct pathway is not relevant for this task. In contrast, both the training regime and the lesion bias affected the naming curve. Similarly to reading, the training regime affected only the intercept of the logistic function and not the slope. The regression results indicate that similarly to reading, even though perhaps to a lesser extent, increased experience delays the point at which naming performance begins to decrease. Finally, the lesion bias had a very strong effect on the slope of the naming curve as well as a considerable effect on the intercept. This is different from the trend seen for reading, where the lesion bias only affected the slope. It suggests that the location of the lesion is especially important for naming; it is responsible for both the initial point of drop in performance and the rate of this drop as the disease progresses. A lesion oriented away from the orthographic input layer and more towards the visual object input has a great impact on naming.

To further investigate how lesion bias affects reading and naming performance, we conducted a simulation where the network was damaged at one location only. Three lesion locations were considered: units in the integrative layer; links between the integrative layer and the visual layer; and links between the integrative layer and the orthographic layer. In order to get comparable results to those obtained in the investigations of effects of lesions reported above,[4] in this final simulation, the lesions progressed over 25 levels, where level x represents a lesion of x% for integrative units and $4x$% for connections between the integrative layer and a visible layer. Thus, the level 25 of lesioning links was a complete obliteration of the connections between the relevant visible layer and the integrative layer.

The results can be seen in Figure 9. This simulation supported the idea that lesioning connections between semantics and the visual layer profoundly impairs naming performance and hardly affects reading performance, while lesioning connections between semantics and the orthographic layer results in substantial reading impairment and very little naming impairment. Finally, lesioning semantic units affects performance on both tasks but naming more so than reading. Notably, these results illustrate that, in the model, performance on each of the two tasks relies most heavily on certain pathways (visual object representation through semantics to phonology for naming and orthographic word representation through semantics and the direct layer to phonology for reading) but it is also influenced by the activation of other available information. This is an essential characteristic of a single, highly interactive system, which integrates information from different modalities and of different types and participates in a wide range of tasks encompassing the semantic and lexical domains. This is the role attributed to the anterior temporal cortex in our account of semantic dementia (Rogers et al., 2006; Rogers et al., 2004a).

---

[4] As explained earlier, in the original simulations, a 5% unbiased lesion involved lesioning 5% of the integrative units plus 5% of the incoming and 5% of the outgoing connections between the integrative layer and each of the four visible layers (adding up to a total of 20% damaged links); an equivalent lesion fully biased towards a specific layer involved lesioning 5% of the integrative units plus 20% of the incoming and 20% of the outgoing connections between the integrative layer and the specified visible layer (and no links between the integrative layer and any of the other visible layers).

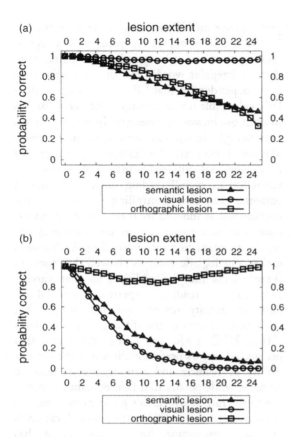

Figure 9. Further investigation of the effect of lesion location on reading and naming: (a) effects on reading; (b) effects on naming.

GENERAL DISCUSSION

In summary, the present computational investigation of the relationship between naming and reading deficits in SD adopted a single-system perspective using a connectionist model that implements semantics. In this model, information from different modalities and types feeds into a single integrative layer. The results from our simulations showed that within such a system, we can replicate the overall relationship between reading and naming seen in SD patients (as reported by Patterson et al., 2006, and Woollams et al., 2007), and we can successfully model data from five SD patients among whom there are cases of both association and dissociation of deficits. The driving force of the account was the manipulation of three network parameters seen as implementing plausible individual differences among the patients. The three factors were experience with reading, capacity of the direct pathway mapping orthography to phonology, and spatial distribution bias of the lesion. Each of these factors contributed significantly and uniquely to the variability in the relationship between naming and reading impairment.

We also captured the role of frequency and regularity in reading. Specifically, we showed that the frequency-by-regularity interaction seen in both the network's and the patients' reading performance can be accounted for by assuming that both frequency and regularity have additive influence on the underlying strength of the correct response to an item, but that this effect is subject to logistic compression.

There are three main points that emerged from our work. First, the pattern of association and dissociation between naming and reading seen in semantic dementia is consistent with our single-system account. The strong relationship between semantic and lexical deficits seen in semantic dementia patients is also found in our computational model, where both reading and naming depend on an intact semantic system; extremely rare patients like E.M. who appear to evidence dissociation between conceptual knowledge and lexical knowledge can, in fact, be accounted for in our single-system model. Second, premorbid and postmorbid individual differences among SD patients are likely to be important in accounting for the variability in patients' performance on semantic and linguistic tasks such as naming and reading. Third, there is a strong need for a thorough investigation of individual differences in temporal lobe atrophy in semantic dementia and how it relates to behavioural performance on semantic and linguistic tasks. These points are reviewed in the following paragraphs.

A single system for conceptual and lexical knowledge

Our simulations show how both an association and a dissociation of function can be produced in a single system. Despite the high correlation between naming and reading of irregular words in our network ($R^2 = .95$)—which is indeed the trend found also in group studies of SD patients (cf. Patterson et al., 2006; Woollams et al., 2007)—we found multiple data fits for patient E.M. who shows little impairment in reading despite her profound naming deficit. While our results do not rule out a two-system perspective, they clearly show that the data from patients like E.M. is not, as others have argued (e.g., Blazely et al., 2005), inconsistent with the view that there is a single, cross-modal, highly interactive system that integrates different types of information (including linguistic information) and participates in a wide range of tasks encompassing the semantic and lexical domains.

Our results also underscore the danger of overfitting due to attributing too much weight to individual patient data. Rather, we need to be able to characterize the distribution and understand the variability in that distribution as a function of individual differences (see also Woollams et al., 2007). If there is in fact an underlying continuum as suggested here and in previous reports, it could be misleading to look at selected few individuals, for example P.C. versus E.M. reported by Blazely et al. (2005).

The importance of individual differences

The present computational study highlights the importance of individual differences in explaining neuropsychological data. Each of the three individual differences factors investigated—reading experience, capacity of the direct pathway mapping orthography to phonology, and bias of the lesion distribution—affected the impairment of reading and/or naming produced by damage, as well as the relationship between these two impairments.

In addition to the variability in overall naming and reading performance in the patient data discussed here, there is also a lot of variability in the reading data when broken down by item type. As mentioned earlier, the general trend in both SD patients and the network is such that performance on HF words is better than that on LF words, performance on words with a regular spelling-to-sound correspondence is better than that on irregular words, and the two effects are not independent so that LF irregulars are particularly vulnerable under damage. The extent of this interaction, however, varies greatly across patients. Interestingly, in our simulations, all three manipulations influenced this interaction, suggesting that individual differences may explain not only variability in overall reading impairment among patients, even after controlling for the semantic impairment as indexed by their naming performance, but also variability in the frequency-by-regularity interaction seen in reading. As discussed earlier, our logistic analyses showed that some of these effects may be additive, so that varying amounts of reading experience and direct pathway capacity, for example, may simply shift the reading curves of the different types of items (HFR, HFE, LFR, and LFE). We found that premorbid factors preferentially affect the susceptibility of reading and naming performance to damage, while postmorbid factors mainly contribute to the rate at which this performance worsens with damage. In addition, the lesion location is especially important for naming as it has considerable impact for the initial point at which performance starts to decline as well as the decline rate.

Individual differences in affected temporal subregions in semantic dementia?

Finally, the current investigation of the role of individual differences in the relationship between naming and reading impairment under semantic damage has suggested that lesion location may be an important factor affecting the exact relationship between performance on semantic and lexical tasks. This is a notion also embraced by the separate systems account (Blazely et al., 2005), which posits that the observed high correlation between semantic and lexical impairment in the majority of SD patients is explained by damage to two anatomically neighbouring but functionally distinct systems. Here we have shown that the specifics of the brain damage can be very relevant to a single systems account as well. Therefore, a thorough investigation looking at individual patients' brain scans and relating region-specific atrophy to task performance would be highly informative to both accounts and possibly relevant to settling the debate between these two opposing views. Combined with demographic data about each patient—including relevant parameters such as years of education, occupation, reading habits, previous assessments of literacy, and so on—this kind of database may be able to address some of the predictions made by our model. One prediction is that premorbid reading experience may explain variability among patients early in the course of the disease, while lesion distribution may explain later variability as the disease progresses.

It may be worth noting, however, that our results do not strongly require an appeal to differences in lesion location to explain most of the available data. In particular, we were able to fit the data from patient E.M. with only a manipulation of the reading experience variable (O:V = 2:1), or with a combination of reading experience and direct pathway size (O:V = 2:1, direct pathway of 30). Among the patients considered here, only patient F.M. could not be fitted without manipulating the lesion distribution variable. This fact, together with the recent success of Woollams et al. (2007) in accounting for the data from a large number of SD cases with a single premorbid individual difference variable, suggests that it not yet clear exactly how important the lesion distribution factor is in explaining variability in the relation of reading and naming performance in semantic dementia.

Limitations of the present investigations
As a final note, we briefly mention several limitations of the present work. First, it has not considered lexical decision (LD), a task used with E.M. and P.C. in Blazeley et al. (2005), but not with the other patients tested. Blazely et al. found that LD was relatively preserved in patient E.M., consistent with their view that there is a separate orthographic lexicon, which is spared in this patient. We acknowledge that an account for patient E.M.'s data from the perspective of our single system account will not be complete until patterns of lexical decision as well as word reading are simulated.

More generally, the present investigation has not considered a wide range of other tasks that have been used with semantic dementia patients. Data from such tasks may further constrain our single-system model, and future research investigating a wide range of patients on a fuller battery of tasks will be important for further progress in understanding the relationship between lexical and semantic processes, in semantic dementia and in general.

CONCLUSION

Our results support the notion that semantic and lexical tasks do not require separate systems; the range of data patterns produced by SD patients is consistent with the idea that both types of tasks can be performed (and can deteriorate at varying rates upon damage) within a single system. Cases of association and dissociation of semantic and lexical deficits may well represent a combination of graded influences rather than any sort of underlying dichotomy. The results are consistent with the view that all SD patients come from a single distribution, the variance of which is a function of individual differences existing prior to brain damage and individual differences in the extent and spatial distribution of the progressive brain damage. Our investigation emphasizes the importance of individual differences among patients and suggests that theoretical and computational accounts of conceptual knowledge and its deterioration in semantic dementia would greatly benefit from future investigations looking at individual patients' brain scans in combination with the best possible information about premorbid biological and experiential factors, relating both region-specific atrophy and premorbid factors to performance in a range of tasks requiring knowledge of words and objects.

Manuscript received 21 May 2007
Revised manuscript received 12 September 2007
Revised manuscript accepted 2 October 2007
First published online 10 January 2008

REFERENCES

Blazely, A., Coltheart, M., & Casey, B. J. (2005). Semantic impairment with and without surface dyslexia: Implications for models of reading, *Cognitive Neuropsychology, 22*, 695–717.

Bozeat, S., Lambon Ralph, M. A., Patterson, K., Garrard, P., & Hodges, J. R. (2000). Non-verbal semantic impairment in semantic dementia. *Neuropsychologia, 38*, 1207–1215.

Brunswick, N., McCrory, E., Price, C. J., Frith, C. D., & Frith, U. (1999). Explicit and implicit processing of words and pseudowords by adult developmental dyslexics: A search for Wernicke's Wortschatz? *Brain, 122*, 1901–1917.

Burnage, G. (1990). CELEX English lexical user guide. In G. Burnage (Ed.), *CELEX—a guide for users*. Nijmegen, The Netherlands: University of Nijmegen, Centre for Lexical Information.

Chan, D., Fox, N. C., Scahill, R. I., Crum, W. R., Whitwell, J. L., Leschziner, G., et al. (2001). Patterns of temporal lobe atrophy in semantic dementia and Alzheimer's disease. *Annals of Neurology, 49*, 433–442.

Cipolotti, L., & Warrington, E. K. (1995). Semantic memory and reading abilities: A case report. *Journal of the International Neuropsychological Society, 1*, 104–110.

Coccia, M., Bartolini, M., Luzzi, S., Provinciali, L., & Lambon Ralph, M. A. (2004). Semantic memory is an amodal, dynamic system: Evidence from the interaction of naming and object use in semantic dementia. *Cognitive Neuropsychology, 21*, 513–527.

Cohen, J. D., Dunbar, K., & McClelland, J. L. (1990). On the control of automatic processes: A parallel-distributed processing account of the Stroop effect. *Psychological Review, 97*, 332–361.

Coltheart, M. (2004). Are there lexicons? *Quarterly Journal of Experimental Psychology, 57*, 1153–1171.

Cortese, M. J., Balota, D. A., Sergent-Marshall, S. D., Buckner, R. L., & Gold, B. T. (2006). Consistency and regularity in past-tense verb generation in healthy ageing, Alzheimer's disease, and semantic dementia. *Cognitive Neuropsychology, 23*, 856–876.

Dell, G. S., Martin, N., & Schwartz, M. F. (2007). A case-series test of the interactive two-step model of lexical access: Predicting word repetition from picture naming. *Journal of Memory and Language, 56*, 490–520.

Funnell, E. (1996). Response biases in oral reading: An account of the co-occurrence of surface dyslexia and semantic dementia. *Quarterly Journal of Experimental Psychology, 49A*, 417–446.

Galton, C. J., Patterson, K., Graham, K., Lambon Ralph, M. A., Williams, G., Antoun, N., et al. (2001). Differing patterns of temporal atrophy in Alzheimer's disease and semantic dementia. *Neurology, 57*, 216–225.

Garrard, P., & Carroll, E. (2006). Lost in semantic space: A multi-modal, non-verbal assessment of feature knowledge in semantic dementia. *Brain, 129*, 1152–1163.

Graham, K. S., Hodges, J. R., & Patterson, K. (1994). The relationship between comprehension and oral reading in progressive fluent aphasia, *Neuropsychologia, 32*, 299–316.

Graham, N. L., Patterson, K., & Hodges, J. R. (2000). The impact of semantic memory impairment on spelling: Evidence from semantic dementia. *Neuropsychologia, 38*, 143–163.

Harm, M. W., & Seidenberg, M. S. (2004). Computing the meaning of words in reading: Cooperative division of labor between visual and phonological processes. *Psychological Review, 111*, 662–720.

Hodges, J. R., Graham, N., & Patterson, K. (1995). Charting the progression in semantic dementia: Implications for the organization of semantic memory. *Memory, 3*, 463–495.

Hodges, J. R., Patterson, K., Oxbury, S., & Funnell, E. (1992). Semantic dementia: Progressive fluent aphasia with temporal lobe atrophy. *Brain, 115*, 1783–1806.

Howard, D., & Patterson, K. (1992). *The Pyramids and Palm Trees Test: A test of semantic access from words and pictures*. Bury St. Edmunds, UK: Thames Valley Test Company.

Kucera, H., & Francis, W. N. (1967). *Computational analysis of present-day American English*. Providence, RI: Brown University Press.

Lambon Ralph, M. A., & Howard, D. (2000). Gogi aphasia or semantic dementia? Simulating and assessing poor verbal comprehension in a case of progressive fluent aphasia. *Cognitive Neuropsychology, 17*, 437–465.

Lambon Ralph, M. A., McClelland, J. L., Patterson, K., Galton, C. J., & Hodges, J. R. (2001). No right to speak? The relationship between object naming and semantic impairment: Neuropsychological evidence and a computational model. *Journal of Cognitive Neuroscience, 13*, 341–356.

Luzzi, S., Snowden, J. S., Neary, D., Coccia, M., Provinciali, L., & Lambon Ralph, M. A. (2007). Distinct patterns of olfactory impairment in Alzheimer's disease, semantic dementia, frontotemporal dementia, and corticobasal degeneration. *Neuropsychologia, 45*, 1823–1831.

McCrory, E. J., Mechelli, A., Frith, U., & Price, C. J. (2005). More than words: A common neural basis for reading and naming deficits in developmental dyslexia? *Brain, 128*, 261–267.

McKay, A., Castles, A., Davis, C., & Savage, G. (2007). The impact of progressive semantic loss on reading aloud. *Cognitive Neuropsychology, 24*, 162–186.

Mummery, C. J., Patterson, K., Price, C. J., Ashburner, J., Frackowiak, R. S. J., & Hodges, J. R. (2000). A voxel-based study of semantic dementia: Relationship between temporal lobe atrophy and semantic memory. *Annals of Neurology, 47*, 36–45.

Patterson, K., & Hodges, J. (1992). Deterioration of word meaning: Implications for reading. *Neuropsychologia, 30*, 1025–1040.

Patterson, K., & Hodges, J. (2000). Semantic dementia: One window on the structure and organisation of semantic memory. In F. Boller & J. Grafman (Eds.), *Handbook of neuropsychology: Memory and its disorders* (2nd ed., Vol. 2, pp. 313–333). Amsterdam: Elsevier Science.

Patterson, K., Lambon Ralph, M. A., Hodges, J. R., & McClelland, J. L. (2001). Deficits in irregular past-tense verb morphology associated with degraded semantic knowledge. *Neuropsychologia, 39*, 709–724.

Patterson, K., Lambon Ralph, M. A., Jefferies, E., Woollams, A., Jones, R., Hodges, J. R., et al. (2006). "Pre-semantic" cognition in semantic dementia: Six deficits in search of an explanation. *Journal of Cognitive Neuroscience, 18*, 169–183.

Patterson, K., Suzuki, T., Wydell, T., & Sasanuma, S. (1995). Progressive aphasia and surface alexia in Japanese. *Neurocase, 1*, 155–165.

Plaut, D. C. (1997). Structure and function in the lexical system: Insights from distributed models of word reading and lexical decision. *Language and Cognitive Processes, 12*, 767–808.

Plaut, D. C. (2002). Graded modality-specific specialization in semantics: A computational account of optic aphasia. *Cognitive Neuropsychology, 19*, 603–639.

Plaut, D. C., McClelland, J. L., Seidenberg, M. S., & Patterson, K. (1996). Understanding normal and impaired word reading: Computational principles in quasi-regular domains. *Psychological Review, 103*, 56–115.

Pugh, K. R., Mencl, W. E., Jenner, A. R., Lee, J. R., Katz, L., Frost, S. J., et al. (2001). Neuroimaging studies of reading development and reading disability. *Learning Disabilities Research & Practice, 16*, 240–249.

Rogers, T. T., Hocking, J., Noppeney, U., Mechelli, A., Gorno-Tempini, M. L., Patterson, K., et al. (2006). The anterior temporal cortex and semantic memory: Reconciling findings from neuropsychology and functional imaging. *Cognitive, Affective, and Behavioral Neuroscience, 6*, 201–213.

Rogers, T. T., Lambon Ralph, M. A., Garrard, P., Bozeat, S., McClelland, J. L., Hodges, J. R., et al. (2004a). The structure and deterioration of semantic memory: A neuropsychological and computational investigation. *Psychological Review, 111*, 205–235.

Rogers, T. T., Lambon Ralph, M. A., Hodges, J. R., & Patterson, K. (2004b). Natural selection: The impact of semantic impairment on lexical and object decision. *Cognitive Neuropsychology, 21*, 331–352.

Rooney, P., Hussar, W., Planty, M., Choy, S., Hampden-Thompson, G., Provasnik, S., et al. (2006). *The condition of education.* Washington, DC: National Center for Education Statistics.

Rosen, H. J., Gorno-Tempini, M. L., Goldman, W. P., Perry, R. J., Schuff, N., Weiner, M., et al. (2002). Patterns of brain atrophy in frontotemporal dementia and semantic dementia. *Neurology, 58*, 198–208.

Schwartz, M. F., Dell, G. S., Martin, N., Gahl, S., & Sobel, P. (2006). A case-series test of the interactive two-step model of lexical access: Evidence from picture naming. *Journal of Memory and Language, 54*, 228–264.

Schwartz, M. F., Saffran, E. M., & Marin, O. S. M. (1980). Fractionating the reading process in dementia: Evidence for word-specific print-to-sound associations. In M. Coltheart, K. Patterson, & J. C. Marshall (Eds.), *Deep dyslexia.* London: Routledge and Kegan Paul.

Seidenberg, M. S., & McClelland, J. L. (1989). A distributed, developmental model of word recognition and naming. *Psychological Review, 96*, 523–568.

Snowden, J. S., Goulding, P. J., & Neary, D. (1989). Semantic dementia: A form of circumscribed cerebral atrophy. *Behavioural Neurobiology, 2*, 167–182.

Snowden, J. S., Neary, D., & Mann, D. M. A. (1996). *Frontotemporal lobar degeneration: Frontotemporal dementia, progressive aphasia, semantic dementia.* New York: Churchill Livingstone.

Snowden, J. S., Thompson, J. C., & Neary, D. (2004). Knowledge of famous faces and names in semantic dementia. *Brain, 127*, 860–872.

Studholme, C., Cardenas, V., Blumenfeld, R., Schuff, N., Rosen, H. J., Miller, B., et al. (2004). Deformation tensor morphometry of semantic dementia with quantitative validation. *NeuroImage, 21*, 1387–1398.

Welbourne, S. R., & Lambon Ralph, M. A. (2005). Exploring the impact of plasticity-related recovery after brain damage in a connectionist model of single-word reading. *Cognitive, Affective, & Behavioral Neuroscience, 5*, 77–92.

Whitwell, J. L., Anderson, V. M., Scahill, R. I., Rossor, M. N., & Fox, N. C. (2004). Longitudinal patterns of regional change on volumetric MRI in frontotemporal lobar degeneration. *Dementia & Geriatric Cognitive Disorders, 17*, 307–310.

Woollams, A., Lambon Ralph, M. A., Plaut, D. C., & Patterson, K. (2007). SD-squared: On the association between semantic dementia and surface dyslexia. *Psychological Review, 114*, 316–339.

APPENDIX A

Visual patterns and action patterns generation

Algorigthm

A total of 240 binary patterns were generated by giving a 1 with probability of .8 at positions marked with " + ", probability .2 at positions marked with "0", and probability 0 at positions marked with "−".

Visual Prototypes

Action Prototypes

APPENDIX B

Phonological patterns and orthographic patterns generation

Algorithm

The CVCC patterns were generated by giving 1 to the vowel marked with "+" and 0s to all other vowels (marked with "−"). Onsets and codas were picked for each item by giving each of the 12 consonants (marked with "0") equal chance (i.e., probability of being selected = 1/12) at each of the three positions (one for the onset, two for the coda). Once the consonants were picked, they were given a 1 while all others were given 0s. Thus, all 240 patterns consisted of 36-item long vectors with only four 1s (one for onset in the first 12 positions, one for vowel in the second 12 positions, and two for coda in the last 12 positions). The 240 unique orthographic patterns were first generated and then matched with the appropriate phonological pattern. The numbers in the first column refer to the number of patterns with that specific vowel.

Phonological Prototypes

no of patterns	onset												vowel										coda											
	b	p	d	t	g	k	m	n	l	f	s	ṡ	ej	æ	aj	I	ow	o	ij	ɩ	b	p	d	t	g	k	m	n	l	f	s	ṡ
37	0	0	0	0	0	0	0	0	0	0	0	0	−	+	−	−	−	−	−	−	0	0	0	0	0	0	0	0	0	0	0	0
2	0	0	0	0	0	0	0	0	0	0	0	0	−	+	−	−	−	−	−	−	0	0	0	0	0	0	0	0	0	0	0	0
2	0	0	0	0	0	0	0	0	0	0	0	0	+	−	−	−	−	−	−	−	0	0	0	0	0	0	0	0	0	0	0	0
14	0	0	0	0	0	0	0	0	0	0	0	0	+	−	−	−	−	−	−	−	0	0	0	0	0	0	0	0	0	0	0	0
5	0	0	0	0	0	0	0	0	0	0	0	0	+	−	−	−	−	−	−	−	0	0	0	0	0	0	0	0	0	0	0	0
37	0	0	0	0	0	0	0	0	0	0	0	0	−	−	−	+	−	−	−	−	0	0	0	0	0	0	0	0	0	0	0	0
2	0	0	0	0	0	0	0	0	0	0	0	0	−	−	−	+	−	−	−	−	0	0	0	0	0	0	0	0	0	0	0	0
2	0	0	0	0	0	0	0	0	0	0	0	0	−	−	+	−	−	−	−	−	0	0	0	0	0	0	0	0	0	0	0	0
14	0	0	0	0	0	0	0	0	0	0	0	0	−	−	+	−	−	−	−	−	0	0	0	0	0	0	0	0	0	0	0	0
5	0	0	0	0	0	0	0	0	0	0	0	0	−	−	+	−	−	−	−	−	0	0	0	0	0	0	0	0	0	0	0	0
37	0	0	0	0	0	0	0	0	0	0	0	0	−	−	−	−	+	−	−	−	0	0	0	0	0	0	0	0	0	0	0	0
2	0	0	0	0	0	0	0	0	0	0	0	0	−	−	−	−	+	−	−	−	0	0	0	0	0	0	0	0	0	0	0	0
2	0	0	0	0	0	0	0	0	0	0	0	0	−	−	−	−	+	−	−	−	0	0	0	0	0	0	0	0	0	0	0	0
14	0	0	0	0	0	0	0	0	0	0	0	0	−	−	−	−	+	−	−	−	0	0	0	0	0	0	0	0	0	0	0	0
5	0	0	0	0	0	0	0	0	0	0	0	0	−	−	−	−	+	−	−	−	0	0	0	0	0	0	0	0	0	0	0	0
37	0	0	0	0	0	0	0	0	0	0	0	0	−	−	−	−	−	−	+	−	0	0	0	0	0	0	0	0	0	0	0	0
2	0	0	0	0	0	0	0	0	0	0	0	0	−	−	−	−	−	−	+	−	0	0	0	0	0	0	0	0	0	0	0	0
2	0	0	0	0	0	0	0	0	0	0	0	0	−	−	−	−	−	+	−	−	0	0	0	0	0	0	0	0	0	0	0	0
14	0	0	0	0	0	0	0	0	0	0	0	0	−	−	−	−	−	+	−	−	0	0	0	0	0	0	0	0	0	0	0	0
5	0	0	0	0	0	0	0	0	0	0	0	0	−	−	−	−	−	+	−	−	0	0	0	0	0	0	0	0	0	0	0	0

Orthographic Prototypes

no of patterns	onset												vowel												coda											
	b	p	d	t	g	k	m	n	l	f	s	sh	a	A	ai	i	I	Y	o	O	oa	e	ea	ie	b	p	d	t	g	k	m	n	l	f	s	sh
37	0	0	0	0	0	0	0	0	0	0	0	0	+	−	−	−	−	−	−	−	−	−	−	−	0	0	0	0	0	0	0	0	0	0	0	0
2	0	0	0	0	0	0	0	0	0	0	0	0	−	+	−	−	−	−	−	−	−	−	−	−	0	0	0	0	0	0	0	0	0	0	0	0
2	0	0	0	0	0	0	0	0	0	0	0	0	+	−	−	−	−	−	−	−	−	−	−	−	0	0	0	0	0	0	0	0	0	0	0	0
14	0	0	0	0	0	0	0	0	0	0	0	0	−	+	−	−	−	−	−	−	−	−	−	−	0	0	0	0	0	0	0	0	0	0	0	0
5	0	0	0	0	0	0	0	0	0	0	0	0	−	−	+	−	−	−	−	−	−	−	−	−	0	0	0	0	0	0	0	0	0	0	0	0
37	0	0	0	0	0	0	0	0	0	0	0	0	−	−	−	+	−	−	−	−	−	−	−	−	0	0	0	0	0	0	0	0	0	0	0	0
2	0	0	0	0	0	0	0	0	0	0	0	0	−	−	−	+	−	−	−	−	−	−	−	−	0	0	0	0	0	0	0	0	0	0	0	0
2	0	0	0	0	0	0	0	0	0	0	0	0	−	−	−	−	+	−	−	−	−	−	−	−	0	0	0	0	0	0	0	0	0	0	0	0
14	0	0	0	0	0	0	0	0	0	0	0	0	−	−	−	−	+	−	−	−	−	−	−	−	0	0	0	0	0	0	0	0	0	0	0	0
5	0	0	0	0	0	0	0	0	0	0	0	0	−	−	−	−	−	+	−	−	−	−	−	−	0	0	0	0	0	0	0	0	0	0	0	0
37	0	0	0	0	0	0	0	0	0	0	0	0	−	−	−	−	−	−	+	−	−	−	−	−	0	0	0	0	0	0	0	0	0	0	0	0
2	0	0	0	0	0	0	0	0	0	0	0	0	−	−	−	−	−	−	+	−	−	−	−	−	0	0	0	0	0	0	0	0	0	0	0	0
2	0	0	0	0	0	0	0	0	0	0	0	0	−	−	−	−	−	−	+	−	−	−	−	−	0	0	0	0	0	0	0	0	0	0	0	0
14	0	0	0	0	0	0	0	0	0	0	0	0	−	−	−	−	−	−	−	+	−	−	−	−	0	0	0	0	0	0	0	0	0	0	0	0
5	0	0	0	0	0	0	0	0	0	0	0	0	−	−	−	−	−	−	−	−	+	−	−	−	0	0	0	0	0	0	0	0	0	0	0	0
37	0	0	0	0	0	0	0	0	0	0	0	0	−	−	−	−	−	−	−	−	−	+	−	−	0	0	0	0	0	0	0	0	0	0	0	0
2	0	0	0	0	0	0	0	0	0	0	0	0	−	−	−	−	−	−	−	−	−	−	+	−	0	0	0	0	0	0	0	0	0	0	0	0
2	0	0	0	0	0	0	0	0	0	0	0	0	−	−	−	−	−	−	−	−	−	−	+	−	0	0	0	0	0	0	0	0	0	0	0	0
14	0	0	0	0	0	0	0	0	0	0	0	0	−	−	−	−	−	−	−	−	−	−	+	−	0	0	0	0	0	0	0	0	0	0	0	0
5	0	0	0	0	0	0	0	0	0	0	0	0	−	−	−	−	−	−	−	−	−	−	−	+	0	0	0	0	0	0	0	0	0	0	0	0

APPENDIX C

Full list of successful fits for the five patients

| Patient | No. fits | Successful fit parameters ||| Statistics ||
		Training O:V	Direct pathway size[a]	Lesion bias	χ^2	p
J.L.	43	1:1	10	unbiased	3.567	.468
				50% vis	0.309	.989
				75% vis	2.300	.681
				100% vis	5.302	.258
			20	100% orth	2.591	.628
				75% orth	2.264	.687
				50% orth	0.120	.998
				unbiased	0.531	.970
				50% vis	4.333	.363
				75% vis	5.171	.270
			30	100% orth	2.591	.628
				75% orth	2.444	.655
				50% orth	1.348	.853
				unbiased	2.229	.694
				50% vis	5.171	.270
		1:2	10	unbiased	6.171	.187
				50% vis	3.818	.431
				75% vis	4.393	.355
				100% vis	5.099	.277
			20	75% orth	5.636	.228
				50% orth	6.171	.187
				unbiased	4.660	.324
				50% vis	0.103	.999
				75% vis	3.256	.516
				100% vis	4.094	.394
			30	75% orth	3.074	.546
				50% orth	2.261	.688
				unbiased	0.872	.929
				50% vis	3.152	.533
				75% vis	3.185	.527
		2:1	10	100% orth	5.737	.220
				75% orth	4.127	.389
				50% orth	2.351	.672
				unbiased	2.052	.726
				50% vis	0.924	.921
			20	100% orth	1.482	.830
				75% orth	0.662	.956
				50% orth	1.501	.826
				unbiased	7.749	.101
				50% vis	7.749	.101
			30	100% orth	0.545	.969
				75% orth	3.066	.547
				50% orth	6.601	.159

(Continued overleaf)

Appendix C (Continued)

Patient	No. fits	Successful fit parameters			Statistics	
		Training O:V	Direct pathway size[a]	Lesion bias	χ^2	p
P.C.	22	1:1	10	50% vis	5.453	.244
				75% vis	5.494	.240
				100% vis	5.784	.216
			20	50% orth	4.481	.345
				unbiased	5.494	.240
				50% vis	5.856	.210
				75% vis	4.929	.295
			30	50% orth	5.065	.281
				unbiased	4.481	.345
		1:2	10	50% vis	6.704	.152
				75% vis	6.797	.147
				100% vis	4.481	.345
			20	50% vis	3.724	.445
				75% vis	6.367	.173
		2:1	10	75% vis	8.457	.076
			20	100% orth	3.782	.436
				75% orth	6.077	.193
				50% orth	5.494	.240
				unbiased	4.929	.295
			30	100% orth	5.694	.223
				75% orth	4.481	.345
				50% orth	6.367	.173
G.C.	18	1:1	10	50% orth	9.155	.057
				unbiased	7.594	.108
				50% vis	4.472	.346
			20	100% orth	7.348	.119
				75% orth	5.930	.204
				50% orth	7.186	.126
		1:2	10	unbiased	6.746	.150
			20	unbiased	8.321	.081
				50% vis	5.477	.242
			30	unbiased	8.985	.062
		2:1	10	75% orth	9.487	.050
				unbiased	9.150	.057
				50% vis	8.335	.080
			20	100% orth	8.671	.070
				75% orth	5.477	.242
				50% orth	7.702	.103
			30	100% orth	6.133	.189
				75% orth	7.282	.122
E.M.	15	1:1	30	50% vis	6.461	.167
				75% vis	5.379	.251
				100% vis	3.091	.543
		1:2	30	75% vis	7.478	.113
				100% vis	7.478	.113

(*Continued overleaf*)

Appendix C (Continued)

Patient	No. fits	Successful fit parameters			Statistics	
		Training O:V	Direct pathway size[a]	Lesion bias	χ^2	p
		2:1	10	75% vis	8.555	.073
				100% vis	7.469	.113
			20	unbiased	4.173	.383
				50% vis	6.461	.167
				75% vis	2.141	.710
				100% vis	2.141	.710
			30	unbiased	6.461	.167
				50% vis	4.178	.383
				75% vis	4.178	.383
				100% vis	3.091	.543
F.M.	7	1:1	30	75% vis	6.072	.194
				100% vis	4.865	.302
		2:1	20	75% vis	4.327	.364
				100% vis	4.485	.344
			30	50% vis	4.865	.302
				75% vis	3.408	.492
				100% vis	2.646	.619

Note: O:V = orthographic-to-visual ratio. vis = visual. orth = orthographic.

Computational modelling of phonological dyslexia: How does the DRC model fare?

Lyndsey Nickels, Britta Biedermann, Max Coltheart, and Steve Saunders
Macquarie Centre for Cognitive Science, Macquarie University, Sydney, Australia

Jeremy J. Tree
University of Exeter, Exeter, UK

This paper investigates the patterns of reading impairment in phonological dyslexia using computational modelling with the dual-route cascaded model of reading (DRC, Coltheart, Rastle, Perry, Langdon, & Ziegler, 2001). Systematic lesioning of nonlexical and phonological processes in DRC demonstrates that different lesions and severity of those lesions can reproduce features of phonological dyslexia including impaired reading of nonwords, relatively spared reading of words, an advantage for reading pseudohomophones. Using the same stimuli for model and for patients, lesions to DRC were also used to simulate the reading accuracy shown by three individuals with acquired phonological dyslexia. No single lesion could replicate the reading performance of all three individuals. In order to simulate reading accuracy for one individual a phonological impairment was necessary (addition of noise to the phoneme units), and for the remaining two individuals an impairment to nonlexical reading procedures (increasing the time interval between each new letter being processed) was necessary. We argue that no single locus of impairment (neither phonological nor nonlexical) can account for the reading impairments of all individuals with phonological dyslexia. Instead, different individuals have different impairments (and combinations of impairments) that together provide the spectrum of patterns found in phonological dyslexia.

Phonological dyslexia is a reading disorder that has as its defining symptoms poor reading of nonwords with relatively unimpaired reading of real words. This disorder has been relatively well investigated, and several cases have been reported in some detail. These cases include both those individuals who have never had "normal" patterns of reading (developmental phonological dyslexia; e.g., Howard & Best, 1996; Temple & Marshall, 1983) and those who were previously skilled readers prior to brain damage (acquired phonological dyslexia; e.g., Derouesne & Beauvois, 1985; see Table 1 for a summary). The pattern of reading impairment shown in phonological dyslexia has been interpreted within theories of skilled reading, and more recently

---

Correspondence should be addressed to Lyndsey Nickels, Macquarie Centre for Cognitive Science (MACCS), Macquarie University, Sydney, NSW 2109, Australia (E-mail: lnickels@maccs.mq.edu.au).

During preparation of this paper Lyndsey Nickels was funded by an Australian Research Council QEII fellowship, and Max Coltheart by an Australian Research Council Federation fellowship. We thank David Howard and Marco Zorzi for helpful comments on an earlier version of this paper.

Table 1. *Summary of cases with phonological dyslexia where pseudohomophone reading was explicitly tested*

Case	Authors	Word reading[a]	NW reading[a]	PSH effect	Vis Sim effect
M.J.K.[b]	Howard & Best (1996)	96	50	yes	yes
H.M.[b]	Temple & Marshall (1983)	84	22	yes	yes
A.M.	Patterson (1982)	94	8	yes	yes
L.B.	Derouesne & Beauvois (1985)	95	48	yes	yes
R.G.	Derouesne & Beauvois (1979), Beauvois & Derouesne (1979)	100	25	yes	no
T.Y.	Sasanuma et al. (1996)	99	40	yes	N/A
A.D.	Cuetos, Valle-Arroyo, & Suarez (1996)	89	35	yes (trend)	N/A
K.T.	Patterson et al. (1996)	91	0	yes	N/A
B.K.	Berndt, Haendiges, Mitchum, & Wayland (1996)	98	40	yes	N/A
B.B.O.	Patterson & Marcel (1992)	90+	33	yes	N/A
R.T.I.	Patterson & Marcel (1992)	90+	30	yes	N/A
T.W.A.	Patterson & Marcel (1992)	90+	17	yes	N/A
H.C.	Berndt et al. (1996)	90	12	yes	N/A
D.P.R.	Patterson & Marcel (1992)	90+	10	yes	N/A
J.D.	Berndt et al. (1996)	90	8	yes	N/A
C.J.	Funnell (1987), Patterson (2000)	95	21	no	N/A
A.N.	Goodall & Phillips (1995)	85	30	no	N/A
M.V.	Bub, Black, Howell, & Kertesz (1987)	88	42	no	N/A
W.B.A.	Patterson & Marcel (1992)	90+	77	no	N/A
W.E.	Berndt et al. (1996)	99	65	no	N/A
M.C.	Tainturier & Rapp (2003)	100	56	no	N/A
J.H.	Berndt et al. (1996)	98	42	no	N/A
W.B.	Funnell (1983)	93	0	no	N/A

Note: Word and nonword reading will be from lists of different difficulties and hence not strictly comparable across cases. NW = nonword. PSH effect: Pseudohomophones read significantly more accurately than nonwords. Vis Sim effect: Pseudohomophones that are visually similar to the word corresponding to their phonological form are read significantly more accurately than pseudohomophones that are less visually similar.
[a]Percentage correct. [b]These cases are developmental.

computational modelling of the disorder has also been attempted.

The "classical" dual-route model of reading (e.g., Coltheart, 1996, 2006) incorporates one (nonlexical) route that can read nonwords and all regular words and another (direct lexical) route that can read aloud all words (regular and exception).[1] This dual-route model has been implemented computationally in the dual-route cascaded (DRC) model of reading (Coltheart, Curtis, Atkins, & Haller, 1993; Coltheart, Rastle, Perry, Langdon, & Ziegler, 2001; see Figure 1). Within the dual-route framework, phonological dyslexia is generally interpreted as an impairment of the nonlexical route, which, by definition, results in impaired nonword reading but without any impact on word reading. It follows that simulation of phonological dyslexia within the DRC model is trivial: If the nonlexical route no longer activates phoneme representations, word reading remains error free but nonword reading is impossible. Of course, this "extreme" phonological dyslexia is rarely, if ever, observed, and so the challenge for computational modelling is to simulate less severe reading impairments. Coltheart, Langdon, and Haller (1996) did

---

[1] This model also proposes an additional route for reading words via their semantic representations. This route is not implemented in the DRC computational implementation of the dual-route model.

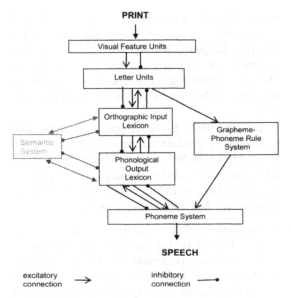

Figure 1. *The dual-route cascaded model of reading. Shown on the right-hand side of the figure is the nonlexical route, which translates print to sound, from left to right, one letter at a time. The grapheme–phoneme rule system activates a series of phonemes in the phoneme system according to rule-governed correspondences. The lexical route is depicted on the left-hand side of the figure. This route comprises the orthographic input lexicon and the phonological output lexicon, which contain nodes representing, respectively, the orthographic and phonological forms of all "known" words. The lexical routine is able to read correctly all (and only) words that the model has in its vocabulary by activating the component phonemes in the phoneme system. The components in grey (the semantic system and the links to and from it) are not currently implemented.*

just this. They demonstrated not only that the DRC model, appropriately lesioned, can easily simulate a less extreme nonword reading deficit, but also that the reading of this lesioned model showed some of the more subtle features of the reading performance of a particular phonological dyslexic, L.B. (Derouesne & Beauvois, 1985). That is, both L.B. and DRC when lesioned showed a pseudohomophone advantage: better reading performance when a novel letter string corresponds to a known phonological form (e.g., brane) than when it corresponds to a novel phonological form (e.g., brone). Not only did L.B. show a pseudohomophone advantage, but the occurrence of such an advantage depended on the similarity of the letter string to the underlying word (an interaction with orthographic similarity). L.B. showed a pseudohomophone advantage (compared to control nonwords) for stimuli that were similar in spelling to the underlying words (e.g., koat −coat) but not for those that were less similar (e.g., kote−coat) as did DRC when lesioned.

While important, this early work using DRC must still be regarded as extremely preliminary. In particular, while the general pattern was similar, overall the simulated reading performance was lower in accuracy than that of L.B. In addition, and even more critically, as L.B. was a French speaker, the simulations of phonological dyslexia could not use the exact stimuli used with this patient. It is vital for simulations to demonstrate that not only can the computational model reproduce the accuracy and pattern of behaviour of the patient, but also that this can be achieved using the same stimuli. Perry, Ziegler, and Zorzi (2007) simulated phonological dyslexic reading using CDP+, a modified version of Zorzi, Houghton, and Butterworth's (1998) connectionist dual-process (CDP) model. Like Coltheart et al. (1996) they demonstrated that when lesioned CDP+ could replicate the pattern shown by L.B. Once again, however, the strength of the simulation is limited by the use of different stimuli in model and patient.

Harm and Seidenberg (2001) have also performed computational modelling of phonological dyslexia using a version of the "triangle" connectionist model of reading (e.g., Plaut, McClelland, Seidenberg, & Patterson, 1996; Seidenberg & McClelland, 1989; for a review of different versions of this model see Coltheart, 2005). The architecture of their version of this model is shown in Figure 2. They concentrated on the "phonological impairment hypothesis" of phonological dyslexia (Farah, Stowe, & Levinson, 1996; Harm & Seidenberg, 1999; Manis, Seidenberg, Doi, McBride-Chang, & Peterson, 1996; Patterson & Marcel, 1992; Patterson, Suzuki, & Wydell, 1996; Sasanuma, Ito, Patterson, & Ito, 1996; Seidenberg, 1995).

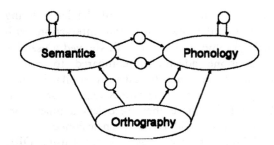

Figure 2. *A version of the triangle model of reading (adapted from Harm & Seidenberg, 2001, Fig. 3). Empty circles represent "hidden" units between orthography and phonology and semantics and "clean up" units for semantics and phonology.*

According to this hypothesis, the impairment of nonword reading is due to a general impairment of phonological processing,[2] which affects nonword reading to a greater extent than word reading. They demonstrated that a phonologically impaired version of the triangle model (where noise was added to the phonological attractors) could broadly simulate the patterns shown by developmental phonological dyslexic M.J. (Howard & Best, 1996). Moreover, this success included simulation of some of the effects attributed by Howard and Best to orthographic factors (e.g., orthographic complexity of nonwords; pseudohomophone similarity effect). However, as for the Coltheart et al. (1996) work, once again, this interesting simulation research falls short. While Harm and Seidenberg did use the identical stimuli to those used with M.J., the overall accuracy of the lesioned model differs from that of the phonological dyslexic person (see Harm & Seidenberg, 2001, Table 1). In addition, while it is certainly the case that some individuals with phonological dyslexia have general phonological impairments (characterized by, for example, poor nonword repetition and poor segmentation skills; see Table 1, earlier, for a summary), there are now a number of cases where there is no corresponding phonological impairment (e.g., Caccappolo-van Vliet, Miozzo, & Stern, 2004a, 2004b; Tree & Kay, in press; see Coltheart, 2006, for discussion). Hence a phonological impairment cannot be the only mechanism by which phonological dyslexia arises.

In sum, while the attempts at simulation of phonological dyslexia to date (Coltheart et al, 1996; Harm & Seidenberg, 2001; Perry et al, 2007) can be regarded as useful preliminary investigations, there is a clear need for further simulation work. Any such simulation must:

1. Simulate reading behaviour using the same stimuli as those for the phonological dyslexic readers whose performance is being simulated.
2. Demonstrate that the computational model and the phonological dyslexic readers perform at similar levels of accuracy and, ideally, that performance of the computational model is sufficiently similar to that of the phonological dyslexic readers for there to be no statistical difference.
3. Be able to account for a variety of patterns of reading behaviour (e.g., differences in severity; presence/absence of phonological impairments; presence/absence of pseudohomophone advantage; see Table 1).

Here we present the results of further explorations of the simulation of phonological dyslexia through lesioning of the DRC model of reading (Coltheart et al., 2001). We first motivate the choice of parameters to lesion to impair reading performance, so that reading performance is affected in such a way as to produce the relative impairment in nonword reading that is typical of phonological dyslexia. Then we examine the effects of systematic lesioning of those parameters to examine the range of performance that DRC can simulate. Finally, we present data from three individuals with phonological dyslexia and determine how well

---

[2] This impairment of phonological processing can take many forms—it can be reflected in phonological errors in all word production tasks, or be restricted to phonological errors only in those tasks argued to be sensitive to such impairments such as repetition of lists of nonwords, phoneme segmentation, blending, and deletion tasks. For further discussion see Tree and Kay (in press).

DRC can simulate the reading behaviour of all three.

SYSTEMATIC LESIONING OF THE DRC MODEL

As described above, the defining feature of phonological dyslexia is impaired nonword reading. Therefore, in our attempts to simulate this disorder we need to consider which parameters of the DRC model, when varied, might be expected to selectively impair nonword reading.

This clearly excludes from consideration those parameters that are associated with the lexical route: the strength of connections between letter units and the orthographic lexicon, the orthographic lexicon, connections between the orthographic and phonological lexicons, the phonological lexicon, and the connections between the phonological lexicon and the phoneme units. In addition, while it is possible that impairments to the visual feature units or letter units might impair nonword reading to a greater extent than word reading, this level of impairment has been associated with pure alexia (letter-by-letter reading; e.g., Arguin & Bub, 1993). As discussed above, one prominent theory of phonological dyslexia proposes a phonological impairment, which results in greater difficulty with nonword reading than word reading. Hence, despite the fact that this component is used for both word and nonword reading, we consider lesions of the phoneme system, which could be considered one cause of such a phonological impairment. Specifically we investigate the effects of phoneme decay and phoneme noise on reading.

First, we examine the effects of lesions to the nonlexical pathway. There are three DRC parameters specific to this route: grapheme–phoneme correspondence rule (GPC) onset, GPC phoneme excitation, and GPC interletter interval (ILI). We discuss each in turn.

General simulation methodology

Stimuli

The stimuli used were those that had been used in testing all three of the phonological dyslexic readers described later. They comprised a set of monosyllabic words and nonwords. All stimuli are provided in the Appendix.

Words. These were 156 monosyllables drawn from an unpublished set of stimuli devised by David Howard (Howard & Franklin, 1988) and comprised regular and irregular words of high and low imageability.

Nonwords. The 217 monosyllabic nonwords were the monosyllables from a list used by Howard and Best (1996). They were divided into two sets: those that, while pronounceable, did not correspond to the phonology of an English word[3] when read by the grapheme–phoneme correspondence rules used in DRC (e.g., BEEL, BRABB, DREAN; labelled "nonwords", $n = 106$) and those that did correspond to the phonology of an English word (e.g., CHEEZE, AKE; labelled pseudohomophones, $n = 111$). These strict criteria led to some of the original Howard and Best stimuli being excluded from the analyses reported here, because, for example, some of the stimuli labelled as nonwords were letter strings that corresponded to items that were (rare) words in CELEX and therefore words in DRC's vocabulary. In addition, the pseudohomophones were subdivided into two sets: those that were orthographic neighbours of their word homophone (labelled high-similarity pseudohomophones, e.g., CHEEZE; $n = 29$) and those that were not orthographic neighbours (labelled low-similarity pseudohomophones, e.g., AKE, $n = 82$). This is a different (more stringent) classification of similarity to that of Howard and Best, and hence the numbers of stimuli in each set differ to those reported by Howard and Best.

---

[3] Where an English word was defined as a monosyllabic word in CELEX (Baayen, Piepenbrock, & van Rijn, 1993).

With its standard parameters as described below, the DRC model reads all stimuli accurately and in less than 500 cycles.

DRC model

The version of the DRC model we used in the simulations reported here was Version 1.1.4, using Language Set 1.1.2. This version had been improved in a number of minor ways from that of Coltheart et al. (2001) and differs in a number of mostly insignificant ways from that of Coltheart and colleagues. The model we used (Version 1.1.4) can be downloaded from http://www.maccs.mq.edu.au/~ssaunder/PDsims.

This site also contains a document describing the differences between the DRC model we used and the DRC model used by Coltheart et al. (2001), the differences between the language versions, and the stimuli used in our simulations. While detailed testing of the DRC1.1.4 model is still in progress, we have found that it correctly reproduces the benchmark effects simulated by the DRC model described by Coltheart et al. (2001): effects of frequency, regularity, position of regularity, neighbourhood size, pseudohomophony, lexicality, and length, and interactions of frequency with regularity, and lexicality with length, as well as strategy effects and the whammy effect.

The alterations to the DRC model meant that the default parameters for the model also needed some alterations from those reported by Coltheart et al. (2001) in order to make the new model behave in the same way as the original one. The default parameters for our version of the DRC model are given in Table 2. In order to simulate reading with no time pressure we require the parameter minimum naming phonology to be .9. This parameter specifies the minimum level of activation that must be reached by a phoneme in each position of the output (including the position of the first blank phoneme). We used a maximum number of cycles of 1,000—that is, if an item had not reached the minimum naming phonology threshold at this point, the response was considered to be an error (equivalent to a "no

Table 2. *DRC 1.1.4 standard parameters*

Parameter type	Parameter name	Standard setting
General	ActivationRate	.2
	FrequencyScale	.05
	MinReadingPhonology	.9
Feature level	FeatureLetterExcitation	.005
	FeatureLetterInhibition	.15
Letter level	LetterOrthlexExcitation	.07
	LetterOrthlexInhibition	.456
	LetterLateralInhibition	0
Orthographic lexicon (orthlex)	OrthlexPhonlexExcitation	.25
	OrthlexPhonlexInhibition	0
	OrthlexLetterExcitation	.3
	OrthlexLetterInhibition	0
	OrthlexLateralInhibition	.06
	OrthlexNoise	0
Phonological lexicon (phonlex)	PhonlexPhonemeExcitation	.1
	PhonlexPhonemeInhibition	0
	PhonlexOrthlexExcitation	.25
	PhonlexOrthlexInhibition	0
	PhonlexLateralInhibition	.07
	PhonlexNoise	0
Phoneme level	PhonemePhonlexExcitation	.04
	PhonemePhonlexInhibition	.16
	PhonemeLateralInhibition	.15
	PhonemeNoise	0
	PhonemeDecay	0
GPC route	GPCPhonemeExcitation	.038
	GPCInterletterInterval	13
	GPConset	22

Note: DRC 1.1.4 = Version 1.1.4 of the dual-route cascaded model.

response"). In these cases, we examined whether or not the sequence of phonemes that were most highly activated corresponded to the target sequence. In all cases reported below, except where otherwise noted, all targets that were not named (correctly or incorrectly) in 1,000 cycles had a string of phonemes that did not correspond to the target as the most active.

In speeded reading, normal subjects read words in less than 1/2 second, and DRC in 100 cycles. Hence 1,000 cycles corresponds to around 5 seconds. When testing the phonological dyslexic cases reported here, in order for testing to be manageable for both the people with phonological dyslexia and the experimenters, the time given for reading of each stimulus was no more than 5 seconds.

In all simulations we first used an extreme modification of the parameter value, to determine whether further simulation was warranted (see GPC onset for an example where only limited further simulation was required). This was then followed by systematic lesioning first using large steps in the manipulations of value of the parameter (what counts as large varies from parameter to parameter). Then areas of the parameter range where there were large changes in reading performance were investigated using smaller steps (see GPC ILI for an example of this). Effects of lexicality, pseudohomophony, and visual similarity on DRC's performance were evaluated statistically using Fisher exact test for deterministic simulations (where every simulation will always produce the same result) and for individual runs with simulations involving noise. Effects of these factors on DRC's performance on lesions involving noise were also examined across all 10 runs using a combined S test (Leach, 1979).

Modifying parameters of the nonlexical route

GPC onset

The nonlexical route is not immediately activated by letter units. The GPC onset parameter controls how many cycles will elapse before the first letter contributes activation to the nonlexical route. (This helps balance the relative strengths of the lexical and nonlexical routes.) If processing of a nonword by the nonlexical route is delayed by increasing the value of this parameter, it is plausible that a real-word neighbour of the target might become sufficiently activated to cause error. We therefore investigated how DRC performed when reading the word, nonword, and pseudohomophone stimuli when we changed the value of GPC onset from its default of 22 cycles to an extreme value of 400 cycles (as noted above, all stimuli are read accurately by the unlesioned model in less than 500 cycles and many in less than 400 cycles). Even with such an extreme manipulation, DRC only made one error. It incorrectly read the nonword SKILED as the phonological word /skIld/ (skilled). This error was present for values of GPC onset between 52 and 75 cycles,

with no further change in the model's accuracy after that point, although the number of cycles required to produce an output increased. The reason for this, perhaps surprising, lack of impact on nonword reading accuracy of even the most extreme manipulation of GPC onset lies in the default parameter settings of DRC. Under these parameter settings, due to strong inhibitory links from the letter level to the orthographic lexicon, presentation of a nonword rarely results in any word being activated in the orthographic lexicon and hence in the phonological lexicon. Thus, in the absence of any erroneous activation from the phonological lexicon to the phonemes, even with extreme delays to processing via the GPC route, the target phonemes of the nonword are still the most active.

In sum, it is evident that manipulating the lag between presentation of a stimulus (activation of the letter units) and the start of processing by the grapheme–phoneme correspondence rules is not a plausible method for reproducing phonological dyslexia.

GPC interletter interval

The nonlexical route processes letters serially, left to right. The GPC interletter interval (GPC ILI) parameter sets the number of cycles that intervene between the processing of each letter by the grapheme–phoneme rules (for example if GPC ILI is put to 0, all letters are processed at the same time). This was the parameter that Coltheart et al. (1996) manipulated to simulate L.B.'s phonological dyslexia. The default value is 13. Once again, we began with an extreme lesion (400 cycles) at which point all words are still read correctly, while all nonwords and pseudohomophones are incorrect. We then systematically explored the parameter range, first with large steps (25 cycles) and then determining those points at which critical change happened and examining these regions using smaller steps (5, 2, or 1). Figure 3 summarizes these simulations.

Manipulation of GPC ILI results in overt errors for nonwords and pseudohomophones. In other words, a series of phonemes including at least one nontarget phoneme reaches criterion

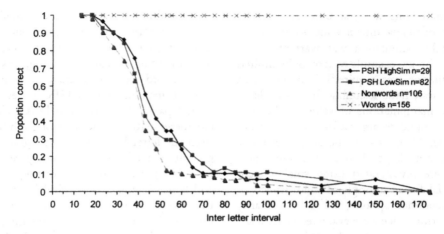

Figure 3. The effects of increasing the GPC interletter interval parameter on the accuracy of DRC's reading of words, nonwords, and high- and low-similarity pseudohomophones (PSH).

for output (minimum naming phonology of .9). However, it is clear that the effects on the different classes of nonword stimuli are neither linear nor predictable. Words remain correctly read throughout the parameter range. There is first a significant difference between words and nonwords at an interletter interval of 23 cycles (Fisher exact, two-tailed, $p < .001$) All nonwords and pseudohomophones reach floor by an interletter interval of 175 cycles. While in general nonwords are read less accurately than pseudohomophones, there are several regions in the parameter range where there is no significant difference in performance, despite performance being both off ceiling and not at floor. There is a significant difference in performance when GPC ILI ranges from 50 to 60 cycles (all comparisons, Fisher exact, one-tailed, $p < .02$). However, there are also other points in the parameter range where there is a significant pseudohomophone advantage including GPC ILI of 33 cycles (Fisher exact, one-tailed, $p = .046$) and GPC ILI of 44–45 cycles (Fisher exact, one-tailed, 44 cycles, $p = .026$; 45 cycles, $p = .042$). Correlation confirms that there is no systematic relationship between accuracy and the size of the advantage for pseudohomophones. This advantage is not related to overall nonword accuracy (including pseudohomophones, Pearson's correlation = .19, two-tailed, $p < .1$),

or nonword accuracy (excluding pseudohomophones, Pearson's correlation = .094, two-tailed, $p < .1$). While the correlation between pseudohomophone accuracy and the size of the pseudohomophone advantage is close to significance across all simulations (GPC ILI 13–400; Pearson's correlation = 2.45, two-tailed, $p = .061$), excluding those simulations where performance on nonwords and pseudohomophones is at ceiling or at floor, no hint of a relationship remains (Pearson's correlation = − .004, two-tailed, $p = .982$).

While at many points in the parameter range there is numerical advantage for pseudohomophones that are highly similar to their phonological "base" words, at no point is this significant (Fisher exact test, one-tailed, $p > .05$, all comparisons). In part this may be due to the relatively small number of high similarity items included ($n = 29$).

In sum, manipulation of the GPC interletter interval produces interesting and nonlinear patterns of reading impairment for nonwords. However, no significant effects of similarity of the pseudohomophone to its phonological base word emerged. Feedback from the lexical route to the phoneme level is more helpful for pseudohomophones than nonwords; hence pseudohomophones are generally read aloud more accurately. The role of the lexical route is confirmed by

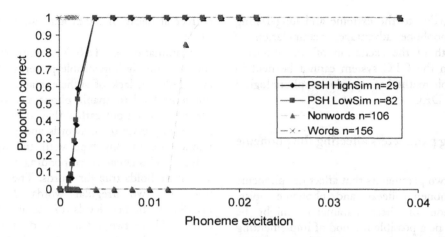

Figure 4. *The effects of decreasing the phoneme excitation parameter on the accuracy of DRC's reading of words, nonwords, and high- and low-similarity pseudohomophones (PSH).*

simulations where the weights on the excitatory links between the phonological lexicon and the phoneme nodes are set to zero, resulting in no input from the lexical route. Under these conditions, nonwords and pseudohomophones are equally affected by the manipulations of GPC interletter interval.

GPC phoneme excitation

This parameter specifies the strength of the input from the GPC system and the phoneme system. The higher GPC phoneme excitation, the quicker the activation builds within the phoneme system. The default value is .038. Figure 4 shows the effects of decreasing the phoneme excitation. Note that in contrast to GPC ILI (Figure 3, earlier) and the other simulations, lower values at the left of the figure represent a more severe lesion.

Reducing the strength of GPC phoneme excitation has no effect on reading accuracy until the value falls below .016. At this point nonword reading accuracy falls rapidly to floor by a value of .012. However, the strength of GPC phoneme excitation has to fall a great deal further (to below .006) before pseudohomophone reading is affected. This is a far more extreme pseudohomophone advantage than any reported in the literature, and seems unlikely ever to be observed in patients.

Closer examination of the output of DRC during this simulation reveals that the vast majority of responses to nonwords and pseudohomophones are in fact the equivalent of "no responses": cases where the threshold for producing a response had not been reached at the limit of 1,000 cycles. Nevertheless, the most active phonemes almost always corresponded to the target. Manipulating GPC phoneme excitation affects accuracy of nonwords and then pseudohomophones but only two overt errors are ever produced at the most severe lesions (.0004 and below). The pseudohomophone WROWNED (round) is produced as "drowned", and the nonword THACKED is produced as "thanked". The explanation for the lack of overt errors lies once again in the fact that, due to the default parameter settings, a letter string that corresponds to a nonword rarely results in activation of any word neighbours in the phonological lexicon. Hence, the only activation that will reach the phoneme level initially will be that from the GPC route, which is reduced due to the effects of the manipulation of GPC phoneme excitation parameter. Although there will be feedback from the phoneme level to the phonological lexicon, inhibition between nodes in the phonological lexicon will generally "damp down" activation and therefore prevent more than minimal activation of nontarget phonemes.

In sum, due to the extreme and long-lasting pseudohomophone advantage, manipulation of the strength of the excitation of the phoneme nodes from the GPC system cannot be held to be a plausible method of reproducing phonological dyslexia in DRC.

Modifying parameters affecting the phoneme level

There are two parameters that affect the phoneme system: phoneme decay and phoneme noise. Manipulation of these parameters might be thought to be a possible method of implementing the phonological impairment hypothesis in DRC.

Phoneme decay

Phoneme decay is a parameter that reduces the level of activation of the phoneme nodes by a fixed percentage between each cycle. It has a default value of zero. Figure 5 shows the effect of increasing the value of phoneme decay. There is no effect on reading accuracy until a value of .0008, at which point nonword reading falls quickly to floor. However, as for GPC phoneme excitation reported earlier, pseudohomophone reading remains implausibly unimpaired for some considerable time, before falling to floor with levels of decay of .0032 or higher. In addition, word reading shows impairment before pseudohomophones, with accuracy falling to around 50% correct at decay of .0023 and falling to floor at .0031.

Examination of DRC's output reveals that these seemingly implausible patterns of performance reflect a lack of sufficient activation at the phoneme level to enable phonemes to reach the criterion for output rather than overt errors. All of the responses to nonwords and pseudohomophones are of this type with the most active string of phonemes corresponding to the target. The same holds true for words. The only exceptions are two irregular words (PIQUE and HEIR) at higher levels of decay (.0023 and above). These two words also do not result in overt errors but the most activated phonemes do not correspond to the target phonemes.

In summary, manipulations of phoneme decay can be excluded as a means of simulating phonological dyslexia due to the implausible response pattern with its major feature being an extreme pseudohomophone advantage (pseudohomophones at ceiling and nonwords at floor).

Phoneme noise

The second parameter that can affect the phoneme system is phoneme noise. This allows random noise to be added to the activation of every phoneme node after the node's activation has been computed on the basis of activation from its inputs. This noise is sampled randomly from a normal distribution with a mean of zero and a

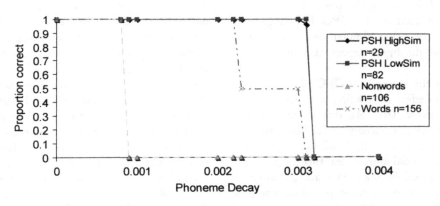

Figure 5. *The effects of increasing the phoneme decay parameter on the accuracy of DRC's reading of words, nonwords, and high- and low-similarity pseudohomophones (PSH).*

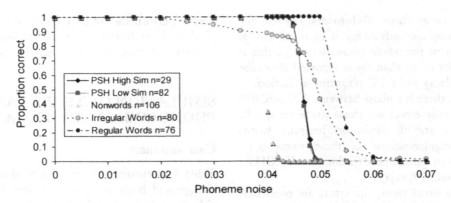

Figure 6. The effects on increasing the phoneme noise parameter on the accuracy of DRC's reading of words, nonwords, and high- and low-similarity pseudohomophones (PSH). The figure represents the average of 10 simulations.

standard deviation equal to the noise parameter. The default value of the noise parameter is zero: With this value for the parameter, the amount of noise added to a computed activation is always zero. As the noise added is random, there will be variation in the amount of noise and hence in the exact performance of the model on any single simulation. (This is unlike the previous simulations, which will always produce the same results.) Hence, for these simulations we present the average accuracy of 10 simulations at each point (see Figure 6).

There is little effect of manipulating phoneme noise on nonword reading until after a value of .035, at which point accuracy drops off rapidly. Nonwords are significantly worse than words from .04: phoneme noise = .04, combined S-test, $z = -32.71$, one-tailed, $p < .0001$; phoneme noise = .07, combined S-test, $z = 2.61$, one-tailed, $p = .005$. However, no individual run shows a significant advantage for words after a value of noise of .055: values of noise .060 and greater, Fisher exact test, one-tailed, $p > .05$ all comparisons. This is followed relatively soon after by the accuracy of pseudohomophones decreasing. There is a significant pseudohomophone advantage from values of noise of .040 to .049 (inclusive): combined S-test, $z > 3.80$, one-tailed, $p < .0001$; all comparisons. Examining the 10 individual simulation runs of DRC, every run shows a significant pseudohomophone advantage with values of noise from .040 to .048 (inclusive): Fisher exact test, one-tailed, $p < .03$, all comparisons. In contrast, there is only one point in the parameter range where there is a significant difference in accuracy between high- and low-similarity pseudohomophones—when phoneme noise has a value of .048: combined S-test, $z = -1.70$, one-tailed, $p = .044$. However, none of the 10 individual simulations show a significant visual similarity effect (Fisher exact tests, $p > .05$, all 10 simulations). Finally, as the noise levels increase still further, the accuracy of words also shows increasing impairment. Reading accuracy for irregular words is impaired first, followed by that of regular words. DRC shows a significant advantage for regular words with phoneme noise lesions from .025 to .055 inclusive: phoneme noise = .025, combined S-test, $z = 5.10$, one-tailed, $p < .001$; phoneme noise = .055, combined S-test, $z = 8.8$, one-tailed, $p < .001$. Every individual run of a lesion type shows a significant advantage for regular words from .035 to .055, inclusive (Fisher exact test, one-tailed, $p < .05$, all comparisons), with 2 (of the 10) runs showing significant effects when phoneme noise is .03 (Fisher exact test, one-tailed, $p = .040$, both runs).

There are two features of this simulation that are of slight concern. First, once again there is a parameter range (from .041 to .046) where the pseudohomophone advantage is extreme, but in the context of the whole parameter range this is a far smaller range than those reported above for phoneme decay and GPC phoneme excitation.

Second, there is a phase between .020 and .030 when the only errors are those made on words. The errors are all made on irregular words and are regularizations of these items (e.g., PALM/paːm/pronounced/pælm/; YACHT/jɒt/pronounced /jætʃt/).

In these simulations, the errors are overwhelmingly those where no overt response is produced. However, unlike the cases discussed earlier, here, the correct string of phonemes is not activated.

In summary, adding noise to the phoneme nodes produces impaired nonword and pseudohomophone reading as is typical of phonological dyslexia. In addition, at higher levels of noise, word reading also shows increasing levels of impairment, as is found in some (but not all) individuals with phonological dyslexia.

Summary of systematic lesioning

Systematic lesioning of the DRC model has shown that manipulation of some of the parameters produces patterns of reading behaviour that do not resemble any of the phonological dyslexic readers reported in the literature. Changing one parameter, GPC onset, failed to affect reading in any substantial way. Clearly, while not of concern, this lesion cannot be a means of simulating reading impairment. However, variation of two other parameters—GPC excitation and phoneme decay—produced patterns of performance (an extreme pseudohomophone advantage) that have never been observed in people with phonological dyslexia and in our view are unlikely to ever appear.

In contrast, manipulating GPC interletter interval and phoneme noise both affected reading accuracy in ways that have been observed in the reading performance of people with phonological dyslexia. However, this general observation is not sufficient. Can DRC simulate the precise performance of individuals with phonological dyslexia tested on the same stimuli? We address this issue using three single case studies.

SIMULATION OF THREE CASES OF PHONOLOGICAL DYSLEXIA

Case summary

Table 3 summarizes the biographical details and background language testing of the three individuals whose impaired reading we have sought to simulate. J.H. became aphasic following a stroke; his speech is well formed and fluent with some hesitations. He has extremely mild anomia with occasional word-finding difficulties in spontaneous speech. J.H. has intact general cognitive functioning (further details of J.H. can be found in Tree & Kay, in press). G.S.W. has a progressive language disorder which at post mortem was found to be the result of Alzheimer's pathology, though at the time of testing his cognitive functioning was intact, and his primary symptom was a severe anomia, presenting as circumlocutions (not phonological errors) in the context of fluent speech and unimpaired comprehension. N.J. has a longstanding nonfluent aphasia with output that would be characterized as agrammatic, but also has good cognitive function and comprehension (further details can be found in Inglis, 1999). While both J.H. and G.S.W. have good repetition of both words and nonwords, N.J. shows a slight impairment with words and clearly impaired nonword repetition. This would suggest that N.J. has the characteristics of a phonological impairment discussed earlier, while J.H. and G.S.W. have unimpaired phonological processing (for detailed discussion of this issue with respect to J.H., see Tree & Kay, in press).

Reading

All three were tested on (amongst many other lists) the same stimuli as those that were used in

Table 3. *Background language assessment for three cases of phonological dyslexia*

	n	J.H.	G.S.W.	N.J.
Age		62	71	68
Gender		*Male*	*Male*	*Male*
Previous occupation		*Manager*	*Manager*	*Journalist*
Aetiology (onset year)		*CVA (2002)*	*DAT*	*CVA (1983)*
Lesion		*Left anterior circulation infarct*	*Mild–moderate generalized atrophy*	*Right parietal infarct*
Comprehension				
Word–picture matching				
Spoken(PALPA 47)	40	—	0.98	1.00
Written (PALPA 48)	40	—	0.95	0.95
Pyramids and Palm Trees, 3 picture version	52	0.94	—	0.96
Synonym judgements				
Spoken (PALPA 49)	60	.87	0.95	0.93
Written (PALPA 50)	60		0.90	0.97
Test for Reception of Grammar	80	0.94	0.91	—
Picture naming				
Graded Naming Test	30	0.7	—	—
Boston Naming Test	60	—	0.48	0.52
Repetition (PALPA 9)				
Words	80	1.00	1.00	0.93
Nonwords	80	.98	.93	0.71
Reading				
Words (Regular & Irregular)				
PALPA 35	60	1.00	0.97	—
Coltheart & Leahy (1996)	60	—	0.95	0.90
Nonwords (PALPA 36)	24	0.54	0.17	0.04

Note: CVA = cerebrovascular accident. DAT = dementia of the Alzheimer's type. PALPA = Psycholinguistic Assessment of Language Processing in Aphasia (Kay, Lesser, & Coltheart, 1992). Pyramids and Palm Trees (Howard & Patterson, 1992). Test for Reception of Grammar (Bishop, 1982). Graded Naming Test (McKenna & Warrington, 1983). Boston Naming Test (Kaplan, Goodglass, & Weintraub, 1983).

the systematic lesioning of DRC described above. The results are shown in Table 4.[4]

The critical facts for the purposes of this paper are that all three men show the defining features of phonological dyslexia. All three have poor nonword reading in the context of relatively well-preserved word reading. Only G.S.W. and N.J. show a significant advantage for reading of pseudohomophones over control nonwords on this list. J.H. and G.S.W. show no significant difference between high- and low-similarity pseudohomophones with these stimuli, but N.J. does show a significant advantage for reading high-similarity pseudohomophones. None of these individuals show effects of regularity on word reading.

Simulation

For all three individuals we compared the simulations with the DRC computational model of reading reported above with the levels of performance shown by the patients, aiming to identify those that showed the "best fit". This procedure involved, first, visual inspection of the results of systematic lesioning above, focusing on the lesioning where either GPC interletter interval or

---

[4] While we have used a different classification of the pseudohomophones to that of Howard and Best (1996), the proportions correct in each category for the patients are remarkably similar across both classifications.

Table 4. *Reading performance of three phonological dyslexic cases for the lists used for simulation with DRC*

	n	J.H.	G.S.W.	N.J.
Words (Howard im × freq list)	156	1.00	0.91	0.76
Regular words	80	1.00	0.88	0.76
Irregular words	76	1.00	0.94	0.76
Regular vs. irregular words				
Fisher exact test, one-tailed, *p*		1.00	.174	.570
Nonwords	106	0.52	0.07	0.00
PSH	111	0.60	0.23	0.10
Nonwords vs. PSH				
Fisher exact test, one-tailed *p*		.137	.001	.001
High-similarity PSH	29	0.66	0.31	0.21
Low-similarity PSH	82	0.58	0.20	0.06
High- vs. low-similarity PSH				
Fisher exact test, one-tailed, *p*		.330	.155	.029

Note: DRC = dual-route cascaded model; im = imageability; freq = frequency. PSH = pseudohomophones.

phoneme noise was manipulated. The performance of the patients was compared to the lesioned model (for GPC interletter interval lesions and independently phoneme noise lesions), first focusing on nonword accuracy and then examining whether accuracy of pseudohomophones and words was "in the right ball park". Then, having determined which range of lesions were most similar to those of the patients, we determined which of these lesions produced the best fit on the basis of minimization of chi-square across the stimulus categories (nonwords, high-similarity pseudohomophones, low-similarity pseudohomophones, and words; Dell et al., 1997[5]), aiming to achieve both a nonsignificant overall chi-square but also no significant difference between DRC and patients for individual categories: McNemar's test for deterministic simulations, a series of McNemar's tests with each run for simulations including noise, combined with a Wilcoxon test looking at DRC's average accuracy per item compared to the patients. For the simulations involving noise where the model is not deterministic, having determined the best fit on the basis of 10 simulations, we then reran the closest simulations 20 times for final calculation of chi-square.

In all three cases we were able to identify lesioned versions of DRC where patient and simulation were not significantly different in their reading of nonwords or high-similarity or low-similarity pseudohomophones. We discuss each case in turn.

J.H.

Comparing J.H.'s reading pattern to the parameter ranges for phoneme noise (Figure 6 above), it is clear that at levels of phoneme noise close to .04, when DRC's nonword reading is at the same level as that of J.H. (52% correct), DRC's pseudohomophone reading is far superior (around 100% correct for DRC, cf. 60% correct for J.H.). Hence, lesions of phoneme noise were rejected as a plausible means of simulating J.H.'s phonological dyslexia. In contrast, when manipulation of GPC interletter interval (Figure 3 above) results in nonword reading of around 50% correct, at an interletter interval of around 40 cycles, pseudohomophone reading is slightly superior, and words remain at ceiling. This match from visual inspection was statistically evaluated. Total chi-square comparing J.H. and DRC was at a minimum when the GPC interletter interval parameter was set to 40 cycles (with all other parameters at their default values), as shown in Figure 7: $\chi^2(2) = 0.378$, $p = .827$. Not only was there no significant difference overall but there was also no significant difference between DRC and J.H.'s reading performance on any of the lists—words, nonwords, or pseudohomophones (all comparisons, McNemar's test, $p > .5$, two-tailed). The fit between J.H.'s

---

[5] If performance on any category is at ceiling or floor, chi-square is no longer valid, and hence this category was removed from the calculation.

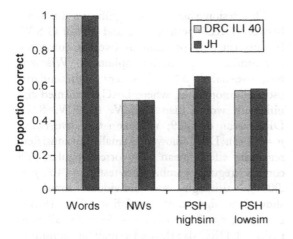

Figure 7. *Comparison of the performance of J.H. and DRC with GPC interletter interval (ILI) parameter increased to 40 cycles.*

performance and that of DRC with this lesion is remarkable—the only difference is that DRC names correctly two fewer high-similarity pseudohomophone stimuli and one fewer low-similarity pseudohomophones than J.H. Neither J.H. nor DRC shows a significant pseudohomophone advantage, nor a significant visual similarity effect, with these stimuli.

G.S.W.

As for J.H., visual inspection of the phoneme noise lesioned parameter range showed that when DRC's nonword reading was equivalent to that of G.S.W. (proportion correct = .07), pseudohomophones were far more accurate (DRC around 100% correct compared to G.S.W. 23% correct). Hence phoneme noise was rejected as a plausible means of simulating G.S.W.'s phonological dyslexia. However, examination of the GPC interletter interval parameter range showed that with an interletter interval of around 50–65, performance on nonwords and pseudohomophones approximated that of G.S.W. Once again, minimization of chi-square was used: An interletter interval of 61 cycles produced the best match to G.S.W.'s performance (Figure 8), although the overall chi-square was significant: $\chi^2(3) = 15.473$, $p = .001$. However, when performance was examined across nonwords and high- and low-similarity pseudohomophones alone (excluding words), once again 61 cycles produced the best match, with no significant difference between DRC and G.S.W.: $\chi^2(2) = 2.833$, $p = .243$. Individual comparisons confirmed that DRC's reading of nonwords and pseudohomophones was not significantly different to that of G.S.W. (all comparisons, McNemar's test, $p > .05$, two-tailed). Like G.S.W., DRC with GPC interletter interval increased to 61 cycles showed a significant pseudohomophone advantage (Fisher exact test, one-tailed, $p = .005$), but no significant effect of visual similarity (Fisher exact test, one-tailed, $p = .441$).

However, the simulation fails to capture one aspect of G.S.W.'s performance: DRC's word reading remained error free and significantly better than that of G.S.W. It is clear that with a lesion to a single parameter, DRC is unable to capture G.S.W.'s performance. However, in conventional (noncomputational) cognitive neuropsychology, multiple points of impairment are frequently proposed for a particular individual in order to account for the, often complex, patterns of behaviour. Such an account would not assume a priori that all of G.S.W.'s language behaviour could be attributed to the impairment to the sublexical route (which causes his poor nonword

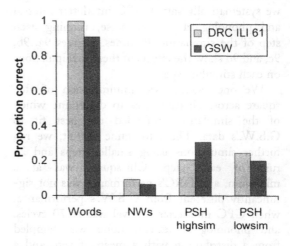

Figure 8. *Comparison of the performance of G.S.W. and DRC with GPC interletter interval (ILI) parameter increased to 61 cycles.*

reading). A lesion involving only modification of the GPC interletter interval parameter could not account for the fact that G.S.W. has a marked anomia despite having unimpaired performance on assessments of semantic processing. The account given for such an anomia would be generally agreed to be an impairment at the level of the phonological output lexicon or the links between the semantic system and the output lexicon (e.g., Caramazza & Hillis, 1990; Nickels, 1997, 2001; Raymer & Gonzalez Rothi, 2002). G.S.W. shows an effect of imageability on reading: stimuli from Howard and Franklin, 1988; high imageability 95%, low imageability 81%, $\chi^2(1) = 9.572$, $p = .002$. It follows that either of these levels of impairment could be implicated in both his anomia and his reading impairment. However, as DRC does not have an implemented semantic system further simulations are by necessity restricted to manipulations of parameters affecting the phonological output lexicon. We therefore explored further simulations where DRC's reading performance was examined when not only GPC interletter interval was increased, but also noise was added to the computation of activation levels of each node in the phonological lexicon (to simulate an anomia).

Following exploration using a subset of the stimuli to establish the relevant parameter range, we systematically varied GPC interletter interval and phonological lexicon noise, running each step of the simulation 10 times. Figures 9a, 9b, 9c, and 9d show the effects of these manipulations on each stimulus type.

We once again used minimization of chi-square across all categories to determine which of the simulations provided the best fit to G.S.W.'s data. Then, to refine the fit, we ran further simulations using smaller steps and 20 runs of each step. Chi-square was at a minimum, and DRC's performance was not significantly different from G.S.W.'s performance, when GPC interletter interval was at 70 cycles, and phonological lexicon noise was sampled from a distribution with a mean of zero and a standard deviation of .07875; see Figure 10a; $\chi^2(3) = 7.51$, $p = .057$.

This lesion showed no significant difference between DRC's performance and that of G.S.W. for any category of stimulus (words, nonwords, low-similarity pseudohomophones; Wilcoxon test, two-tailed, $p > .05$) except high-similarity pseudohomophones, where DRC performed significantly worse than G.S.W. (G.S.W. 8/29; DRC mean 4.25/29; Wilcoxon test, two-tailed, $p = .043$). DRC showed a small but consistent regularity effect (mean 92% correct regular, 87% correct irregular, combined S-test, $z = 4.8$, $p < .0001$), although no individual simulation showed a significant regularity effect (Fisher exact test, $z = 0.13-1.55$, $p = .45 - .06$, all comparisons). DRC also showed a small but significant visual similarity effect but in the reverse direction (mean 15% correct high similarity, 20% correct low similarity; combined S-test, $z = 2.98$, $p = .001$), but once again no individual simulation was significant (Fisher exact test, $z = 0.07-1.58$, $p = .47 - .06$, all comparisons). Finally, DRC showed a significant pseudohomophone advantage (combined S-test, $z = 6.22$, $p < .0001$) with four individual simulations also showing a significant advantage (Fisher exact test, $z > 1.90$, $p < .03$).

Although this lesion provided the lowest chi-square (with other lesions around this area also showing nonsignificant chi-square and similar patterns), one other lesion is of interest. When GPC interletter interval was at 67 cycles, and phonological lexicon noise was .0795, overall chi-square was significant; see Figure 10b; $\chi^2(4) = 8.74$, $p = .033$, although no stimulus category showed a significant difference between G.S.W.'s performance and DRC's mean item accuracy (Wilcoxon, two-tailed, $p > .05$). However, this simulation led to 25% (5/20) individual runs showing a significant difference between G.S.W. and DRC in nonword accuracy (G.S.W., 7/106; DRC mean, 15.35/106; McNemar's test, $p < .05$). This reflects the balancing act that we encountered in simulating G.S.W.'s performance using the combination of these two variables. Adding noise to the phonological lexicon not only reduces word-reading accuracy but also improves nonword reading and impairs high-similarity pseudohomophone reading. Hence, when noise is

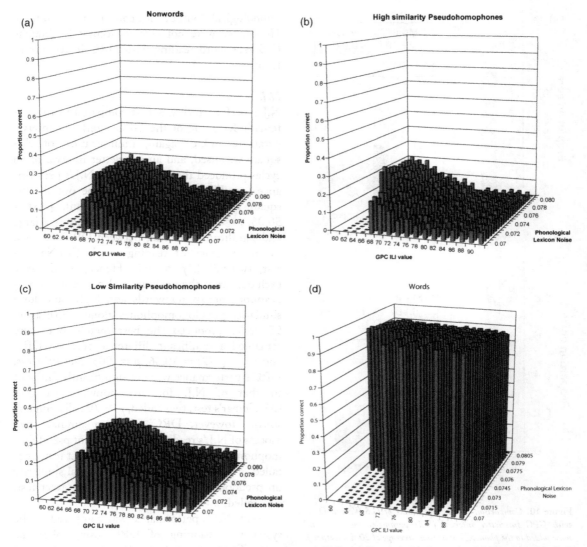

Figure 9. *Summary of simulations varying both GPC interletter interval (ILI) and phonological lexicon noise. (a) Nonword stimuli. (b) High-similarity pseudohomophone stimuli. (c) Low-similarity pseudohomophone stimuli. (d) Word stimuli (note: For clarity of effects, the elevation on this figure is different from that of 9a–9c).*

added GPC interletter interval must also be increased to reduce DRC's nonword reading—however, increasing GPC interletter interval sufficiently to simulate nonword reading results in high-similarity pseudohomophones being excessively impaired compared to G.S.W. There is no point in the parameter range where both G.S.W.'s nonword and his high-similarity pseudohomophone reading can be simulated.

In summary, G.S.W.'s reading could not be adequately simulated with a single lesion to the sublexical route: While nonword and pseudohomophone reading were simulated, word reading was not. However, his poor picture-naming performance motivated the addition of an additional lesion at the level of the phonological lexicon or access to this lexicon from semantics. DRC is only able to simulate the former

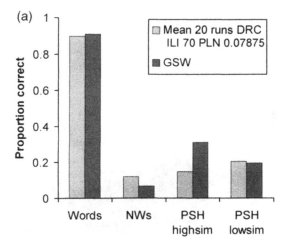

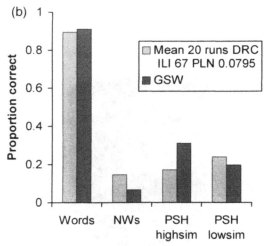

Figure 10. *Comparison of the performance of G.S.W. and DRC with GPC interletter interval (ILI) parameter increased and noise added to the phonological lexicon (average of 20 simulations).*

possibility; the addition of noise to the phonological lexicon resulted in a pattern that was not significantly different overall, but there was a significant difference for one category of stimuli—high-similarity pseudohomophones. While a different lexical lesion (e.g., from semantics to the phonological lexicon) could be better able to simulate G.S.W.'s anomia, it is unlikely that this would affect word reading substantially (as the route from orthographic input lexicon to phonological output lexicon remains intact). Hence, we were not able to accurately simulate G.S.W.'s word reading with DRC in its current form.

N.J.

N.J.'s performance was first compared to the systematic lesioning of the GPC interletter interval parameter. Once again, minimization of chi-square was used, and an interletter interval of 95 cycles produced the best match to N.J.'s performance (see Figure 11). However, the overall chi-square was large and highly significant; $\chi^2(3) = 50.06$, $p < .0001$. It is clear that there is a large and significant difference between DRC and N.J. in the accuracy of reading words (McNemar's test, two-tailed, $p < .05$). Hence, words were excluded from the analysis, and performance was examined across nonwords and high- and low-similarity pseudohomophones alone. Once again 95 cycles produced the best match, but there remained a significant difference between DRC and N.J., $\chi^2(2) = 10.66$, $p = .005$. Nevertheless, DRC's performance was not significantly different to that of N.J. for any nonword category (McNemar's test, two-tailed, $p > .05$, all comparisons). However, DRC failed to simulate two aspects of N.J.'s reading: the significant pseudohomophone advantage (DRC: Fisher exact test, one-tailed, $p = .099$) and the effect of visual similarity on pseudohomophones (DRC: Fisher exact test, one-tailed, $p = .466$).

Next, N.J.'s performance was compared to the systematic lesioning of DRC using phoneme noise. The best match was found when phoneme noise was set to a value of .048 (see Figure 12). There was no significant difference between N.J.'s and DRC's performance overall, $\chi^2(3) = 6.60$, $p = .086$. This simulation also showed no significant difference in performance between DRC and N.J. for nonwords (N.J., 0/106; DRC, mean 0/106, SD 0) and high-similarity pseudohomophones (N.J., 6/29; DRC, mean 4.4/29, SD 1.52; individual runs, McNemar's test, two-tailed, $p > .05$, all comparisons; average of 20 runs, Wilcoxon matched pairs, two-tailed, $p = .320$). No single run of DRC showed a significant

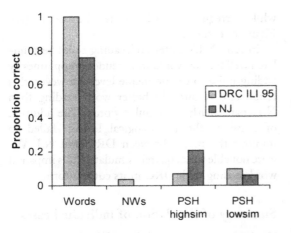

Figure 11. *Comparison of the performance of N.J. and DRC with GPC interletter interval (ILI) parameter increased to 95 cycles.*

difference for low-similarity pseudohomophones (N.J., 5/82; DRC, mean 8.7/82; SD 2.20; individual runs, McNemar's test, two-tailed, $p > .05$, all comparisons) although the average of 20 runs was significantly different to N.J.'s performance (Wilcoxon matched pairs, two-tailed, $p < .05$). Like N.J., DRC showed a significant pseudohomophone advantage overall and for every individual run (DRC, mean 0% correct nonwords, 12% correct pseudohomophones, combined S-test, $z = 16.27$, $p < .0001$; individual runs:

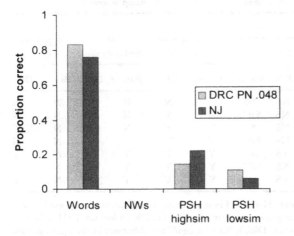

Figure 12. *Comparison of the performance of N.J. and DRC with the phoneme noise (PN) parameter set to 0.048 (average of 20 simulations).*

Fisher exact test, $z > 2.45$, $p < .008$) and a significant effect of visual similarity overall (mean 15% correct high similarity, 11% correct low similarity, combined S-test, $z = -2.82$, $p = .002$) and for two individual runs (Fisher exact test, $p > 1.69$, $p < .045$).

DRC's accuracy for words (83%) was close to that of N.J. (76%). This difference was not significant overall (N.J., 119/156; DRC, mean 129.85, SD 2.87; average of 20 runs, Wilcoxon matched pairs, two-tailed, $p = .140$). N.J.'s performance was significantly different to that of 3 of the 20 individual runs of DRC (McNemar's test, two-tailed, $p < .05$). In addition, unlike N.J., DRC showed a highly significant regularity effect, overall and for every individual run (mean 100% correct regular, 67% correct irregular, combined S-test, $z = -24.38$, $p < .0001$; individual runs, Fisher exact test, $z > 4.89$, $p < .0001$). This difference is further reflected in the fact that while DRC's irregular word reading is not significantly different from that of N.J. (individual runs, McNemar's test, two-tailed, $p > .05$, all comparisons; average of 20 runs, Wilcoxon matched pairs, two-tailed, $p = .068$), N.J.'s regular word reading is far worse than that of DRC (individual runs, McNemar's test, two-tailed, $p < .0001$, all comparisons; average of 20 runs, Wilcoxon matched pairs, two-tailed, $p < .001$).

Thus, while manipulating phoneme noise provided a better overall simulation of N.J.'s performance than manipulating GPC interletter interval, both simulations showed marked differences in performance, including significantly better word reading than N.J. Like G.S.W., N.J. is impaired on the Boston Naming Test. While some of N.J.'s errors are phonological errors as would be predicted by a phoneme level impairment, others are semantically related or perhaps (by virtue of his agrammatism) single word circumlocutions. It is most likely that these are the result of a high-level semantic impairment as on more stringent tests of semantics to those reported here (e.g., abstract word–picture matching, Shallice & McGill, personal communication) N.J. performs outside normal limits. He also shows an imageability effect in word reading (Howard &

Franklin, 1988; high imageability 77%, low imageability 55%, Fisher exact test, two-tailed, $z = 3.5192$, $p = .0004$). Unfortunately, until semantic representations are implemented in DRC it will not be possible to simulate N.J.'s anomia precisely. Nevertheless, we explored adding noise to the phonological lexicon (as we had with G.S.W.) in addition to manipulating phoneme noise, to simulate N.J.'s anomia. The best fit was provided when phoneme noise was .048, and phonological lexicon noise was .002; however, it did not result in a better fit (as judged by overall chi-square) than phoneme noise alone, $\chi^2(3) = 6.96$, $p = .073$. There was little difference in the comparison for word reading overall between N.J. and DRC compared to the pure phoneme noise lesion alone (4 runs showed a significant difference, McNemar's test, two-tailed, $p < .05$; average 20 runs, Wilcoxon $p = .222$). Both regular (all 20 runs showed a significant difference, McNemar's test, two-tailed, $p < .0001$; average 20 runs, Wilcoxon $p = .0001$), and irregular words showed a significant difference (3 runs showed a significant difference, McNemar's test, two-tailed, $p < .05$; average 20 runs, Wilcoxon $p = .032$). As before, DRC showed a marked regularity effect—with regular words remaining at ceiling while irregular words were impaired (see Figure 6, earlier).

In sum, N.J.'s pattern of reading could be simulated well for nonwords and pseudohomophones by adding noise to the phoneme level. However, this lesion also resulted in better word reading than N.J., particularly for regular words. The addition of noise to the phonological lexicon failed to improve the match between DRC and N.J. We were not able to adequately simulate N.J.'s impaired word reading with DRC in its current form.

Summary of simulation of individual cases

We have explored the ability of the DRC computational model of reading to simulate the patterns of reading shown by three individuals with phonological dyslexia. These individuals show a range of different behaviours typical of the literature. A summary of the effects shown by the patients and the relevant DRC simulations is provided in Table 5. We demonstrated that a single lesion in the DRC model could successfully simulate the key characteristic of impaired reading of nonwords and pseudohomophones using identical stimuli, with word reading remaining relatively less impaired. In addition, we demonstrated that the

Table 5. *Comparison of performance of lesioned versions of the DRC model and three patients with phonological dyslexia*

		Chi-square					Pseudohomophone advantage		Visual similarity effect		Regularity effect	
Patient	Lesion	Overall	Nonwords	High sim PSH	Low sim PSH	Words	Patient	DRC	Patient	DRC	Patient	DRC
J.H.	ILI 40	NS	NS	NS	NS	NS	N	N	N	N	N	N
G.S.W.	ILI 61	SIG	NS	NS	NS	SIG	Y	Y	N	N	N	N
	ILI 68 + PLN 0.07875	NS	NS	SIG	NS	NS	Y	Y	N	N	N	Y/N
N.J.	ILI 61	SIG	NS	NS	NS	SIG	Y	N	Y	N	N	N
	PN 0.048	NS	NS	NS	NS	SIG	Y	Y	Y	Y	N	Y
	PN 0.048 + PLN 0.002	NS	NS	NS	NS	SIG	Y	Y	Y	Y	N	Y
	PN 0.048 + PLN 0.004	NS	NS	NS	NS	NS	Y	Y	Y	N/Y	N	Y

Note: DRC model = dual-route cascaded model; ILI = GPC interletter interval; PN = phoneme noise; PLN = phonological lexicon noise; high sim PSH = high-similarity pseudohomophones (neighbours of their base words in DRC); low sim PSH = low-similarity pseudohomophones (not neighbours of their base words in DRC); NS = no significant difference in chi-square statistic between DRC and patient; SIG = significant difference in chi-square statistic between DRC and patient; N = no significant effect shown; Y = significant effect shown. For DRC Y/N or N/Y reflects the fact that for noise lesions, the overall pattern may have been different to that of individual runs.

different patterns of effects that were shown by the patients across nonwords and high- and low-similarity pseudohomophones could also be simulated by DRC. However, there was no single parameter that could account for the reading of all three individuals: The successful simulation required manipulation of a parameter associated with the nonlexical route in two cases (GPC interletter interval; J.H., G.S.W.) and a parameter associated with the phoneme level for the other case (phoneme noise; N.J.). The fact that different lesions were required is consistent with the data from assessment: N.J. showed features of a phonological impairment and required a phoneme level lesion (phoneme noise), while J.H. and G.S.W. showed no evidence of a phonological impairment and were successfully simulated using an impairment to the sublexical route (GPC interletter interval).

While DRC was able to simulate nonword and pseudohomophone reading successfully, word reading was less successfully simulated. Two of the individuals showed reduced accuracy in word reading. However, these individuals also had a co-occurring anomia, and hence an additional impairment causing impaired activation of lexical entries in the phonological output lexicon is probable. The cause of this impaired activation could be at the semantic level, in the activation of the lexicon from semantics, or at the level of the lexicon itself. Only the last of these can be implemented in DRC. This lesion (phonological lexicon noise) improved the "fit" in one case (G.S.W.) but disparities still remained between DRC and patient performance.

GENERAL DISCUSSION

We have presented the results of further explorations of the simulation of phonological dyslexia through lesioning of the DRC model of reading (Coltheart et al., 2001). We first motivated the choice of parameters lesioned so that reading performance might be affected in such a way as to produce the relative impairment in nonword reading that is typical of phonological dyslexia.

These parameters were of two types—those affecting the nonlexical reading mechanism (GPC onset; GPC interletter interval; GPC phoneme excitation) and those affecting the phoneme level (phoneme decay and phoneme noise). We then examined the effects on reading performance of systematic lesioning of those parameters.

GPC onset

Increasing the number of cycles that are waited before the first letter becomes activated in the nonlexical route had virtually no effect on reading accuracy, and hence GPC onset was rejected as a plausible mechanism for simulating phonological dyslexia.

GPC phoneme excitation

This parameter manipulates the strength with which GPC output activates the phoneme system. Reducing the strength of this parameter resulted in few overt responses; incorrect phoneme strings were activated but not sufficiently to reach the criterion for production. The major feature of this manipulation was an extreme pseudohomophone advantage: Pseudohomophones remained error free while nonwords were at floor for a large portion of the parameter space. As such an extreme pattern has not been reported in the literature, and in our view is unlikely to occur, we suggest that manipulation of the strength of the excitation of the phoneme nodes from the GPC rules cannot reproduce phonological dyslexia in DRC.

Phoneme decay

Reducing the level of activation of the phoneme nodes by an increasingly large percentage between each cycle resulted in few overt responses; incorrect phoneme strings were activated but not sufficiently to reach the criterion for production. Once again, the major feature of this manipulation was an extreme pseudohomophone advantage: We note above that such an extreme pattern is unlikely to occur in people with phonological dyslexia. We therefore suggest that, in DRC, a phoneme decay lesion cannot reproduce phonological dyslexia.

GPC interletter interval
This was the parameter that Coltheart et al. (1996) manipulated to simulate L.B.'s phonological dyslexia. We also found that manipulation of the number of cycles that intervene between the processing of each letter by the grapheme–phoneme rules produced patterns of reading behaviour that closely mirror those shown by individuals with phonological dyslexia. Words remain unimpaired, while nonword and pseudohomophone reading slowly declines in accuracy. In addition, while at some points in the parameter space pseudohomophones are found to be read significantly better than nonwords, at other points there is no significant difference. This mirrors the fact that both patterns are found in the literature. However, no significant effect of the visual similarity between pseudohomophones and their base words was found at any point in the parameter range. We return to this point below.

Phoneme noise
Adding random noise to the activation of the phoneme nodes also produces patterns of reading behaviour that reflect the patterns seen in phonological dyslexia: Nonwords are generally more impaired than words, and at some points in the parameter space there is a significant advantage for pseudohomophones over nonwords and a small but significant effect of visual similarity for pseudohomophones. However, at higher levels of noise this lesion also affects word reading; hence, a phoneme noise lesion cannot simulate the pattern of phonological dyslexia where nonword and pseudohomophone reading is severely impaired but word reading remains relatively unimpaired. In addition, word reading shows a strong effect of regularity—regular words remain unimpaired while irregular words are impaired. This is not an effect that has been reported in cases of phonological dyslexia (although it is not always tested). We discuss this in further detail below.

In summary, these systematic investigations have demonstrated the range of performance that lesioning the DRC model can account for. In addition, more complex manipulations of multiple parameters could illuminate further patterns. For example, while there are several manipulations that show significant pseudohomophone advantages, few showed a significant advantage for pseudohomophones that are orthographic neighbours of their base word (high-similarity pseudohomophones) using these stimuli. However, it is possible that combinations of "lesioned" parameters might result in such a pattern. We discuss the (lack of) effects of similarity in further detail below.

Simulation of the reading performance of three cases of phonological dyslexia

In addition to the systematic exploration of the lesioned parameter space, we set out to determine whether DRC could simulate the reading behaviour of particular individuals with phonological dyslexia. We argued that there were three requirements for simulations of phonological dyslexia, all of which we fulfilled. First, simulations must use the same stimuli as those for the phonological dyslexic readers whose performance is being simulated. Second, performance of the computational model and the phonological dyslexic readers should be similar, and ideally there should be no statistically significant difference in the pattern of performance between model and phonological dyslexic readers: For all three patients there was (at least) one simulation that resulted in no significant difference between DRC and the patients for chi-square across all categories of stimuli. Finally, we argued that the simulations should be able to account for a variety of patterns of reading behaviour, including, for example, differences in severity, presence/absence of phonological impairments, or presence/absence of pseudohomophone advantage. The systematic lesioning demonstrated that DRC could indeed account for a variety of different behaviours, and this was extended in the case studies we presented. The individuals showed a range of severity in nonword and pseudohomophone reading impairment and varied as to whether a significant pseudohomophone advantage or a visual similarity effect was present. Nonetheless, DRC was able to successfully replicate the sublexical reading performance of all three.

We now consider these simulations in further detail. Firstly, we consider just the results with nonwords and pseudohomophones. For all three patients, it was possible for DRC to simulate performance levels of patients on nonwords, high-similarity pseudohomophones, and low-similarity pseudohomophones exactly, in the sense that neither the overall chi-square across the three categories, nor the comparison of DRC with patient for any one of the categories, was ever significant. For G.S.W., this was done by setting GPC interletter interval to 61: Here both G.S.W. and DRC showed a pseudohomophone advantage but no visual similarity effect. For J.H. this was done by setting GPC interletter interval to 40: Here neither J.H. nor DRC showed a pseudohomophone advantage or a visual similarity effect. With N.J., manipulation of the parameter GPC interletter interval did not produce a successful simulation, but manipulation of phoneme noise did: Here both N.J. and DRC showed a pseudohomophone advantage and also an effect of visual similarity. Hence these simulations captured very well the quantitative and qualitative aspects of the reading of nonwords and pseudohomophones in all three patients.

Where the simulations have failed is in their efforts to simulate imperfect word reading (present in two patients, G.S.W. and N.J.).

For G.S.W., introducing noise to the phonological lexicon (in addition to lengthening GPC interletter interval) did cause DRC to make errors with words and produced a simulation in which over the four categories of stimuli the overall chi-square test of the difference in performance between G.S.W. and DRC was not significant; however, this simulation was unsatisfactory in three ways. First, here DRC showed a small but significant accuracy advantage for regular words over irregular words, and G.S.W. did not; second, now DRC differed significantly from G.S.W. in accuracy of reading high-similarity pseudohomophones; third, now DRC showed a visual similarity effect, problematic for two reasons—G.S.W. did not show such an effect, and the DRC effect is in the wrong direction.

For N.J., the phoneme noise manipulation, although it produced extremely accurate simulations of performance for the nonwords and the two types of pseudohomophone, also incorrectly generated a regularity advantage for word-reading accuracy.

The occurrence of a regularity effect in the these simulations with G.S.W. and N.J. is not surprising. Introducing noise within the phonological lexicon will impair the operation of the lexical route but not the operation of the nonlexical route. Regular words enjoy support from the nonlexical route that irregular words do not, and this support would help counteract the effects of the noisy computations within the lexical route. Introducing noise within the phoneme system would also be expected to harm irregular words more then regular words because regular words enjoy two sources of activation to every one of their correct phonemes, whereas for irregular words at least one phoneme is getting incorrect activation (from the nonlexical route).

The problem to be solved in future work is therefore clear: What form of lesioning of DRC can there be that would cause words to be read wrongly and yet would not introduce a regularity advantage? That is the aspect of G.S.W.'s and N.J.'s reading that we have failed to simulate.

Phonological dyslexia and phonological impairment

The "phonological hypothesis" of phonological dyslexia, at least in its strong form, argues that the cause of the reading impairment in phonological dyslexia is a phonological impairment. Because of the differences in their processing demands, this phonological impairment affects nonword reading more than word reading and similarly impairs nonword reading more than nonword repetition. The simulations we performed demonstrated that a phonological impairment (addition of noise to the activation of the phoneme units) can indeed simulate the patterns observed in phonological dyslexia. Furthermore, such a lesion impairs nonword reading more than word reading. We demonstrated that for one phonological dyslexic individual, N.J., an impairment at this level could precisely simulate his performance. N.J. has impaired nonword repetition, as is predicted by a phonological impairment, but that nonword repetition is not as severely impaired as nonword reading. Hence, our data entirely support the fact that for some individuals with phonological dyslexia, a phonological impairment is the cause of their poor nonword reading.

However, our simulations using DRC have also demonstrated that phonological dyslexia can be the result of nonphonological impairments—within the dual-route theory these are impairments to the nonlexical reading process (as has been shown in the past, e.g., Coltheart et al., 1996). We could not simulate the performance of two phonological dyslexic individuals, J.H. and G.S.W., with a phonological impairment—the lesion required in order to simulate their nonword reading performance would have resulted in significantly more accurate pseudohomophone reading performance than either showed. In contrast, impairment to the nonlexical routine (in the form of a lengthened GPC interletter interval) could simulate their nonword and pseudohomophone reading precisely. For J.H., his unimpaired word reading was also successfully simulated, although for G.S.W. there was an additional phonological lexicon impairment (motivated by his poor naming ability).

We argue that no single level of impairment (neither phonological nor nonlexical) can account for the reading impairments of all individuals with phonological dyslexia, rather that different individuals will have different impairments (and combinations of impairments) that together provide the spectrum of patterns found in phonological dyslexia.

Challenges and future directions

While the simulations reported above have successfully demonstrated a number of features of phonological dyslexia, there are a number of features that remain to be explored further.

First, few of the lesioned simulations using DRC showed effects of visual similarity on performance: Pseudohomophones that were not neighbours of their basewords (low-similarity pseudohomophones, e.g., DAW) were generally no less accurate than those that were neighbours of their basewords (high-similarity pseudohomophones, e.g., DETT). Although it is possible that the lack of significance was due to the relatively small numbers of high-similarity stimuli, it is important to note that the absence of effects of visual similarity effect in the majority of the simulations is not (currently) a problem. DRC does show a visual similarity effect with (some) manipulations of phoneme noise. Moreover, the patient who showed an effect of visual similarity on performance was best simulated by the lesion that also resulted in a similarity effect (phoneme noise = 0.048).

Of course, if individuals are found who show visual similarity effects with these stimuli (classified as we have), but with different degrees of severity or different relative patterns of nonword and pseudohomophone reading to N.J., then the challenge would be for DRC to simulate these effects. The fact that other data show different patterns may be dependent on several factors including the definition of visual similarity and the extent to which stimuli are matched on other variables (see for discussion Harm & Seidenberg, 2001). It is not the aim of this paper to argue for whether these effects exist, or indeed whether they are truly orthographic in nature. Our aim is simply to demonstrate that DRC can replicate the patterns shown by particular individuals with phonological dyslexia on a particular set of stimuli using a particular definition of visual similarity.

There are other factors that have also been argued to influence patient performance which have not been addressed in our simulations. For example, Beauvois and Derouesne (1979) also showed an effect of "graphemic complexity" on nonword reading (complex graphemes being those where more than one letter corresponds to a single phoneme e.g., CH). In two of their phonological dyslexic patients, this variable affected nonword reading accuracy, but pseudohomophony did not; in the other two patients, there was no effect of graphemic complexity, but there was an effect of pseudohomophony. It remains to be seen whether future simulation using the DRC model could capture this double dissociation. Furthermore, some but not all phonological dyslexic readers show effects of how concrete or abstract a word is on word-reading accuracy (Coltheart, 1996)—N.J. is such an individual. Effects of concreteness are generally attributed to the semantic system. Thus, simulation of these effects will necessitate the implementation of the semantic route within the DRC model.

In addition, the focus of simulations of acquired dyslexia, to date, has been on replication by computational models of the relative level of reading accuracy of the dyslexic subjects. However, accuracy is not the only variable of interest when examining the reading patterns of dyslexic subjects: Error type is equally important (e.g., visual, semantic, or regularization errors) as is the degree of similarity between the target and the error. Yet in the reports of simulations there has been only cursory mention of error types. For example, in their discussion of simulation of surface dyslexia Coltheart et al. (1996, p. 29) note that "All the errors made by the lesioned model were regularization errors". Perry et al. (2007) also determine the rate of regularization errors in their simulations of surface dyslexia. However, neither Coltheart et al. (1996) nor Perry et al. (2007) examine error types in the simulation of phonological dyslexia. Unless the (lesioned) model can be shown to reproduce the actual error types produced by acquired dyslexic subjects, and also the relative rates of occurrence of these error types, it cannot be said to have fully simulated the dyslexics' performance. While DRC has successfully simulated the reading accuracy of J.H., G.S.W., and N.J., it falls short in replicating the nature of the errors. For example, while the overt errors produced by DRC are overwhelmingly real words (GPC ILI lesions: average proportion of errors 86% words, 14% nonwords), the phonological dyslexic individuals tend to produce relatively large numbers of nonword errors (G.S.W. 40%, J.H. 44%, N.J. 62% nonwords). Clearly, there remains some way to go before DRC can be said to entirely replicate the behaviour of the patients. As is the norm in cognitive neuropsychology, the discrepancy in performance between models and patients can be used to inform our understanding of both.

Finally, this paper has explicitly focused on testing the adequacy of the DRC computational model of reading. However, similar simulations have been performed using other computational models of reading aloud: the PDP "triangle model" (Plaut et al., 1996; see http://www.cnbc.cmu.edu/~plaut/PMSP.data) and the CDP+ model (Perry et al., 2007). As discussed earlier, the triangle model has been applied to the simulation of phonological dyslexia using the assumption that this form of acquired dyslexia is always caused by an impairment at the phonological level. The data provided here suggest that this is unlikely to always be the case. The CDP+ model (Perry et al., 2007) also simulated phonological dyslexia but without using stimuli identical to that of the patients—we have argued here that this is critical. Hence, the way is open for further work with both of these models to investigate whether they can perform as well as or better then the DRC model in simulating the data from our three patients and other patients with phonological dyslexia.

Manuscript received 30 November 2006
Revised manuscript received 12 June 2007
Revised manuscript accepted 15 June 2007
First published online 26 September 2007

REFERENCES

Arguin, M., & Bub, D. N. (1993). Single-character processing in a case of pure alexia. *Neuropsychologica*, *31*, 435–458.

Baayen, R. H., Piepenbrock, R. H., & van Rijn, H. (1993). The CELEX Lexical Database [CD-ROM]. Philadelphia: University of Pennsylvania, Linguistic Data Consortium.

Beauvois, M. F., & Derouesne, J. (1979). Phonological alexia: Three dissociations. *Journal of Neurology, Neurosurgery & Psychiatry, 42*, 1115–1124.

Berndt, R. S., Haendiges, A. N., Mitchum, C. C., & Wayland, S. C. (1996). An investigation of nonlexical reading impairments. *Cognitive Neuropsychology, 13*, 763–801.

Bishop, D. V. (1982). *TROG: Test for reception of grammar.* Manchester, UK: University of Manchester.

Bub, D., Black, S., Howell, J., & Kertesz, A. (1987). Speech output processes and reading. In M. Coltheart, G. Satori, & R. Job (Eds.), *The cognitive neuropsychology of language.* London: Lawrence Erlbaum Associates.

Caccappolo-van Vliet, E., Miozzo, M., & Stern, Y. (2004a). Phonological dyslexia: A test case for reading models. *Psychological Science, 15*, 583–590.

Caccappolo-van Vliet, E., Miozzo, M., & Stern, Y. (2004b). Phonological dyslexia without phonological impairment? *Cognitive Neuropsychology, 21*, 820–839.

Caramazza, A., and Hillis, A. E. (1990). Where do semantic errors come from? *Cortex, 26*, 95–122.

Coltheart, M. (Ed.). (1996). Phonological dyslexia [Special issue]. *Cognitive Neuropsychology, 13*, 749–940.

Coltheart, M. (2005). Modelling reading: The dual route approach. In M. J. Snowling & C. Hulme (Eds.), *The science of reading.* Oxford, UK: Blackwell Publishing.

Coltheart, M. (2006). Acquired dyslexias and the computational modelling of reading. *Cognitive Neuropsychology, 23*, 96–109.

Coltheart, M., Curtis, B., Atkins, P., & Haller, M. (1993). Models of reading aloud: Dual route and parallel-distributed-processing approaches. *Psychological Review, 100*, 586–608.

Coltheart, M., Langdon, R., & Haller, M. (1996). Computational cognitive neuropsychology. In B. Dodd, L. Worral, & R. Campbell (Eds.), *Evaluating theories of language: Evidence from disordered communication.* London: Whurr Publishers.

Coltheart, M., & Leahy, J. (1996). Assessment of lexical and nonlexical reading abilities in children: Some normative data. *Australian Journal of Psychology, 48*, 136–140.

Coltheart, M., Rastle, K., Perry, C., Langdon, R., & Ziegler, J. (2001). DRC: A dual route cascaded model of visual word recognition and reading aloud. *Psychological Review, 108*, 204–256.

Cuetos, F., Valle-Arroyo, F., & Suarez, M.-P. (1996). A case of phonological dyslexia in Spanish. *Cognitive Neuropsychology, 13*, 1–24.

Dell, G. S., Schwartz, M. F., Martin, N., Suffran, E. M., & Gagnon, D. A. (1997). Lexical access in normal and aphasic speech. *Psychological Review, 104*, 801–838.

Derouesne, J., & Beauvois, M. F. (1979). Phonological processing in reading: Data from alexia. *Journal of Neurology, Neurosurgery and Psychiatry, 42*, 1125–1132.

Derouesne, J., & Beauvois, M. F. (1985). The "phonemic" stage in the nonlexical reading process: Evidence from a case of phonological alexia. In K. Patterson, J. C. Marshall, & M. Coltheart (Eds.), *Surface dyslexia* (pp. 399–457). Hove, UK: Lawrence Erlbaum Associates.

Farah, M. J., Stowe, R. M, & Levinson, K. L. (1996). Phonological dyslexia: Loss of a reading specific component of the cognitive architecture? *Cognitive Neuropsychology, 13*, 849–868.

Funnell, E. (1983). Phonological processes in reading: New evidence from acquired dyslexia. *British Journal of Psychology, 74*, 159–180.

Funnell, E. (1987). Morphological errors in acquired dyslexia: A case of mistaken identity. *Quarterly Journal of Experimental Psychology, 39A*, 497–539.

Goodall, W. C., & Phillips, W. A. (1995). Three routes from print to sound: Evidence from a case of acquired dyslexia. *Cognitive Neuropsychology, 12*, 113–147.

Harm, M. W., & Seidenberg, M. S. (1999). Reading acquisition, phonology, and dyslexia: Insights from a connectionist model, *Psychological Review, 106*, 491–528.

Harm, M. W., & Seidenberg, M. S. (2001). Are there orthographic impairments in phonological dyslexia? *Cognitive Neuropsychology, 18*, 71–92.

Howard, D., & Best, W. (1996). Developmental phonological dyslexia: Real word reading can be completely normal. *Cognitive Neuropsychology, 13*, 887–934.

Howard, D., & Patterson, K. (1992). *Pyramids and Palm Trees: A test of semantic access from pictures and words.* Bury St Edmunds, UK: Thames Valley Test Company.

Howard, D., & Franklin, S. (1988). *Missing the meaning?: A cognitive neuropsychological study of processing of words by an aphasic patient.* Cambridge, Massachusetts: MIT Press.

Inglis, A. L. (1999). The complexity of "asyntactic" comprehension: Investigations of an unusual dissociation between passives and object relatives. *Journal of Neurolinguistics, 12*, 41–77.

Kaplan, E. F., Goodglass, H., & Weintraub, S. (1983). *The Boston Naming Test.* Philadelphia: Lea & Febiger.

Kay, J., Lesser, R., & Coltheart, M. (1992). *Psycholinguistic assessment of language processing in aphasia*. London: Lawrence Erlbaum Associates.

Leach, C. (1979). *Introduction to statistics: A nonparametric approach for the social sciences*. New York: Wiley.

Manis, F. R., Seidenberg, M. S., Doi, L., McBride-Chang, C., & Peterson, A. (1996). On the basis of two subtypes of developmental dyslexia. *Cognition, 58*, 157–195.

McKenna, P., & Warrington, E. K. (1983). *The Graded Naming Test*. Windsor, UK: NFER-Nelson.

Nickels, L. A. (1997). *Words fail me: Spoken word production and its breakdown in aphasia*. Hove, UK: Psychology Press.

Nickels, L. A. (2001). Producing spoken words. In B. Rapp (Ed.), *A handbook of cognitive psychology*. New York: Psychology Press.

Patterson, K. (1982). The relation between reading and phonological coding: Further neuropsychological observations. In A. W. Ellis (Ed.), *Normality and pathology in cognitive functioning* (pp. 77–111), London: Academic Press.

Patterson, K. (2000). Phonological alexia: The case of the singing detective. In E. Funnell (Ed.), *Case studies in the neuropsychology of reading* (pp. 57–83). Hove, UK: Lawrence Erlbaum Associates.

Patterson, K., & Marcel, A. (1992). Phonological ALEXIA or PHONOLOGICAL alexia? In J. Alegria, D. Holender, J. Junca de Morais, & M. Moreau (Eds.), *Analytic approaches to human cognition* (pp. 259–274). Amsterdam: North Holland.

Patterson, K., Suzuki, T., & Wydell, T. N. (1996). Interpreting a case of Japanese phonological dyslexia. *Cognitive Neuropsychology, 13*, 803–822.

Perry, C., Ziegler, J. C., & Zorzi, M. (2007). Nested incremental modeling in the development of computational theories: The CDP+ model of reading aloud. *Psychological Review*.

Plaut, D. C., McClelland, J. L., Seidenberg, M. S., & Patterson, K. (1996). Understanding normal and impaired word reading: Computational principles in quasi-regular domains. *Psychological Review, 103*, 56–115.

Raymer, A. M., & Gonzalez-Rothi, L. J. (2002). Clinical diagnosis and treatment of naming disorders. In A. E. Hillis (Ed.), *The handbook of adult language disorders*. Hove, UK: Psychology Press.

Sasanuma, S., Ito, H., Patterson, K., & Ito, T. (1996). Phonological alexia in Japanese: A case study. *Cognitive Neuropsychology, 13*, 823–848.

Seidenberg, M. S. (1995). Visual word recognition: An overview. In P. Eimas & J. L. Miller (Eds.), *Handbook of perception and cognition: Language*. New York: Academic Press.

Seidenberg, M. S., & McClelland, J. L. (1989). A distributed, developmental model of word recognition. *Psychological Review, 96*, 523–568.

Tainturier, M., & Rapp, B. (2003). Is a single graphemic buffer used in reading and spelling? *Aphasiology, 17*, 537–562.

Temple, C., & Marshall, J. (1983). A case study of developmental phonological dyslexia. *British Journal of Psychology, 74*, 517–533.

Tree, J. T., & Kay, J. (in press). Phonological dyslexia and phonological impairment: An exception to the rule? *Neuropsychologia*.

Zorzi, M., Houghton, G., & Butterworth, B. (1998). Two routes or one in reading aloud? A connectionist dual-process model. *Journal of Experimental Psychology: Human Perception and Performance, 24*, 1131–1161.

APPENDIX

List of stimuli

Nonwords

arl	arth	beel
blarce	blowned	brabb
broap	chaut	clarnt
dorle	drean	drede
drok	enck	firce
ghyte	gich	gleek
glud	gredd	grek
guk	heej	jirb
kence	kessed	kipe
kirm	knaik	knait
lunce	murm	nanned
neak	neech	nong
norl	nowth	nunth

ortch	pamp	pawce	chork	daw	dich
peath	ped	pene	drabb	duk	faice
plame	pliph	ploo	fawce	frend	ghoast
plown	poom	porlt	glarce	grede	hed
possed	prak	prunt	highnd	horlt	inck
raun	rem	rorn	jooce	jurm	kain
rowce	saice	sar	kaiv	karf	kene
scrore	sellth	serce	kepped	kirce	klame
sharme	sharnce	sheal	kleigh	kliph	kloo
shirch	shrord	skiled	knek	koak	koan
skreat	slomp	slowt	korl	kossed	krool
spairce	speeze	starsk	kwak	kyned	lanned
stawn	stend	strair	lardge	mowce	nighce
strea	strort	tain	perce	pessed	phacked
taiv	tarf	tarm	phar	pharme	pharst
tepped	thacked	thar	pheal	phined	phlarsk
tharst	thined	thocks	phocks	phond	phrea
thond	thork	townd	phrord	phyne	pigg
trool	tult	tweigh	rainge	rec	rong
tyned	uke	vooce	roth	sarm	seej
wainge	weace	whoast	shaut	skairce	skawn
wighce	woth	yec	skowt	skwair	strore
			toom	url	urth
			wraik	wrait	wredd
			wroap	wrok	wrowned
			wunce		

High-similarity pseudohomophones

bleek	meak
cheeze	mowth
chirch	munth
deel	reech
dett	streat
frunt	swomp
grean	teath
hellth	tence
hownd	thwort
jem	tipe
kamp	tirm
kar	virb
klown	waun
kult	whyte
leace	

Regular words

bad	best
blade	boot
came	cite
coke	cult
dark	dear
dirge	ditch
dog	drum
dull	fault
flag	fond
fraud	got
graph	green
guess	gun
hale	hand
hawk	heat
herd	horse
join	keen

Low-similarity pseudohomophones

ake	artch	bayce
blud	borle	chiled

kept	kiss	chalk	cold
lamb	lawn	dead	debt
less	lure	done	dough
mink	mood	dread	eye
moon	nail	false	flood
nest	night	foot	ghost
pare	park	give	glove
plant	plead	gold	gone
plug	prince	grass	grow
queen	red	grown	head
ridge	save	heir	hose
saw	seat	key	know
seen	side	lose	love
sing	sloe	low	meant
song	square	mild	monk
stain	steam	palm	pear
stool	thorn	pique	post
till	trip	push	put
trout	truck	quart	real
trust	vain	realm	shoe
vest	vine	shone	sign
wheat	wife	slow	snow
		son	soul
		soup	steak
		swamp	thwart
		tomb	tongue

Irregular words

aisle	ate	vague	vase
aunt	bear	want	war
beau	blood	warn	wash
book	bowl	watt	wolf
bread	break	wood	wool
brief	build	worm	worse
bush	cause	wrath	yacht

Visuospatial planning in the travelling salesperson problem: A connectionist account of normal and impaired performance

Simone Cutini
University of Padova, Padua, Italy

Andrea Di Ferdinando
National Research Council, Rome, Italy

Demis Basso
University of Pavia, Pavia, Italy, and University of Pisa, Pisa, Italy

Patrizia Silvia Bisiacchi and Marco Zorzi
University of Padova, Padua, Italy

Planning is a fundamental cognitive function frequently employed in common daily activities. The Travelling Salesperson Problem (TSP), in which participants decide what order between a number of locations optimizes total travel distance, is a paradigm that allows the study of planning and strategy choice. In the TSP, subjects adopt visuo-spatial heuristics to perform the task and operate a continuous monitoring to adapt their behaviour. We present a connectionist model of the TSP that simulates bottom-up and top-down influences observed in the execution of the task. The model accounts for the continuous monitoring observed in healthy participants, and, after a simulated lesion, it also accounts for the decrease of heuristic switching observed in frontal patients and in normal subjects under repetitive transcranial magnetic stimulation (rTMS) over frontal lobe.

Planning is a fundamental cognitive function that is frequently employed in common daily activities. It involves the ability to produce mental representations of future behaviour prior to acting and to reason about its consequences in order to properly choose among the possible courses of action (G. Cohen, 1988). As a complex form of human problem solving, planning requires the cooperation between several cognitive processes, including strategy formation, coordination of mental functions, recognition of goal attainment and storage of representations that can guide behaviour from the initial to the goal state (Carlin et al., 2000).

Correspondence should be addressed to Marco Zorzi, Dipartimento di Psicologia Generale, University of Padova, via Venezia 8, 35131 Padua, Italy (E-mail: marco.zorzi@unipd.it).

This study was supported by grants from Ministero dell'Istruzione Università e Ricerca (MIUR) (P.S.B. and M.Z.) and the University of Padova (M.Z.). D.B. was supported by Grant FIRB RBNE018ET9_003. We are grateful to Rick Cooper and to one anonymous reviewer for their helpful comments and suggestions.

Planning is often carried out in small units during task performance, rather than in a distinct stage devoted to building an entire plan before its execution (e.g., Basso, Bisiacchi, Cotelli, & Farinello, 2001; Phillips, Wynn, McPherson, & Gilhooly, 2001). Planning requires an incremental process in most real-world situations due to limitations in working memory and control processes. The incremental aspect of planning implies that the plan made before the execution is mainly incomplete or inconsistent (e.g., Hayes-Roth & Hayes-Roth, 1979). Initial decisions can be later modified to develop an efficient strategy—that is, an opportunistic combination of simple schemas that can be activated or inhibited when needed. Indeed, human planning is based on cognitive heuristics (Hayes-Roth & Hayes-Roth, 1979; Hirtle & Gärling, 1992; Murakoshi & Kawai, 2000) that can be defined as behavioural schemas that approximate the correct solution using fewer cognitive resources than does performing an exhaustive algorithm. An efficient strategy requires continuous monitoring during task performance in order to allow for on-line changes of heuristic.

The Tower of Hanoi (ToH), since its introduction as a task to study planning from the information-processing perspective (Simon, 1973), and the Tower of London (ToL; Shallice, 1982) are the most widely used tools to assess planning in cognitive studies. The ToH is a complex problem-solving task that has demonstrated sensitivity to prefrontal lobe function and dysfunction (e.g., Goel & Grafman, 1995). The specific executive processes recruited for successful performance (or, conversely, impaired in prefrontal dysfunction) have been a subject of debate, but it is generally agreed that this task taps planning, working memory, and inhibition (e.g., Goel & Grafman, 1995; Roberts & Pennington, 1996). The ToL, derived from the ToH, has gained high popularity among neuropsychologists. Indeed, the results obtained with the ToL led Shallice and his colleagues (Norman & Shallice, 1986; Shallice, 1982) to the development of their influential theory of executive functions. The ToL has proved extremely valuable for investigating executive functions and their disorders following brain damage, and it has been employed in a wide range of studies. However, a number of potential shortcomings of the ToH/ToL have emerged in the recent years with regard to the planning component of the task. First, although sensitive to frontal lobe damage, the ToL has been questioned with regard to its ability to reliably measure planning skills (Kafer & Hunter, 1997). Second, instructions and cueing given to the participants (e.g., on-line planning vs. full mental plan, or prior information about the minimum number of moves; Phillips et al., 2001; Unterrainer, Rahm, Leonhart, Ruff, & Halsband, 2003), forward-thinking (Owen, Downes, Sahakian, Polkey, & Robbins, 1990; Ward & Allport, 1997), and problem structuring (Goel & Grafman, 1995, 2000; Kaller, Unterrainer, Rahm, & Halsband, 2004) seem to strongly influence task performance.

A task that strongly involves planning and is also representative of many real-world situations is the Travelling Salesperson Problem (TSP): Given a space in which a set of interconnected towns is represented by locations on a map, the task consists in finding an itinerary that visits each town exactly once, returning to the starting town, ensuring that total travelled distance is as short as possible. The TSP is a paradigmatic example of nonpolynomial combinatorial optimization (Lawler, Lenstra, Rinnooy Kan, & Shmoys, 1985) that has been extensively studied by mathematicians and computer scientists but much less by psychologists. Nevertheless, there has been a growing interest in the analysis of human performance in TSP-like problems (Cadwallader, 1975; Gärling, 1989, 1994). The TSP task is thought to be a suitable tool to investigate planning because it can be solved with multiple close-to-optimal solutions that can be evaluated with respect to the single perfect solution (MacGregor & Ormerod, 1996). More specifically, it is reasonable to assume that the TSP involves spatial planning, a type of problem solving that requires optimizing the performance against several constraints, based on spatial elements in the environment. In comparison with other planning tasks, spatial planning requires a stronger interaction between central and peripheral processes: Visual, attentional, and motor issues play a fundamental role, in addition to reasoning, for determining the final behaviour.

Previous studies employing a visually presented TSP (MacGregor & Ormerod, 1996; Polivanova, 1974; Vickers, Butavicius, Lee, & Medvedev, 2001) have revealed that human performance is determined by global perceptual properties to which the visual system is naturally attuned. These properties have been shown to influence the choice of spatially based heuristics that are used to perform TSP tours (Barr & Feigenbaum, 1981; Hirtle & Jonides, 1985; MacGregor & Ormerod, 1996; McNamara, 1992). A variant of the TSP, first proposed by Hirtle and Gärling (1992), introduces a distinction between start- and end-point so that participants have to perform an open path instead of a loop. Behavioural data collected using a computerized version of the open-ended TSP, the Maps Test (Basso, 2005; Basso et al., 2001), showed that three distinct spatially based heuristics are mainly used by human participants to perform the TSP task: the nearest neighbour (NN) heuristic (Barr & Feigenbaum, 1981), the straight-line heuristic (Hirtle & Gärling, 1992), and the direction heuristic (Basso et al., 2001). The first states that each location is recursively chosen on the basis of the minimum local distance from the current position. The straight-line heuristic states that a set of collinear points will be taken in order along the line, rather than starting in the middle. This heuristic has been observed in specific partial configurations, in which points approximately formed a line; it has been frequently observed in conjunction with heuristics based on following a specific direction, such as the direction heuristic. The latter takes place when subjects start from a location placed on a border and reach the next locations following one of the main spatial axes (horizontal or vertical) and a direction (up or down for vertical axis, left or right for horizontal axis). It has been introduced as a modification from the zig-zag heuristic described by Hirtle and Gärling (1992), because a definition provided on the basis of human reference points has been proven to be more suitable in the description of the performance (Bryant, Tversky, & Franklin, 1992). In the Maps test (Basso et al., 2001), the starting city is located typically in the upper left corner, and the end city is located in the bottom right corner. Thus, the horizontal movement was described as representative of a direction right heuristic (DR), whereas the vertical movement was described as a direction down heuristic (DD). The same configuration of TSP is used in the present study to allow us a direct comparison with the behavioural data. Figure 1 shows an example of application of the three heuristics (NN, DR, and DD) considered in the present study.

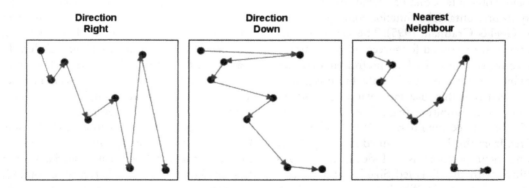

Figure 1. *The figure shows three different tours of the same TSP pattern. Each tour is representative of the use of a unique heuristic along the whole pathway. These heuristics have been implemented in the model using three different saliency maps that bias the choice of the order in which cities are visited.*

The fundamental role of planning in the TSP is confirmed by studies that investigated the effect of lesions or transient neurodisruption of the prefrontal cortex upon performance in the Maps test (Basso et al., 2001; Basso et al., 2006). One key aspect of the TSP task regards the coordination of different heuristics. The use of a single heuristic is inappropriate for most of the maps, and a change of heuristic is necessary to obtain a close-to-optimal solution. Indeed, this is what Basso et al. (2001) observed in the performance of healthy participants. However, the ability to change heuristic during the pathway to optimize performance was markedly impaired in frontal traumatic brain injured (fTBI) patients. A similar pattern of impaired performance was shown by healthy adults under inhibitory repetitive transcranial magnetic stimulation (rTMS) stimulation on the prefrontal cortex (PFC; Basso et al., 2006). Both frontal patients and healthy participants under rTMS did not show the normal pattern of continuous planning: Instead of switching heuristic during the execution of the task, they seemed to apply simple strategies based on only one heuristic (see Figure 2). These results are consistent with the notion that the PFC is a crucial brain area for planning processes and strategy formation (for recent neuroimaging evidence, see Fincham, Carter, van Veen, Stenger, & Anderson, 2002; Newman, Carpenter, Varma, & Just, 2003) and that its lesion is associated with planning deficits (Grafman, 1989, 1995; Lezak, 1995; Shallice, 1982, 1988).

One possible explanation for the finding that lesion or reversible neurodisruption of the PFC leads to a planning deficit in the Maps test is that this region would be crucial for the inhibition of the current heuristic (Basso et al., 2001) whenever a change is necessary to achieve a close-to-optimal performance. That is, the heuristic chosen at the beginning of the task was likely to be kept until the end with no signs of any further consideration of the possible alternative options. These findings are consistent with the presence of perseverative behaviour in frontal patients (Duncan, 1986; Luria, 1980). This behavioural rigidity has been explained in the attention to action (ATA) model by Norman and Shallice (1986; see Cooper & Shallice, 2000, for a computational model) as a

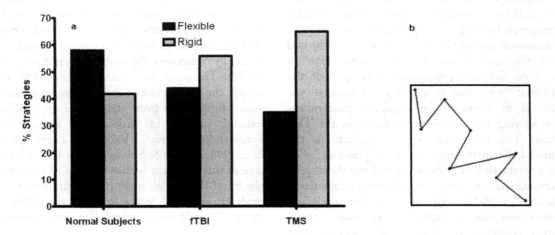

Figure 2. (a) Percentage of strategies used in the open version of the TSP task (data replotted from Basso et al., 2001). From left to right: normal subjects, traumatic frontal lobe brain-injured patients (fTBI), and healthy participants under repetitive transcranial magnetic stimulation (rTMS). Flexible strategies imply the use of at least two different heuristics to perform a given tour. Rigid strategies are the result of using a single heuristic for the whole tour. The results highlight that while normal subjects often use flexible strategies, subjects under rTMS and traumatic frontal lobe brain injured patients use rigid strategies more often than flexible strategies. (b) An example of the open-version TSP.

disruption of the supervisory attentional system (SAS). The SAS is thought to perform the inhibition of the behavioural schema automatically selected for the execution and the switch to another schema that emerged as more suitable to the actual situation. In the study of Basso and colleagues (2001), the impairment observed in fTBI patients was interpreted as a failure in controlling and modifying the plan in the execution phase, rather than pure lack of planning. According to this account, patients achieved an acceptable solution because the contention scheduling process was preserved. They therefore selected an appropriate heuristic based on the initial spatial analysis of the TSP configuration. However, a SAS failure did not allow them to modify the initial plan to optimize the execution of the task. As a consequence, their performance was far from optimal because the behavioural rigidity prevented heuristic switches. Therefore, the main drawback of this deficit is a lower level of optimization, which is indexed by longer tours in comparison to the performance of healthy controls.

In summary, there are three fundamental aspects of the TSP task that deserve consideration: (a) the incremental aspect of spatial planning, (b) the presence of visuo-spatial heuristics triggered by bottom-up processes that influence behaviour during the execution of the task, and (c) the crucial role of the frontal lobe to endorse flexible performance. The goal of the present work was to develop a computational model to simulate the cognitive mechanisms underlying the human performance in the TSP task. The main aim was to replicate in the model the incremental aspect of planning, with the interaction of bottom-up and top-down processes, and its disruption following a simulated lesion. A challenging aspect of our modelling enterprise was to implement all these features in a connectionist model that dispenses with the use of explicit rules to guide behaviour. The descriptive adequacy of the model was tested in terms of its fit to the behavioural data from both healthy participants and patients with frontal lobe lesions.

A CONNECTIONIST MODEL OF THE TSP

The computational model is composed by three interconnected modules, with a broad hierarchical organization and feedback connections, which loosely simulate the occipito-parieto-frontal circuit involved in the TSP task (see Figure 3). These components comprise: (a) a visual module, in which the input pattern is processed by Gabor filters (Jones & Palmer, 1987) to simulate the processes responsible for visuo-spatial analysis and perceptual grouping; (b) a competitive selection module that simulates the internal dynamics for the choice of the heuristic; (c) a spatial module encoding the to-be-visited locations and controlling the execution of the pathway in a sequential manner. Moreover, the presence of saliency maps, recurrent connections, and inhibitory mechanisms allows us to simulate the incremental aspect of visuo-spatial planning and the interaction of bottom-up and top-down processes.

Descriptive overview

In building the model we adopted a nested incremental modelling approach (see Perry, Ziegler, & Zorzi, 2007). This strategy, often neglected in psychology, consists in building a new computational model by combining the best features of previous models. Therefore, two main components of our model, the visual module and the spatial module, were simply taken from state-of-the-art computational models of vision and action (Di Ferdinando, Casarotti, Vallar, & Zorzi, 2005; Lee, 1996; Pouget & Snyder, 2000). One advantage of this approach is that, in spite of the complexity of the model, most of the parameters are predetermined and do not influence the ability of the model to fit the human data in this particular task.

Input to the model consists of a digital image displaying the points that constitute the TSP configuration. The patterns reproduced those used for the computerized version of the TSP task (the Maps test; Basso et al., 2001), where the starting

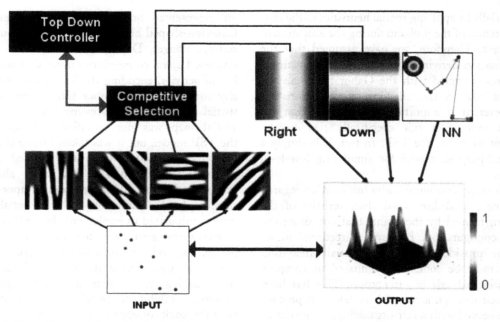

Figure 3. *The architecture of the model. The figure shows the different modules as well as their connectivity.*

point is located in the top-left corner, and the endpoint is located in the bottom-right corner of the display. The output consists in a sequence of spatial commands, each encoding the next goal position in space (that is, the position of the next point to be visited). Thus, the model simulates both spatial and temporal aspects of task execution.

One important component of our modelling enterprise was to provide a computational account of the generation of spatial heuristics and of their influence on the planning process. Perceptual mechanisms clearly assume a critical function as the source of bottom-up influence in the generation of spatial heuristics and their successful use. MacGregor and Ormerod (1996) argued that the detection of the minimum path is an innate and natural tendency determined by the human visual system. Along with their suggestion, we hypothesized that the selection of the most appropriate heuristic for a given pattern is highly determined by its spatial configuration. A pattern elicits a particular response depending on contextual information, such as the strength of spatial relationships between the constitutive elements. This hypothesis is therefore linked to perceptual organization. Perceptual organization can be defined as the ability to impose structural organization on sensory data, so as to group sensory primitives arising from a common underlying cause (Carreira et al., 1998).

The neural substrates of perceptual grouping reside in the primary visual areas of the cortex. Simple cells in area V1 respond as linear spatio-temporal filters, and their receptive fields have been successfully modelled with Gabor filters (Daugman, 1988; Jones & Palmer, 1987; Lee, 1996), a set of Gaussian kernels modulated by a sinusoidal planewave. In our model the input patterns are processed with a set of Gabor filters to provide a computational account of the neural mechanisms involved in perceptual grouping (also see Carreira et al., 1998). Gabor filter processing provides the extraction of the salient features of the patterns, in particular their orientation. Humans solve the visually presented TSP essentially by applying spatial heuristics to the representation of the problem during the execution of the task. Therefore, we have assumed that the information deriving from the salient directional features extracted with the Gabor filters plays a crucial role in the selection of the heuristics. However, it is important to point out that the visual module is not specifically tied to the current model of the TSP. In fact, it is simply a general-purpose model for simulating low-level vision.

Visual processing provides information regarding the spatial-directional characteristics of the pattern formed by the points that constitute the TSP configuration. However, directional information provided by different visual orientation maps must be somehow compared to compute the principal axis of orientation. This has been achieved through a competitive selection process, implemented with a self-organizing, competitive-learning network. Competitive learning (Rumelhart & Zipser, 1985) sorts patterns sharing similar properties into the same category, and it can be viewed as a clustering technique. The network, presented with the input features detected by the visual-processing module, discovered three main categories of input images. The final version of the competitive network had therefore three output nodes, each encoding one specific image category. Each category was then associated to one of the three spatial heuristics.

Heuristics are selected by the competitive process based on bottom-up, salient perceptual information, but they must be turned into a signal that biases the execution of the pathway. The biasing signal in the model is provided by a saliency map, which is simply a gradient of activation influencing the spatial target map. Thus, the three heuristics (NN, DR, and DD) have been implemented in terms of different saliency maps. Activation of the spatial target map is driven by the retinal (input) image but it is modulated by the saliency map, so that a particular area is enhanced according to the selected heuristic: the upper region for DD heuristic, the left region for DR heuristic, and the space surrounding the last city visited for the NN heuristic. Spatial locations are represented on the spatial target map by Gaussian-shaped hills of activity (i.e., population coding; Pouget, Dayan, & Zemel, 2000, for a review). Lateral connections ensure that only one hill of activity, encoding the location of the next city to be visited, becomes fully active on the spatial map during processing. Note that the spatial map was not specifically designed for the TSP model, but it was taken from a previous computational model of visually guided movements (Di Ferdinando et al., 2005; also see Pouget & Snyder, 2000, for a similar approach); accordingly, no parameters of the spatial map were manipulated to implement the TSP model.

Every time a city is visited, the corresponding population code is subsequently suppressed in the spatial target map so that it will not be selected again during the sequential selection process. Moreover, inhibition spreads to the input map via a feedback connection to decrease the saliency of the visited city (i.e., its activation in the input map is reduced to 50%). As a consequence, Gabor filter reprocessing at the next time-step has the potential of triggering a different heuristic.

The sequential behaviour of the model arises from the competitive dynamics that are intrinsic in the spatial map, whereas the specific order in which cities are selected depends on biasing the competition through an activation gradient (i.e., the saliency map). The idea that sequentially ordered behaviour involves a stage of parallel activation of a set of responses has a long history and indeed was central to Lashley's (1951) influential arguments against associative chaining (see Houghton & Hartley, 1995, for discussion). Note that biased activation competition is central to the competitive queuing approach to serial order (Houghton, 1990), which has proven very effective to simulate sequentially ordered behaviour in both normal and pathological conditions (see Houghton & Hartley, 1995, for a review, and Botvinick & Plaut, 2004, 2006, for an alternative approach).

The capacity to change heuristic during the execution of the task—and thus to produce flexible behaviour—is guaranteed by the top-down controller (TDC), which simply has the ability to reset the activation of the three heuristic units in the competitive selection module. There are at least two competing hypotheses regarding the on-line control of heuristic choice. The first hypothesis is that participants adopt a constant replanning approach, in which a new heuristic is chosen at each step regardless of the past choices (e.g., Koenig, Furcy, & Bauer, 2002). The second hypothesis is that the switching is driven by a mismatch detection mechanism that triggers replanning only if the currently selected heuristic is making poor progress (e.g., Onaindía, Sapena, Sebastia, & Marzal, 2001). We tested the two accounts in different versions of the model to assess whether one of them would provide a better fit to the human data. Thus, in the constant replanning model the competitive selection module (i.e., the active heuristic) is reset after each step during the execution of the pathway. In contrast, the mismatch detection model performs a new step based on the heuristic used in the previous step, and the TDC resets the competitive selection module only when a mismatch between the current heuristic and the optimal heuristic (determined by reprocessing the visual input up to the level of the competitive selection module) is detected.

Implementation of the model

Visual processing of the TSP patterns

The input to the visual module consists of a 161 × 161 pixels image representing the pattern. Each city is represented by a black circle with a diameter of 8 pixels coded with ones, whereas empty space is coded with zeros. The image is then processed by a family of Gabor filters (see Appendix for mathematical details). Gabor filters are band-pass filters with tuneable centre frequency, orientation, and bandwidth, which can model the response of simple cells in the primary visual cortex (Lee, 1996). A set of eight Gabor filters tuned to different orientations was used to convolve the input image to obtain eight orientation maps. The use of a small number of filters was motivated by the nature of the task and by the need of simplifying the model (see Appendix for further discussion).

To calculate the strength of the directional features extracted by the different filters, we collected the highest value from each orientation map. This corresponds to a nonlinear MAX operation (see Riesenhuber & Poggio, 1999) over the units belonging to the same map, which effectively provides orientation information that is invariant of spatial position. Moreover, the structure of the visual module is consistent with the hypothesis of Field (1994) that oriented edge detectors constitute a sparse representation of the images. This means that for any image, only a few of the features are needed to represent that particular image, and that over an ensemble of images a particular feature will seldom be significantly active.

Competitive selection among heuristics

The output of the visual module is sent to a competitive network (Rumelhart & Zipser, 1985) that provides an unsupervised categorization of the input pattern based on its visuospatial (i.e., directional) properties. The input layer, composed of eight units, encoded the normalized highest value of the eight visual maps—that is, the strength of a particular orientation axis. The output layer encodes the categories discovered in the training data by the competitive learning algorithm (see Appendix for details). Each output unit of the competitive network sends inhibitory connections to all other output units and one excitatory connection onto itself. This implements a winner-takes-all mechanism ensuring that only one output unit becomes active for a given input. The output units of the competitive network are named "heuristic units" because each unit is later associated to one specific spatial heuristic (see below).

The training set consisted of 100 images with patterns of 6 to 10 cities; each pattern was generated using a pseudorandom procedure that produced a structure consistent with the TSP configurations used by Basso et al. (2001). The network discovered three categories of input images. Inserting more than three units in the competitive layer did not produce substantial changes in the results, as most of the patterns (95%) were still classified by three units. We associated each category (i.e., output unit) to one specific spatial heuristic. We observed that most of the participants executing the TSP task tended to select the direction right (DR) heuristic when the cities were principally distributed along the diagonal axis from top-left to bottom-right, while the direction down (DD) heuristic was often chosen when the cities were principally distributed along the opposite diagonal axis. In intermediate or ambiguous situations, subjects tended to use the nearest-neighbour (NN) heuristic. Notably, two output units of the competitive network after learning were mainly driven by the visual maps tuned to 45° and 135°, respectively. The 45° orientation corresponds to a top-left to bottom-right direction, whereas the 135° orientation corresponds to a top-right to bottom-left direction in the input image. Accordingly, we connected the two units to the DR and DD heuristics, respectively. The last output unit was not driven by any specific orientation map, suggesting that the patterns that it responds to are not characterized by a predominant orientation axis. Accordingly, it was connected to the NN heuristic, which is typically used by participants when confronted with TSP configurations whose spatial layouts lack a clear directional component.

Saliency maps

The three heuristics are implemented by different saliency maps that bias the execution of the pathway with a specific gradient of activity. Each saliency map has the same size as the spatial map (see below), and each unit in the spatial map is activated by the corresponding unit of the saliency map. The saliency map of the NN heuristic is implemented as a Gaussian-shaped hill of activity centred on the last visited city, whereas the saliency maps of the DR and DD heuristics consist of linear gradients that cover the entire visual space (Figure 3). The effect of a saliency map on the spatial map is to relatively enhance the activation of one city by reducing (in accordance with the specific gradient) the activation of the other cities on the map. The competition among units in the spatial map (see below) produces a single winning location that corresponds to the most salient city, which constitutes the next target.

All saliency maps consist in a gradient of activation with a value of 0.3 in the position of maximum enhancement. Thus, the DR saliency map has a value of 0.3 at the extreme left side that decreases linearly to zero at the extreme right side. The DD saliency map employs an equivalent gradient from the upper to the lower side of the spatial target map. Finally, the NN saliency map is represented by a broad Gaussian-shaped hill of activity centred on the last visited city, with a peak of 0.3 and a width of 15°.

Human participants in the open-ended TSP used by Basso and colleagues (2001) were instructed to start with the top-left point and finish with the bottom-right point. This constraint is implemented in the model through a small gradient of activation that provides a "default" bias to the spatial map. That is, the upper left corner is enhanced by 0.05, and the biasing activation decreases linearly to 0 at the bottom right corner. This small bias ensures that the tours performed by the model always start with the top-left point and finish with the bottom-right point but it is completely orthogonal to the (stronger) biases caused by the heuristic saliency maps.

Spatial target map

The spatial target map is composed of 21 × 21 units with lateral connections. Activation of the spatial target map is driven by the retinal (input) image but it is modulated by the saliency map (see Appendix for mathematical details). Spatial plans are represented at population code level (see Figure 4). Each city is represented by a Gaussian-shaped hill of activity, and the competition between units belonging to different populations is resolved over time in favour of one single population. The next city to be visited is therefore represented by the winning population. Its exact location is decoded through a simple vector method (Salinas & Abbott, 1995).

Note that goal locations are coded in retinal coordinates on the spatial map. This frame of reference, appropriate only for eye movements, was chosen for the sake of simplicity. A coordinate

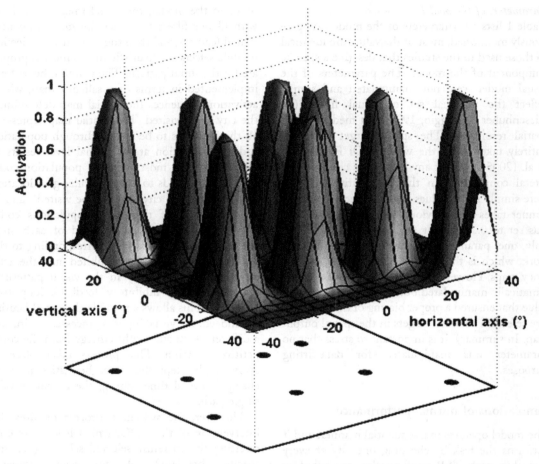

Figure 4. *The activation of the spatial map for one 8-point TSP pattern resulting from the retinal input only (i.e., a biasing signal from the saliency map is not present). Each location activates a population of units that is defined by a broad Gaussian-shaped hill. The different populations compete until there is only one winning population (while all the others are inhibited). This is the next location to be visited.*

transformation into a head-centred or hand-centred motor system would simply require the addition of one intermediate layer of "basis function" units that combine, in a multiplicative way, the retinal signal with the posture signals encoding the position of the eye and the hand (see Pouget & Snyder, 2000, for a review).

Top-down controller

The top-down controller (TDC) provides the required flexibility of the model to make it capable of a change of heuristic during the execution of the task. In the constant replanning version, the TDC resets the competitive selection module after each step. This means that a "new" heuristic must be selected before each step. In contrast, the mismatch detection version of the TDC triggers a reset only when the heuristic used to perform the last step is not optimal. More specifically, a change of heuristic is made possible only after the execution of one step in which the active heuristic did not match the optimal heuristic indicated by visual analysis. Thus, the mismatch detection TDC can switch the heuristic at least one step later than the constant replanning TDC.

Parameters of the model

Table 1 lists all parameters of the model. As previously mentioned, most of the values are identical to those used in the studies that describe a specific component of the model. The parameters of the visual model were not manipulated and simply reflect the minimal set of visual filters (cf. Riesenhuber & Poggio, 1999) at a medium-scale spatial resolution. The spatial target map was entirely taken from the work of Di Ferdinando et al. (2005) without any parameter change. The lateral connections in the competitive network were simply set to values that resulted in efficient winner-takes-all behaviour, and the learning rate was set to 0.1 without any manipulation. Thus, only one parameter is specific to the current work, which is the peak of activation in the saliency maps. However, this parameter was not systematically manipulated but it was simply set to a value that ensured a proper biasing of the competitive selection between targets in the spatial output map. In summary, it is important to stress that no parameter was manipulated for data-fitting purposes.

Simulations of normal performance

The model operates in a sequential manner, and it performs the task by choosing one city at every step. For each TSP configuration presented as input to the model, the visual image is analysed with Gabor filters to detect the most influential spatial features, and then the competitive selection module selects the heuristic that is most appropriate for the input pattern. The winning heuristic is implemented in terms of a saliency map, whose activation influences the spatial map determining the city to be visited. The spatial map represents all the locations to be visited through population codes; competition at the spatial level results in selection of the most activated population code, which corresponds to one particular goal location (the forthcoming city that will be visited), and in the inhibition of the other populations codes (all other locations). At the end of each step, the units in the spatial map corresponding to the selected (visited) city are inhibited, and the activation of the same city in the visual pattern is reduced via the inhibitory feedback loop (see Figure 3). This allows a possible change of heuristic: Indeed, the visual input is processed again, and a different heuristic might emerge from the competitive selection. This process takes place at every single step; therefore, heuristics may be changed several times during the execution of a single path.

However, the switching process requires the intervention of the TDC, which has the role of resetting the currently selected schema (i.e., the specific heuristic). A top-down influence

Table 1. *List of the parameters used in the model*

	Parameter	Value	Taken from
Visual module	x	0	Riesenhuber & Poggio, 1999
	y	0	Riesenhuber & Poggio, 1999
	ω_o (radial frequency)	.57 radians per unit length	
	θ (wavelet orientation)	0, $1/4\pi$, $1/2\pi$ and $3/4\pi$ radians	Riesenhuber & Poggio, 1999
	k	$K \approx \pi$	Lee, 1999
Competitive selection module	η (learning rate)	0.1	
Spatial module	σ (width of the Gaussian)	5°	Di Ferdinando et al., 2005
	A_E	10	Di Ferdinando et al., 2005
	σ_E	15	Di Ferdinando et al., 2005
	A_I	9	Di Ferdinando et al., 2005
	σ_I	105	Di Ferdinando et al., 2005
	Saliency maps	Peak activation of 0.3	

Note: See text for explanation.

becomes clearly visible in the most difficult tasks (i.e., for a large number of cities) where it provides flexibility to the behaviour. If the previously selected heuristic is not appropriate on the basis of the spatial analysis of the remaining unvisited locations, the TDC allows an on-line change to the plan. As previously mentioned, we evaluated the performance of the model using the two different versions of the TDC (constant replanning vs. mismatch detection). Moreover, to investigate whether the incremental aspect of planning is a necessary component to adequately describe human performance, we evaluated a version of the model in which one single heuristic was used for the execution of the entire path. In summary, we compared five different versions of the model: (a) constant replanning model, (b) mismatch detection model, (c) fixed DD model, (d) fixed DR model, and (e) fixed NN model.

These five models were tested on eight different TSP patterns. These were the most frequently tested maps across several experiments performed by Basso et al. (2001) and Basso (2005), so that the performance of each model could be compared with the behavioural data. We collected the tours executed by the model in its different versions for a comparison with those executed by the healthy adults (the number of participants used for this analysis was 140). We chose to inspect the tours at a global level, instead of analysing the single movements during the execution of the tour. Note that the comparison between model and human data at the level of single step is not a stringent one because the likelihood of finding the same single step is much higher than the likelihood of finding the same whole pathway. For each pattern, we compared the tour produced by the model with the tours performed by human participants and ranked the model's tour according to the frequencies observed in the human data.

Results

Table 2 reports the ranks for each tour and model version. A rank of 1 indicates that the tour performed by the model corresponds to the most frequently observed tour across human participants. Some pathways were not classifiable (N.C.) because they did not match any of the tours observed across our sample of human participants. In the case of Pattern 8, none of the models was able to provide a classifiable solution. It is worth noting, however, that the human solutions to Pattern 8 (constituted by 11 locations) was so widely variable that their ranking would be unreliable. The number of possible solutions increases exponentially with the number of locations to be visited; this turns into a greater variability of performance because there is also an increased number of close-to-optimal solutions. This contention is supported by a strong positive correlation ($r = .83$, $p < .005$) between the number of points in a map and the number of different solutions provided by human participants.

Inspection of Table 2 reveals that most of the pathways chosen by the constant replanning model correspond to the most frequently observed tours in the experiments of Basso and colleagues (2001; Basso, 2005). For half of the patterns, the tour executed by the constant replanning model matched the most frequent tour observed in healthy participants. Overall, six out of eight pathways were the first or second most frequent tour in the human data. This is a valuable result, considering that the open-ended TSP is a (non polynomial) NP-complete problem, which has an exponential increase of possible solutions in relation to the number of points. A nonparametric Friedman analysis of variance (ANOVA) on the rank of the tours produced by the five models revealed a significant effect of model version, $\chi^2(4) = 13.143$; $p < .05$. The mean ranks were 1.94, 2.94, 2.88, 4.31, and 2.94 for constant replanning, mismatch detection, fixed NN, fixed DR, and fixed DD, respectively. Pairwise comparisons showed that performance of the DR model was worse than any other model, but no other comparison reached the significance level. However, it is worth noting that the constant replanning model showed the best mean rank. The mean rank of the mismatch detection model was identical to that of the fixed DD model.

A qualitative analysis of the tours performed by the different models confirms that the constant replanning model offers the best fit to the human

Table 2. *Ranks and frequencies of the tours chosen by all versions of the model for each pattern in a comparison with the human data of Basso et al., 2001; Basso, 2005*

Map	Ranking and Percentage				
	Constant Replanning	Mismatch Detection	NN	DR	DD
1	2 (16.8)	2 (16.8)	2 (16.8)	3 (5.46)	1 (68)
2	1 (38.66)	1 (38.66)	3 (14.71)	7 (2.52)	1 (38.66)
3	1 (50)	1 (50)	1 (50)	3 (10)	1 (50)
4	1 (25.6)	2 (18.9)	2 (18.9)	7 (2.9)	2 (18.9)
5	2 (23.1)	6 (2.5)	6 (2.5)	3 (15.5)	N.C.
6	1 (11.3)	1 (11.3)	1 (11.3)	10 (2.1)	7 (5.5)
7	6 (11.3)	N.C.	12 (1.3)	N.C.	18 (0.4)
8	N.C.	N.C.	N.C.	N.C.	N.C.

Note: Each pattern depicted in the first column. A rank of 1 indicates that the pathway chosen by the model corresponds to that most frequently observed across human participants. N.C. (not classifiable) indicates that the tour performed by the model has never been observed across the sample of human participants. NN = nearest neighbour. DR = direction right. DD = direction down.

performance. Specifically, both the mismatch detection and the fixed NN models produced two crossed tours, whereas the constant replanning model did not produce any crossed tour (note that the fixed DD and fixed DR cannot, by definition, produce any crossing). The occurrence of crossings in the tours produced by human participants is extremely rare. Indeed, van Rooij, Stege, and Schactman (2003) hypothesized that humans try to avoid crossed lines when solving the TSP because they are sensitive to the fact that tours with crossed lines are nonoptimal (or, alternatively, that optimal tours have no crossings). Although this position has been criticized by MacGregor, Ormerod, and Chronicle (2004), it is generally agreed that optimal solutions have no crossings.

In summary, the constant replanning model is superior to the simpler models based on single heuristics, as well as to the model that allows for heuristic changes through a mismatch detection mechanism. Thus, having established that the constant replanning model provides the best fit to the data on healthy human participants, we investigated the effect of a lesion to the TDC to assess its ability to account for the impaired performance shown by fTBI patients.

Simulations of impaired performance

Simulation of the impaired performance of frontal patients was obtained by lesioning the TDC in the constant replanning model. The TDC was impaired by lowering its capacity to reset the competitive selection module. Lesions of different degrees of severity were simulated by progressively increasing the inefficiency of the top-down controller from 10% to 70%. A set of 10 frontally damaged networks was obtained by setting the lesion severity to 10%, 15%, 20%, 25%, 30%, 35%, 40%, 50%, 60%, and 70%.

The tours performed by the lesioned model were compared with those observed in fTBI patients. Tour rankings were computed as for the simulations of unimpaired performance. Moreover, we carried out an analysis of the degree of flexibility exhibited by the model by looking at the selection of heuristics during the execution of the task. In previous studies the classification of the heuristic used to move from one city to the next at each step in the pathway was obtained considering the distance between that city and all other unvisited cities (see Basso et al., 2001). If the next selected city was the closest on the horizontal axis, the move was considered as the result of a DR heuristic. Alternatively, if the next city was the closest on the vertical axis, the move was considered as the result of a DD heuristic. Finally, if the next city was the closest in terms of absolute distance (i.e., regardless of the direction), the move was considered representative of a NN heuristic. In the model, the choice of heuristic was directly assessed by recording the winning unit in the competitive module at every step. The presence of multiple heuristics in solving a given TSP configuration was taken as an index of flexible behaviour. Specifically, a flexible strategy was defined as a problem solution in which the participants (or the model) operated at least one heuristic switch; otherwise, the strategy was classified as rigid. Therefore, we assessed the flexibility of the lesioned model in comparison to the unimpaired model and its effect on tour optimization. Performance of 10 different "normal participants" was obtained by introducing some variability in the competitive process that leads to heuristic selection for both the simulations. Gaussian noise (mean 0, variance .05) was added at each processing step to the heuristic nodes. Performance on each map was therefore collected for each of the 10 different runs of the model.

Results

Each tour performed by the model after TDC lesions was ranked according to the patients' data, and the modal rank was calculated for each pattern. The tours of the impaired model were generally consistent with the performance of the frontal patients (see Table 3).

A comparison of the type of strategy (flexible vs. rigid) employed by the normal model and the lesioned model revealed a significant difference, $\chi^2(1) = 13.97$, $p < .001$. Rigid strategies were more frequent than flexible strategies in the lesioned model, whereas the unimpaired model showed the opposite trend. Overall, this pattern mirrors the results obtained by Basso et al. (2001) in their study of healthy participants and frontal patients (see Figure 5).

Figure 6 presents a comparison of two representative pathways performed by the constant replanning model and the lesioned model (30%

Table 3. *Ranks and frequencies of the tours performed by the lesioned model, for each pattern (depicted in the first column) in a comparison with the human data of frontally damaged patients (Basso et al., 2001)*

MAP								
RANK	2	1	2	3	3.5	3	1	N.C.

Note: Each pattern depicted in column head.

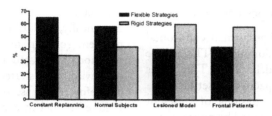

Figure 5. *Overall strategy chosen by the normal models and by the lesioned models, compared to the strategies of healthy participants and frontal patients. A strategy was classified as flexible if the heuristic was changed at least once during the execution of a given pathway.*

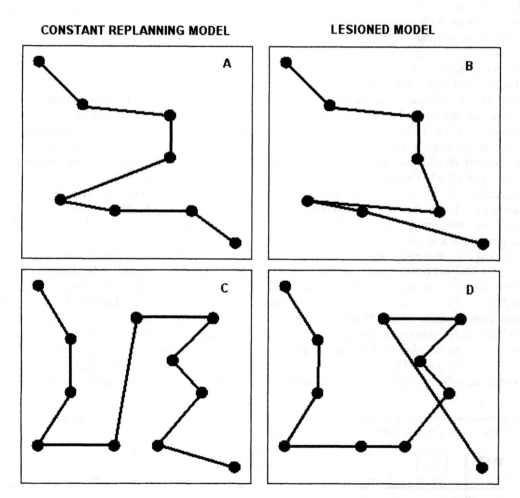

Figure 6. *Tours performed by the model on Maps 4 and 8. The left panels (A and C) show the performance of the normal model, whereas the right panels (B and D) show the pathways executed by a 30% lesioned model. Note that the tour depicted in D contains a crossing, which is a classical sign of nonoptimization and is rarely observed in neurologically intact participants.*

lesion). As can be noted, the pathways were markedly different because of the lack of heuristic changes. The tour executed by the lesioned model contains a crossing, which is a clear sign of nonoptimal performance (as discussed in the previous section).

Another fundamental difference between normal and impaired model is revealed by their different levels of optimization. As suggested by Graham, Joshi, and Pizlo (2000), an appropriate measure of the level of optimization is the ratio of the tour length (RTL), which is the ratio between length of the tour performed by the subject and the length of the shortest tour. In the present study (as in Basso et al., 2006), the RTL index for a given pathway X was computed as the ratio of excess tour length to optimal tour length:

$$RTL(X) = [\text{tour length}(X) - \text{optimal tour length}(X)]/\text{optimal tour length}(X)$$

Mean RTLs for normal versus impaired model were significantly different (0.051 vs. 0.117, respectively; $t = -26.84$, $p < .001$), showing that TDC damage results in a lower level of optimization. These result mirror those of Basso et al. (2001), who found that the optimization level of frontal patients was significantly inferior to that of healthy controls (see Figure 7).

GENERAL DISCUSSION

The TSP is a famous problem-solving task which gained notoriety about two centuries ago among mathematicians and physicists as one of the most fascinating optimization problems (for a review see Schrijver, 2005). Nevertheless, in the latest years there has been a growing interest for the TSP among cognitive scientists. Mathematicians and computer scientists have developed a large number of algorithms for solving the TSP that give an approximation of the optimal solution in a reasonable amount of time. Our model differs fundamentally from these studies in its purpose, because we

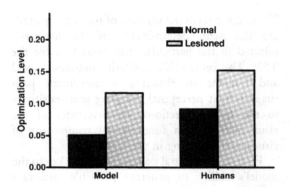

Figure 7. Mean ratio of the tour length (RTL) for model and human participants, indexing the optimization level achieved in the TSP task. From left to right: normal model (dark grey), lesioned model (light grey), neurologically intact participants (dark grey), and frontal patients (light grey). Human data from Basso et al., 2001.

have focused our attention on the simulation of the human cognitive processes involved in the solution of the TSP rather than on the optimization aspects of the problem. Indeed, humans facing the TSP problem carry out the task in a sequential manner, showing the ability to change heuristic during the pathway when needed to optimize their performance (Basso et al., 2001).

The simulations presented in this paper closely mirrored human performance in both normal and pathological conditions. This suggests that the model is able to capture the basic cognitive processes involved in the human solution of the TSP. The core of the model's ability to perform visuospatial planning resides in the bottom-up selection of a visuospatial heuristic in the competitive selection module. The spatial analysis performed by Gabor filters is the source of bottom-up influences in the model. The competitive network receives input from the visual module, and it provides an unsupervised categorization of the input pattern based on the spatial-directional characteristics of the pattern formed by the points that constitute the TSP configuration. Categorization into three classes emerged spontaneously during learning (through an unsupervised Hebbian learning algorithm) as a result of the exposure to a sample of TSP patterns.

Thus, the directional features of the input pattern are the main determinants of the heuristics selected in the particular path used to solve the TSP. The remarkable similarity between model and humans in choosing a movement path suggests that perceptual grouping and sensitivity to the spatial-directional characteristics of the visual pattern is a fundamental component of visuospatial planning in the TSP.

From a behavioural point of view, the key to the model's ability to generate plausible pathways resides in two main features: the selection of the most appropriate heuristic given the contextual information and the incremental monitoring process, which allows a change of heuristic when the ongoing one fails to fit to the sensorial information. Indeed, the most intriguing characteristic of the model regards its capacity to switch between heuristics. This is a fundamental characteristic that gives psychological plausibility to the model. Human participants execute the TSP in an iterative manner; the incremental process is less resource demanding than global planning because subjects do not need to generate a comprehensive plan resolving the entire situation but only the next appropriate action.

The hypothesis that the performance of neurologically intact participants is crucially dependent on incremental planning and on the interaction of bottom-up and top-down processes is highlighted by the comparison between five versions of the model that differed only for the strategic component. First, the use of a single, fixed heuristic proved to be inadequate for the solution of the most complex problems. Fixed-heuristic versions of the model performed plausible tours when confronted with maps containing a small number of points, but their performance broke down as the number of points increased. Specifically, we observed pathways that did not match any of the tours produced by human participants. This result confirms that a flexible use of heuristics is a fundamental aspect of human performance in the TSP (cf. Basso et al., 2001).

Flexible behaviour, however, requires a monitoring system that allows for heuristic switches. We contrasted two alternative hypotheses regarding the operation of the top-down controller: constant replanning versus mismatch detection. The first hypothesis is that a new heuristic is chosen at each step regardless of the past choices (e.g., Koenig et al., 2002), whereas the second suggests that the switching can take place only if the currently selected heuristic is making poor progress (e.g., Onaindía et al., 2001). The two different implementations of the TDC produced a markedly different performance. First, the pathways executed by the constant replanning model provided a better match to the tours that were most frequently observed across a large number of human participants. Second, and more important, the constant replanning model did not produce any crossed tour, whereas the mismatch detection model executed two crossed tours. The latter indicate a nonoptimal performance and are rarely observed in human performance (MacGregor, Chronicle, & Ormerod, 2004; van Rooij et al., 2003). This suggests that a continuous monitoring process, which allows for on-line changes of heuristic whenever the current one is not suitable, is a more viable model of the incremental planning ability displayed by neurologically intact participants.

The importance of flexible, incremental planning is also supported by the empirical data on patients with frontal traumatic brain injury (Basso et al., 2001) as well as normal subjects under rTMS over the frontal lobe (Basso et al., 2006; see Figure 2a). Both the lesion and the reversible neurodisruption of the frontal cortex caused a conspicuous decrease of flexible strategies that incorporate heuristic switches. The same pattern was observed in the simulations when the TDC of the constant replanning model was lesioned in a way that decreased its ability to reset the competitive selection module. Note that the frontal patients still produced acceptable solutions of the TSP in the Basso et al. (2001) study. The damaged model performed in the same way because of the preserved bottom-up mechanism: The simplest TSP problems often do not require a change of heuristic, and thus the performance of the lesioned model is indistinguishable from that of the normal model.

However, in the most complex patterns the intact model efficiently switched heuristic when a change was appropriate, whereas the damaged model often perseverated by keeping active the heuristic selected at the beginning of the pattern. Thus, TDC damage caused a loss of flexibility and adaptivity in the behaviour that turned into a poorer level of optimization.

It is worth noting that the remarkable flexibility of human cognitive control was simulated in the model solely by the interaction between the competitive selection module and the TDC. This reflects the functional role of the PFC hypothesized by J. D. Cohen, Braver, and O'Reilly (1996), who suggest that the PFC maintains the relevant features in an activation-based working memory, providing a top-down support (or biasing) of the corresponding perceptual processing and action selection pathways (also see O'Reilly, Noelle, Braver, & Cohen, 2002).

However, there is an alternative explanation for why heuristic switching might fail after frontal lobe damage. If monitoring is seen as a parallel process that could interrupt behaviour before the application of a heuristic, a monitoring failure would prevent the system to invoke the TDC.[1] This would cause the same loss of flexibility that we attributed to (and modelled as) impaired inhibitory function of the TDC. Thus, further empirical work is necessary to distinguish between these two alternative accounts of the rigid behaviour exhibited by fTBI patients (or healthy participants under rTMS) in the TSP. Notably the monitoring failure account would predict a loss of flexibility in neurologically intact participants when the attentional demands are increased by simultaneously performing a secondary task.

Relation to other models

The most important previous computational model of TSP from a psychological point of view was developed by MacGregor et al. (2000). Their model focuses on the human solution of the closed version of the TSP (see Introduction): It performs the task with a sequential procedure, and it is basically designed to conform in a general way to a convex hull approach. The model of MacGregor and colleagues is entirely driven by conditional rules implemented at each step. One example of its operations is provided by the following list of steps: "Apply the insertion criterion to identify which unconnected interior point is closest to the current arc—apply the insertion criterion to check whether the closest node is closer to any other arc—if not, proceed to Step 5—if it is, move to the end node of the current arc." Although this model represented a great development with respect to the previous conventional attempts to model human performance on TSP, some aspects still seem to require an improvement. Even if the results show a good fit between the model and the human solution, the model of MacGregor is unlikely to produce a particularly good fit to human solutions to highly patterned TSPs. This is because the model does not incorporate a mechanism that is sensitive to factors such as proximity of interior points and regularity of their arrangement. Moreover, recent evidence suggests that the heuristics used to solve the closed version of TSP cannot explain the human performance in the open-ended TSP (Chonicle, MacGregor, Ormerod, & Burr, 2006). Thus, the model of MacGregor et al. (2000), at least in its present form, could not be used to account for the human data on the Maps test of Basso et al. (2001).

It is important to note that a fundamental difference between our model and the model of MacGregor et al. (2000) resides in the nature of the computational mechanisms leading to the solution. In our model, there are no explicit rules that guide the performance, and the perceptual mechanisms simulated with Gabor filters allowed us to account for the perceptual components of the human solution of TSP. To the best of our

---

[1] We thank Rick Cooper for suggesting this view of monitoring as well as the account of rigid behaviour based on a monitoring failure.

knowledge, there is no other model that has successfully simulated human performance in TSP without using explicit rules.

Our model shares several conceptual properties with the attention to action (ATA) model of Norman and Shallice (1986) and the computational model of action planning developed by Cooper and Shallice (2000). The competitive selection module operates in a way that is similar to the contention-scheduling mechanism, whereas the TDC could be regarded as a sort of supervisor attentional system (SAS). In our model, the role of the TDC is to inhibit the previously selected heuristic to promote a flexible behaviour. Notably, a lesion to the TDC resulted in performance characterized by a rigid strategy that lacked heuristic changes, with a pattern that mirrored the behaviour exhibited by frontal patients.

Limitations of the model and future directions

Overall, the model provides a good match to both normal and impaired human performance in the TSP task. One possible criticism, however, is that the complexity of the model and the number of parameters outstrip the complexity of the data to be explained. This is far from being the truth. First of all, the complexity of the model is the result of the assembly of components taken from other computational models that are unrelated to the TSP but are necessary to build a comprehensive model of the task. Indeed, the complex nature of the TSP and the number of different cognitive processes involved called for a nested modelling approach (see Perry et al., 2007). Therefore, two main components of our model, the visual module and the spatial module, were simply taken from state-of-the-art computational models of vision and action (Di Ferdinando et al., 2005; Lee, 1996; Pouget & Snyder, 2000). As a result of this, most of the parameters in the model are not free (see Table 1), and they have an effect only at the module level (i.e., they are not determinant for an optimal solution of the TSP). In fact, the combination of the visual and spatial components simply forms a model of visually guided movements towards visually salient stimuli. Two other components, the competitive selection module and the TDC, are required to produce a solution of the TSP and form the core of the model's ability to perform incremental visuospatial planning.

A second possible criticism regards the complexity of the data to be explained. At a first glance, an analysis of the tours at a global level would seem less accurate than an analysis of the single movements during the execution of the tour. What should be kept in mind, however, is that the overall solution is much more meaningful than the single movements. Indeed, looking at the match between model and human data at the level of single step is not very fruitful, because the probability of finding a matching movement is much higher than the probability of finding the same pathway in its totality. In fact, for a tour with rank "1", the overall pathway of the human participants and that of the model is exactly the same, indicating a maximum concordance between the two solutions. Thus, this approach provides a rigorous and fine-grained analysis of the performance.

Nonetheless, a limitation of the current model is that it cannot capture the variability of human solutions to a single TSP pattern. Modelling individual differences was clearly beyond the scope of the current work, but this issue could now be tackled by combining behavioural and computational investigations. Simulations suggest that the observed variability of human solutions cannot be accounted for by simply adding noise during processing. Thus, individual differences might be captured in the model only by considering different "cognitive styles" (e.g., Witkin & Goodenough, 1981), such as predispositions towards using a particular heuristic (Bisiacchi, Basso, & Cotelli, 1999).

The last possible criticism to the current model concerns its limitation to the open-ended TSP task. In this regard, we note that the extension to the closed-TSP would require minimal modifications of the model. In particular, the two versions of TSP seem to involve different types of heuristics (Chronicle et al., 2006). Moreover, although the model was specifically designed to provide a solution of the TSP, it could be extended to other tasks that require sequential visuo-motor scanning. For example, the Trail-Making Test B (TMT-B: Reitan, 1958) requires alternately connecting digits (1–13) and letters (A–L) that are randomly located on a sheet of paper. The TMT-B is frequently used in neuropsychology to assess the executive function of mental set shifting. A simulation of the TMT-B test would require only few modifications of our model. Finally, the competitive selection and TDC components of our model could be used to simulate other nonspatial tasks that involve cognitive control. One advantage of our nested incremental modelling approach (see Perry et al., 2007) is that these components can be easily untied from the other parts of the model and reused in a different context. Note that only the competitive selection module and the TDC would be essential to account for the rapid switching in dynamic categorization tasks, as in the Wisconsin Card Sorting Test (WCST; Grant & Berg, 1948). However, extension to the WCST would clearly require substantial modifications that range from the nature of input and output representations to the structure of the learning phase (Rougier, Noelle, Braver, Cohen, & O'Reilly, 2005).

CONCLUSIONS

The present work is an effort to simulate the nature of the computational mechanisms underlying the human performance on visually presented TSP. Consistent with the connectionist approach to human cognition, our model dispenses with the use of explicit rules to guide behaviour in a complex problem-solving task. The simulations highlighted the fundamental role of perceptual grouping and sensitivity to the spatial-directional characteristics of the visual pattern in visuospatial planning while performing the TSP. Moreover, the model allowed us to assess the role of incremental planning and to test different hypotheses regarding the on-line monitoring of performance. The behaviour of the model seems to capture the fundamental aspects of human skilled performance and to mirror the impairment and behavioural rigidity typical of frontal lobe patients after a simulated lesion. We believe that the model provides a useful platform for designing new empirical studies that aim at a more fine-grained analysis of human performance in the TSP task because it can be used to make predictions regarding both healthy subjects and clinical populations.

Manuscript received 3 January 2007
Revised manuscript received 26 July 2007
Revised manuscript accepted 1 August 2007
First published online 6 October 2007

REFERENCES

Barr, A., & Feigenbaum, E. A. (1981). *The handbook of artificial intelligence* (Vol. 1). Stanford Los Altos, CA: W. Kaufmann.

Basso, D. (2005). *Involvement of the prefrontal cortex in visuo-spatial planning*. PhD thesis, Department of Psychology, University of Rome "La Sapienza". Available from: http://padis.uniroma1.it/getfile.py?recid=334

Basso, D., Bisiacchi, P. S., Cotelli, M., & Farinello, C. (2001). Planning times during Travelling Salesman's problem: Differences between closed head injury and normal subjects. *Brain and Cognition, 46*, 38–42.

Basso, D., Lotze, M., Vitale, L., Ferreri, F., Bisiacchi, P. S., Olivetti-Belardinelli, M., et al. (2006). The role of prefrontal cortex on visuo-spatial planning: A repetitive-TMS study. *Experimental Brain Research, 171*, 411–415.

Bisiacchi, P. S., Basso, D., & Cotelli, M. (1999). Cognitive strategies for sequential visuo-spatial decisions. In M. Zanforlin & L. Tommasi (Eds.), *Research in perception. Proceedings of the meeting in honour of F. Metelli* (pp. 179–181). Padova, Italy: Logos Press.

Botvinick, M., & Plaut, D. C. (2004). Doing without schema hierarchies: A recurrent connectionist approach to normal and impaired routine sequential action. *Psychological Review, 111*, 395–429.

Botvinick, M., & Plaut, D. C. (2006). Short-term memory for serial order: A recurrent neural network model. *Psychological Review, 113*, 201–233.

Brown, T. H., & Chattarji, S. (1995). Hebbian synaptic plasticity. In M. A. Arbib (Ed.), *The handbook of brain theory and neural networks* (pp. 454–459). Cambridge, MA: The MIT Press.

Bryant, D. J., Tversky, B., & Franklin, N. (1992). Internal and external spatial frameworks for representing described scenes. *Journal of Memory and Language, 31,* 74–98.

Cadwallader, M. (1975). A behavioral model of consumer spatial decision making. *Economic Geography, 51,* 339–349.

Carlin, D., Bonerba, J., Phipps, M., Alexander, G. E., Shapiro, M. B., & Grafman, J. (2000). Planning impairments in frontal lobe dementia and frontal lobe lesion patients. *Neuropsychologia, 38,* 655–665.

Carreira, M. J., Orwell, J., Turnes, R., Boyce, J. F., Cabello, D., & Haddon, J. F. (1998). Perceptual grouping from Gabor filter responses. In P. H. Lewis & M. S. Nixon (Eds.), *Proceedings of the Ninth British Machine Vision Conference* (pp. 336–345).

Chronicle, E. P., MacGregor, J. N., Ormerod, T. C., & Burr, A. (2006). It looks easy! Heuristics for combinatorial optimization problems. *Quarterly Journal of Experimental Psychology, 59,* 783–800.

Cohen, G. (1988). *Memory in the real world.* Hillsdale, NJ: Lawrence Erlbaum Associates.

Cohen, J. D., Braver, T. S., & O'Reilly, R. C. (1996). A computational approach to prefrontal cortex, cognitive control, and schizophrenia: Recent developments and current challenges. *Philosophical Transactions of the Royal Society of London. Series B, 351,* 1515–1527.

Cooper, R., & Shallice, T. (2000). Contention scheduling and the control of routine activities. *Cognitive Neuropsychology, 17,* 297–338.

Daugman, J. (1988). Complete discrete 2D Gabor transform by neural networks for image analysis and compression. *IEEE Transactions on Acoustics, Speech, and Signal Processing, 36,* 169–1179.

Di Ferdinando, A., Casarotti, M., Vallar, G., & Zorzi, M. (2005). Hemispheric asymmetries in the neglect syndrome: A computational study. In A. Cangelosi, G. Bugmann, & R. Borisyuk (Eds.), *Modelling language, cognition and action* (pp. 249–258). Singapore: World Scientific.

Duncan, J. (1986). Disorganization of behaviour after frontal lobe damage. *Cognitive Neuropsychology, 3,* 271–290.

Field, D. J. (1994). What is the goal of sensory coding? *Neural Computation, 4,* 559–601.

Fincham, J. M., Carter, C. S., van Veen, V., Stenger, V. A., & Anderson, J. R. (2002). Neural mechanisms of planning: A computational analysis using event-related fMRI. *Proceedings of the National Academy of Sciences, 99,* 3346–3351.

Gärling, T. (1989). The role of cognitive maps in spatial decisions. *Journal of Environmental Psychology, 9,* 269–278.

Gärling, T. (1994). Processing of time constraints on sequence decisions in a planning task. *European Journal of Cognitive Psychology, 6,* 399–416.

Goel, V., & Grafman, J. (1995). Are the frontal lobes implicated in "planning" functions? Interpreting data from the Tower of Hanoi. *Neuropsychologia, 33,* 623–642.

Goel, V., & Grafman, J. (2000). Role of the right prefrontal cortex in ill-structured planning. *Cognitive Neuropsychology, 17,* 415–436.

Grafman, J. (1989). Plans, actions and mental sets: Managerial knowledge units in the frontal lobes. In E. Perecman (Ed.), *Integrating theory and practice in clinical neuropsychology* (pp. 93–137). Hillsdale, NJ: Lawrence Erlbaum Associates.

Grafman, J. (1995). Similarities and distinctions among current models of prefrontal cortical functions. *Annals of the New York Academy of Sciences, 769,* 337–368.

Graham, S. M., Joshi, A., & Pizlo, Z. (2000). The Traveling Salesman Problem: A hierarchical model. *Memory & Cognition, 28,* 1191–1204.

Grant, D. A., & Berg, E. A. (1948). A behavioural analysis of degree of reinforcement and ease of shifting to new responses in a Weigl-type card-sorting problem. *Journal of Experimental Psychology, 38,* 404–411.

Hayes-Roth, B., & Hayes-Roth, F. (1979). A cognitive model of planning. *Cognitive Science, 3,* 275–310.

Hirtle, S., & Gärling, T. (1992). Heuristic rules for sequential spatial decisions. *Geoforum, 23,* 227–238.

Hirtle, S. C., & Jonides, J. (1985). Evidence of hierarchies in cognitive maps. *Memory and Cognition, 3,* 208–217.

Houghton, G. (1990). The problem of serial order: A neural network model of sequence learning and recall. In R. Dale, C. Mellish, & M. Zock (Eds.), *Current research in natural language generation* (pp. 287–319). London: Academic Press.

Houghton, G., & Hartley, T. (1995). Parallel models of serial behaviour: Lashley revisited. *Psyche, 2*(25). Retrieved September 24, 2006, from: http://psyche.cs.monash.edu.au/v2/psyche-2-25-houghton.html

Jones, J. P., & Palmer, L. A. (1987). An evaluation of the two-dimensional Gabor filter model of simple receptive fields in cat striate cortex. *Journal of Neurophysiology, 58*, 1233–1258.

Kafer, K. L., & Hunter, M. (1997). On testing the validity of planning/problem-solving tasks in a normal population. *Journal of the International Neuropsychological Society, 3*, 108–119.

Kaller, C. P., Unterrainer, J. M., Rahm, B., & Halsband, U. (2004). The impact of problem structure on planning: Insights from the Tower of London task. *Cognitive Brain Research, 20*, 462–472.

Koenig, S., Furcy, D., & Bauer, C. (2002). Heuristic search-based replanning. In M. Ghallab, J. Hertzberg, & P. Traverso (Eds.), *Proceedings of the Sixth International Conference on Artificial Intelligence Planning Systems* (pp. 294–301). Menlo Park, CA: AAAI Press.

Lashley, K. S. (1951). The problem of serial order in behavior. In L. A. Jeffress (Ed.), *Cerebral mechanisms in behavior*. New York: Wiley.

Lawler, E. L., Lenstra, J. K., Rinnooy Kan, A. H. G., & Shmoys, D. B. (1985). *The traveling salesman problem: A guided tour of combinatorial optimization*. New York: John Wiley and Sons.

Lee, T. S. (1996). Image representation using 2D Gabor wavelets. *IEEE Transactions on Pattern Analysis and Machine Intelligence, 18*, 959–971.

Lezak, M. (1995). *Neuropsychological assessment* (3rd ed.). New York: Oxford University Press.

Luria, A. R. (1980). *Higher cortical functions in man*. New York: Basic Books.

MacGregor, J. N., Chronicle, E. P., & Ormerod, T. C. (2004). Convex-hull or crossing-avoidance? Solution heuristics in the traveling salesperson problem. *Memory & Cognition, 32*, 260–270.

MacGregor, J. N., & Ormerod, T. (1996). Human performance on the traveling salesman problem. *Perception & Psychophysics, 58*, 527–539.

MacGregor, J. N., Ormerod, T. C., & Chronicle, E. P. (2000). A model of human performance on the traveling salesperson problem. *Memory & Cognition, 7*, 1183–1190.

McNamara, T. (1992). Spatial representation. *Geoforum, 2*, 139–150.

Murakoshi, S., & Kawai, M. (2000). Use of knowledge and heuristics for wayfinding in an artificial environment. *Environment and Behaviour, 32*, 756–774.

Newman, S. D., Carpenter, P. A., Varma, S., & Just, M. A. (2003). Frontal and parietal participation in problem solving in the Tower of London: fMRI and computational modeling of planning and high-level perception. *Neuropsychologia, 41*, 1668–1682.

Norman, D., & Shallice, T. (1986). Attention to action: Willed and automatic control of behaviour. In R. Davidson, G. Schwartz, & D. Shapiro (Eds.), *Consciousness and self regulation: Advances in research and theory* (Vol. 4, pp. 1–18). New York: Plenum.

Onaindia, E., Sapena, O., Sebastia, L., & Marzal, E. (2001). SimPlanner: An execution-monitoring system for replanning in dynamic worlds. In P. Brazdil & A. Jorge (Eds.), *Proceedings of progress in artificial intelligence knowledge extraction, multi-agent systems, logic programming, and constraint solving* (pp. 393–400). Berlin, Germany: Springer-Verlag.

O'Reilly, R. C., Noelle, D., Braver, T. S., & Cohen, J. D. (2002). Prefrontal cortex and dynamic categorization tasks. Representational organization and neuromodulatory control. *Cerebral Cortex, 12*, 246–257.

Owen, A. M., Downes, J. J., Sahakian, B. J., Polkey, C. E., & Robbins, T. W. (1990). Planning and spatial working memory following frontal lobe lesions in man. *Neuropsychologia, 28*, 1021–1034.

Perry, C., Ziegler, J. C., & Zorzi, M. (2007). Nested incremental modeling in the development of computational theories: The CDP+ model of reading aloud. *Psychological Review, 114*, 273–315.

Phillips, L. H, Wynn, V. E., McPherson, S., & Gilhooly, K. J. (2001). Mental planning and the Tower of London task. *Quarterly Journal of Experimental Psychology, 54A*, 579–598.

Polivanova, N. I. (1974). On some functional and structural features of the visual-intuitive components of a problem-solving process. *Voprosy Psikhologii [Questions of Psychology], 4*, 41–51.

Pouget, A., Dayan, P., & Zemel, R. (2000). Information processing with population codes. *Nature Reviews Neuroscience, 1*, 125–132.

Pouget A., & Snyder, L. H. (2000). Computational approaches to sensorimotor transformations. *Nature Neuroscience, 3*(Suppl.), 1192–1198.

Reitan, R. (1958). Validity of the Trail-Making Test as an indication of organic brain damage. *Perceptual Motor Skills, 8*, 271–276.

Riesenhuber, M., & Poggio, T. (1999). Hierarchical models of object recognition in cortex. *Nature Neuroscience, 2*, 1019–1025.

Roberts, R. J., & Pennington, B. F. (1996). An interactive framework for examining prefrontal cognitive processes. *Developmental Neuropsychology, 12*, 105–126.

Rougier, N. P., Noelle, D., Braver, T. S., Cohen, J. D., & O'Reilly, R. C. (2005). Prefrontal cortex and the flexibility of cognitive control: Rules without symbols. *Proceedings of the National Academy of Sciences, 102*, 7338–7343.

Rumelhart, D. E., & Zipser, D. (1985). Feature discovery by competitive learning. *Cognitive Science, 9*, 75–112.

Salinas, E., & Abbott, L. F. (1995). Transfer of coded information from sensory to motor networks. *Journal of Neuroscience, 15*, 6461–6474.

Schrijver, A. (2005). On the history of combinatorial optimization (till 1960). In K. Aardal, G. L. Nemhauser, & R. Weismantel (Eds.), *Handbook of discrete optimization* (pp. 1–68). Amsterdam: Elsevier.

Shallice, T. (1982). Specific impairments of planning. *Philosophical Transactions of the Royal Society of London, Part B, 298*, 199–209.

Shallice, T. (1988). *From neuropsychology to mental structure*. Cambridge, UK: Cambridge University Press.

Simon, H. A. (1973). The structure of ill-structured problems. *Artificial Intelligence, 4*, 181–202.

Unterrainer, J. M., Rahm, B., Leonhart, R., Ruff, C. C., & Halsband, U. (2003). The Tower of London: The impact of instructions, cueing, and learning on planning abilities. *Cognitive Brain Research, 17*, 675–683.

van Rooij, I., Stege, U., & Schactman, A. (2003). Convex hull and tour crossings in the Euclidean traveling salesperson problem: Implications for human performance studies. *Memory & Cognition, 31*, 215–220.

Vickers, D., Butavicius, M., Lee, M. D., & Medvedev, A. (2001). Human performance on visually presented traveling salesman problems. *Psychological Research, 65*, 34–45.

Ward, G., & Allport, A. (1997). Planning and problem-solving using the five-disc Tower of London task. *The Quarterly Journal of Experimental Psychology, 50A*, 49–78.

Witkin, H. A., & Goodenough, D. R. (1981). *Cognitive styles: Essence and origins*. New York: International Universities Press.

APPENDIX

Mathematical details of the model

Visual module

Visual processing is based on the family of Gabor filters derived by Lee (1996), which satisfies both mathematical and neurophysiological constraints:

$$\psi(x,y,\omega_o,\theta) = \frac{\omega_o}{\sqrt{2\pi}\kappa} \cdot \exp\left\{\left(\frac{\omega_o^2}{8k^2}\right)\right.$$
$$\cdot [4(x \cdot \cos\theta y \cdot \sin\theta)^2 + (-x \cdot \sin\theta + y \cdot \cos\theta)^2]\right\}$$
$$\cdot \left\{\exp[i(\omega_o \cdot x \cot\cos\theta + \omega_o \cdot v \cot\sin\theta] \right.$$
$$\left. - \exp\left(\frac{k^2}{2}\right)\right\} \qquad 1$$

where x and y represent the centre of the wavelet, ω_o is the spatial frequency in radians per unit length, and θ is the wavelet orientation in radians. K is a constant set to π (Lee, 1996). The real and imaginary parts of the complex function produce two filters, referred to as odd and even. In the present work, we varied only the wavelet orientation (0, 1/4;π, 1/2;π, and 3/4;π) for a total of eight filters (four even and four odd), while the spatial frequency was fixed at 0.57 radians. Four orientations constitute the minimal set of filters and are sufficient to provide rotation and size invariance (Riesenhuber & Poggio, 1999). We use a single, low-frequency bandwidth because it is more suitable to detect the main directional features of the entire stimulus. Note that adding more spatial frequencies, and thus more Gabor filter maps, did not improve the performance of the model.

Competitive selection module and top-down controller

Activation of each heuristic unit y_i at time t in the competitive selection module is obtained by summing the feedforward activation from the input layer I_i (visual module) and the recurrent input from the lateral connections in the heuristic layer.

$$y_i^t = I_i + \left(\sum_k y_k^{(t-1)} * w_{ik}\right) \qquad 2$$

where y^{t-1} is the activation of the kth heuristic unit (including itself) at the previous time step ($t - 1$), and w_{ik} indicates the weight of the corresponding lateral connection. The latter are fixed to the values of 0.2 and -0.1 for self-excitatory and lateral inhibitory connections, respectively. The feedforward activation from the visual module to each ith heuristic unit is calculated as follows:

$$I_i = \sum_j w_{ij} x_j \qquad 3$$

where x_j is the activation of the jth input unit, and w_{ij} is the weight of the corresponding connection.

The activation equations are run iteratively until one heuristic unit wins the competition. Note that the relaxation is driven by the lateral connections because I_i remains constant. To speed up the relaxation process we terminate the competition whenever one unit reaches a value of 0.9 (instead of the maximum of 1.0). At that point, the winning unit is set to 1, whereas all other units are set to 0.

During the learning phase, the feedforward weights between jth input units and the winning heuristic unit y are updated according to a Hebbian learning rule (Brown & Chattarji, 1995):

$$\Delta w_j = \eta(x_j w_j) y \qquad 4$$

where η is the learning rate (set to 0.1). Note that competitive learning (Rumelhart & Zipser, 1985) sorts patterns sharing similar properties into the same category, and it can be viewed as a clustering technique.

The effect of the TDC is simply to reset to zero the activation of all heuristic units in the competitive selection module. The efficiency of the TDC in resetting the heuristics nodes is decreased after a simulated lesion. That is, a residual activation (proportional to the severity of the lesion) persists in the heuristic nodes. For example, for a 20% lesion the residual activation of the winning heuristic unit corresponds to 80% of the activation at $t = 1$. The residual activation y of the winning unit is calculated as follows:

$$y = \frac{I_i * L}{100} \qquad 5$$

where L is the severity of the TDC lesion expressed as a percentage. Thus, when L is set to zero there is no residual activation.

Spatial module

Activation of each unit in the spatial target map is calculated as follows:

$$O = f\left[R_i(1 - S_i) + \sum_j W_{ij} O_j\right] \qquad 6$$

where R_i is the input from retinal (input) units (see below) and S_i is the activation value of the ith unit in the saliency map. The rightmost term of the equation computes the recurrent input resulting from the lateral connections W with the other units. Finally, $f(x)$ is a squashing function that bounds the activation in the [0, 1] range:

$$f(x) = \begin{cases} \dfrac{2}{1 + e^{-x}} - 1 & \text{if } x > 0 \\ 0 & \text{otherwise} \end{cases} \qquad 7$$

The retinal input R_i to each unit in the spatial target map is calculated as follows:

$$R_i = \exp\left(-\frac{d_{ri}^2}{2\sigma^2}\right) \qquad 8$$

where d_{ri} is the distance between the centre of the retinal receptive field (r_{xi}, r_{yi}) of the spatial unit and the retinal coordinates (r_x, r_y) of the visual target—that is, $d_{ri}^2 = (r_x - r_{xi})^2 + (r_y - r_{yi})^2$; σ is the width of the Gaussian (set to 5°). The receptive field centres were spread uniformly between $-40°$ and $+40°$ on both x and y axes, with increments of 4°.

The spatial target map contains symmetric lateral connections with fixed-value inhibitory weights that depend on the distance between neurons:

$$W_{ij} = \min\left[0, A_E \exp\left(\frac{d_{ij}^2}{2\sigma_E^2}\right) - A_I \exp\left(-\frac{d_{ij}^2}{2\sigma_I^2}\right)\right] \qquad 9$$

where d_{ij} is the distance between the two neurons. The connections weights cannot have a positive value. A_E and σ_E are always higher than A_I and σ_I, respectively.

The exact location represented by the spatial target map is decoded through a simple vector method (Salinas & Abbott, 1995):

$$(O_x, O_y) = \left(\frac{\sum_i O_i O_{xi}}{\sum_i O_i}, \frac{\sum_i O_i O_{yi}}{\sum_i O_i}\right) \qquad 10$$

where (O_x, O_y) is the location of the planned movement, O_i is the activation value of the ith unit in the spatial target map, and O_{xi} and O_{yi} are the field centre coordinates of the ith unit.

Is compound chaining the serial-order mechanism of spelling? A simple recurrent network investigation

Ariel M. Goldberg and Brenda Rapp
Department of Cognitive Science, Johns Hopkins University, Baltimore, MD, USA

Although considerable progress has been made in determining the cognitive architecture of spelling, less is known about the serial-order mechanism of spelling: the process(es) involved in producing each letter in the proper order. In this study, we investigate *compound chaining* as a theory of the serial-order mechanism of spelling. Chaining theories posit that the retrieval from memory of each element in a sequence is dependent upon the retrieval of previous elements. We examine this issue by comparing the performance of simple recurrent networks (a class of neural networks that we show can operate by chaining) with that of two individuals with acquired dysgraphia affecting the serial-order mechanism of spelling—the graphemic buffer. We compare their performance in terms of the effects of serial position, the effect of length on overall letter accuracy, and the effect of length on the accuracy of specific positions within the word. We find that the networks produce significantly different patterns of performance from those of the dysgraphics, indicating that compound chaining is not an appropriate theory of the serial-order mechanism of spelling.

Keywords: Serial order; Spelling; Graphemic buffer; Simulation; Compound chaining.

Serial behaviour—the act of producing a set of actions in their proper order—is an integral part of cognition. Tasks such as producing a sentence, pronouncing and spelling words, recalling a series of events, and navigating through space are all basic cognitive tasks that rely on the ability to structure and produce actions in a particular order. Uncovering the properties of the representations and processes responsible for serial behaviour has been of interest to psychologists since at least Ebbinghaus (1885) but the endeavour was first truly made prominent by Karl Lashley (1951). In his landmark essay, Lashley drew attention to the centrality of serial order in cognition as well as the computational challenges involved in solving the "problem of serial order". While a significant amount of work since then has been dedicated to understanding the nature of these processes, as Houghton and Hartley (1995) note, the majority of modern theories of cognition take serial order for granted.

Correspondence should be addressed to Ariel M. Goldberg, Department of Cognitive Science, Johns Hopkins University, 3400 North Charles Street, Baltimore, MD 21218, USA (E-mail: goldberg@cogsci.jhu.edu).

We greatly appreciate the support provided by NIH (National Institutes of Health) Grant DC 006740 to the second author. In addition, we would like to thank B.W.N. and R.S.B. for their enthusiasm and tireless work on this project and Paul Smolensky, Don Mathis, Manny Vindiola, Michael McCloskey, and the members of the Johns Hopkins University Neural Networks Research Lab for many valuable theoretical and implementational discussions related to this project.

Theoretical linguistics ... avails itself of such formal objects as ordered sets, strings etc. as primitives, from which to build descriptions of grammars and other abstract objects. In artificial intelligence and computer science, analogous objects plus recursive serial processing are provided by computer programming languages. In such a context, serial order per se will not appear to be any kind of problem at all. (p. 2)

The basic questions are: "How is the order of the elements in a sequence represented?" and "What are the specific characteristics of the mechanisms that ensure that the elements are selected and produced in their proper order?". There have been a number of classes of representational/processing mechanisms that have been proposed and examined as candidates for serial-order systems in a variety of cognitive domains. We examine a theory of serial order referred to as *compound chaining* that falls within the broader class of theories known as *chaining theories* (e.g., Ebbinghaus, 1885; Lashley, 1951). We do so by creating computer simulations of the spelling process that instantiate the core characteristics of compound chaining. Specifically we make use of a type of neural network, known as a *simple recurrent network* (SRN; Jordan, 1986; Elman, 1990), which, it has been argued, achieves serial order through compound chaining (e.g., Glasspool, 1998; Henson, Norris, Page, & Baddeley, 1996; Houghton & Hartley, 1995). We test the compound chaining theory by comparing the performance of SRNs, when they have undergone disruption, with the performance of humans who have acquired spelling deficits as a result of neural injury.

In the following sections of this Introduction we: (a) describe the cognitive architecture of spelling and situate the serial-order mechanism within these processes; (b) review simple and compound chaining and other theories of serial order that have been proposed; (c) discuss the current state of research on the serial-order mechanism of spelling and motivate the use of simple recurrent networks to test a chaining theory of serial order in spelling.

Overview of the functional architecture of spelling

Figure 1 depicts a common functional architecture of the processing involved in spelling (Caramazza,

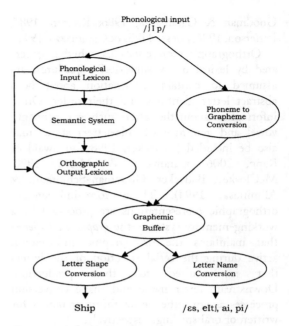

Figure 1. *The cognitive architecture of the spelling system.*

1988; Ellis, 1982; for a review see Rapp, 2002), which will be useful for situating the serial-order demands of the spelling process and the dysgraphic impairments.

According to this framework, the spelling of familiar words is distinguished from the spelling of sublexical elements, and these are carried out by the lexical and phoneme-to-grapheme conversion systems, respectively. The key component of the lexical system is the *orthographic lexicon*, which corresponds to the long-term memory repository of the spellings of familiar words, while the phoneme-to-grapheme conversion system corresponds to the knowledge of the procedures for converting sounds to letters. While the lexical system is critical for the spelling of irregular words, and the phoneme-to-grapheme conversion system is critical for spelling unfamiliar words, both systems may be engaged in spelling all stimuli (Rapp, Epstein, & Tainturier, 2002). Also proposed is a process whereby the representations in the phonological input lexicon can make direct contact with the orthographic output lexicon, bypassing semantics (Baxter & Warrington, 1987;

Goodman & Caramazza, 1986; Kremin, 1987; Patterson, 1986; but see Hillis & Caramazza, 1991).

Orthographic representations, whether generated by lexical or by sublexical procedures, are assumed to contain information about both abstract letter identities and their order. Other information about the letters such as consonant/vowel and geminate (double-letter) status may also be included (Badecker, 1996; Buchwald & Rapp, 2006; Caramazza & Miceli, 1990; McCloskey, Badecker, Goodman-Schulman, & Aliminosa, 1994). These form-independent orthographic representations are processed by a working-memory system—the *graphemic buffer*—that maintains the orthographic information active during the serial selection of the letters that is required for their production. Downstream letter name and shape conversion processes assign either letter forms or names for written or oral spelling, respectively.

We are concerned with deficits affecting the functioning of the graphemic buffering system, which, as a system that ensures that letters are available for serial production, fits the canonical description of a serial-order mechanism. Damage at the level of the graphemic buffer results almost exclusively in errors relating to either the order or the identity of the letters being spelled—for example, deletions (SPRINT → SPINT), substitutions (SPRINT → SPKINT), additions (SPRINT → SPRINWT), movements (SPRINT → SRINTP), and transpositions (SPRINT → SNRIPT).

Damage to the graphemic buffer typically results in performance features that have been associated with other working-memory systems: *length* and *serial position effects*. The length effect is the finding that accuracy decreases as the length of the word increases, and it is present whether accuracy is measured in terms of the number of words or the number of letters spelled correctly at each length (e.g., Buchwald & Rapp, 2008). The length effect as measured by letter accuracy, in particular, indicates that for each element in the sequence, the functioning of the graphemic buffer is influenced by the length of the sequence as a whole. This has often been taken to indicate that the functioning of the buffer involves a limited-capacity resource (such as working memory). The serial position effect refers to the fact that errors tend to have a bow-shaped distribution, with the majority of errors occurring in the middle of words. Furthermore, the curve is often (although not always) asymmetric, with better performance at the beginning than at the end (e.g., Caramazza, Miceli, Villa, & Romani, 1987). The length and serial position effects have been reported in both normal (Jensen, 1962; Wing & Baddeley, 1980) and dysgraphic spellers (e.g., Caramazza & Miceli, 1990; McCloskey et al., 1994). This is an indication that they reflect aspects of the basic functioning of the serial-order mechanism of spelling. In the research we report on here, these two performance patterns form the basis for comparing network and dysgraphic spelling.

Theories of serial order

It is useful to first define a few terms. We take a *sequence* to be an ordered collection of *items*. Thus, a word—as an ordered collection of graphemes or phonemes—corresponds to a sequence. A sequence is stored in memory (either long-term, LTM, or short-term, STM) until it is time to produce it. The production of a sequence involves the production of each item, and this involves two stages: (a) the retrieval/selection of the item from STM or LTM and (b) the generation of that item (writing a letter, pronouncing a phoneme, etc.). The generation may be the actual physical production involving the motor system and involve a "visible" product, or it may involve more abstract intermediate levels of generation that are involved in planning the overt production.

Theories differ with regard to the mechanism by which the retrieval/selection of an item takes place. Certain theories, such as the primacy model (Page & Norris, 1998) and SOB (for "serial-order-in-a-box"; Farrell & Lewandowsky, 2002) propose that when a sequence is to be produced, all of the items in the sequence are simultaneously activated. Items receive less activation the further they are from the beginning of the sequence. Production proceeds by selecting the item with the most activation at the given timestep and then subsequently suppressing its activation. In contrast, for most theories of serial order the retrieval of an item from memory is triggered by a *cue*. Within such frameworks, the production of a sequence ultimately comes down to a problem of cue ordering—a serial-order system must supply the proper cue at the proper time. One of the major divisions among cueing theories of serial order is how exactly this cue ordering is accomplished. Two main classes of theories have been proposed—positional theories and chaining theories. These form the focus of our discussion.

Positional theories
In *positional* theories, an abstract representation of sequence position serves as the cue to item retrieval (Ladd & Woodworth, 1911). The serial-order mechanism iteratively updates a representation of position, which cues the retrieval of another item. For example, Brown, Preece, and Hulme (2000) propose that associations are formed in memory between the items in a sequence and a temporal oscillator, which can be thought of as a sort of clock (see Figure 2). Each item is associated with a different clock state. To produce the sequence, the clock is reset to its initial state and allowed to run. As it proceeds, each clock state cues the retrieval of the associated item in the sequence. Positional theories have variously taken cues to be the states of a temporal oscillator (Brown et al., 2000) or some kind of control signal (e.g., Anderson & Matessa, 1997; Burgess & Hitch, 1992; Henson, 1998; Houghton, 1990; Houghton, Glasspool, & Shallice, 1994; Lee & Estes, 1981).

Positional theories may encode position temporally, ordinally, relative to the beginning and end of the sequence, or nominally (Henson, 1999). For example, some systems utilize a representation of elapsed time for cues (Brown et al., 2000), making these systems sensitive to temporal factors such as the presentation rate of the sequence. Other systems utilize a representation of the item's absolute ordinal distance from the beginning of the sequence (Burgess &

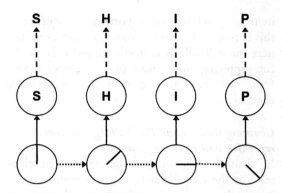

Figure 2. *A schematized depiction of the positional theory proposed by Brown, Preece, and Hulme (2000). The states of a temporal oscillator (depicted here as a clock) cue the retrieval (solid arrows) of the items in a sequence (circled items), which in turn drives the generation of the items (dashed arrows). Each word has its own clock, which moves from state to state (dotted arrow) independently of the rest of the system.*

Hitch, 1992). Some positional systems utilize a representation that encodes an item's position relative to the beginning and end of the sequence (Henson 1998; Houghton 1990). For example, the first item in a 7-item sequence would be encoded as <beginning + 1, end − 7>, indicating that the item is the first item from the left margin of the sequence and the 7th item from the right margin. This encoding scheme differs from the ordinal encoding in that it is sensitive to sequence length. Finally, other theories, termed *frame-and-slot* theories (e.g., Dell, 1986; Dell, Burger, & Svec 1997; MacKay, 1982, 1987; Shattuck-Hufnagel, 1979) hold that items are associated with nominal, rather than numerical, positions (e.g., the onset, nucleus, and coda of a syllable frame). Each of these kinds of representation may differ substantially from each other, and positional theories have exploited these differences to attain and explain various properties of serial behaviour.

A critical and often implicit component of positional theories is that the cue-supplying mechanism is assumed to function independently of the processes that retrieve and produce items. That is, the clock or control signal is assumed to move from one state to the next, regardless of which items are produced. An important consequence of this is that if an item is erroneously retrieved, the next cue will still be correctly supplied. How the cue-supplying mechanism (e.g., a clock) moves from one state to the next is not typically explained.

Chaining theories and the challenges of item repetition and recovery from error

In chaining mechanisms, the items themselves serve as the cues. That is, a representation of an item in the sequence is used to trigger the retrieval of another item in the sequence. In the literature, chaining theories are typically discussed in a context in which a single sequence is being learned and generated, as in short-term memory theories of list learning (Jones, Beaman, & Macken, 1996; Lewandowsky & Murdock, 1989; Richman & Simon, 1994; Wickelgren, 1965; see Henson, 1996, for reviews). However, a number of implementational details are often left unspecified, and it is unclear how the theories would be scaled up to work in a context in which a large number of sequences need to be learned and produced—as is the case in spelling.

One theory, known as *simple chaining*, posits that the cue for each item is the immediately preceding item in the sequence—each item serves as the cue to the next (Figure 3A). To spell a word, for example, one would retrieve the first letter in the word to be spelled. This letter then cues the retrieval of the second letter, and one then simply follows the chain, retrieving/selecting and producing the letter cued by the previous letter.

Although appealing in its simplicity, simple chaining suffers from a number of theoretical drawbacks (Lashley, 1951). First, it is not clear what mechanism leads to the activation of the first item in the sequence. Second, a simple chaining system that utilized *type* item representations would be incapable of producing sequences containing repeated items. For example, in order to spell the word RADAR, associations would have to be stored between both A and D and A and R. As a result, the representation of A would be an ambiguous cue, and the system would be unable to determine whether D or R should be retrieved. The problem is magnified when one attempts to account for a situation in which multiple sequences are stored and retrieved from long-term memory. For example, in order to store RADAR and RATIO, A would have to be associated with (serve as a cue to) both D and R as well as T. We can refer to these as problems with intra- and intersequence item repetition.

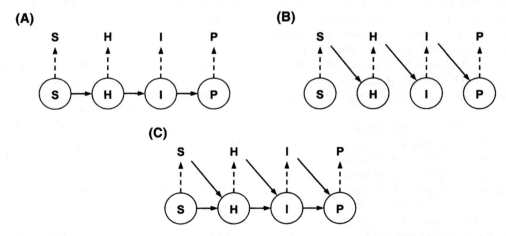

Figure 3. Internal-cue (A), external-cue (B), and hybrid (C) chaining systems. Solid arrows represent retrieval/selection processes, and dashed arrows represent the processes involved in generating the item. For simplicity, the retrieval of items is depicted as being cued by only a single item (simple chaining) although compound chaining posits multi-item cues.

The problem of generating the first element in the sequence could be addressed if we assume that lexical spelling involves activating a word's lexical node in the orthographic lexicon. In that case, the lexical node activates/retrieves/selects the first letter in the word, kick-starting the chain. The lexical nodes (depicted below in square brackets) would thus function somewhat akin to the "plan units" of the SRNs described in Jordan (1986). One way to address the issue of repeated elements (either within or across words), would be to utilize *token* rather than type item representations—for example, [RADAR] → R_1 → A_1 → D_1 → A_2 → R_2; [RATIO] → R_{16} → A_{35} → T_1 → I_5 → O_{11} (see Wickelgren, 1969, for one proposal). Although effective in dealing with the inter- and intrasequence repetition problem, this and other similar solutions are representationally cumbersome.

Simple chaining systems suffer from a more severe limitation, however. Since each retrieved item serves as the sole cue to the retrieval of the next, an error in retrieval would be catastrophic for the system (Lashley, 1951). If, for example, T_1 were retrieved instead of D_1 when spelling the word RADAR, either production would halt because T_1 does not cue the retrieval of any other item in the context of spelling the word RADAR or the cue would trigger the spelling of another word (e.g., RATIO). Since people are typically able to successfully continue spelling a word after having made an error, this represents a quite considerable shortcoming of simple chaining as a theory of the serial-order mechanism of spelling.

A more complex version of this theory known as *compound chaining* has been developed in which multiple items may serve as the cue for an item (e.g., Ebbinghaus, 1885; see Henson, 1996, and Henson et al., 1996, for reviews). In one version proposed by Ebbinghaus, each item in a sequence is cued by all of the preceding items. Thus, the word RADAR would be stored in memory as follows: The lexical node for RADAR would activate R_1, R_1 would serve as the cue to A_1, then $R_1 + A_1$ would serve as the cue to D_1, $R_1 + A_1 + D_1$ would serve as the cue to A_2, and so on. The multi-item cueing could be construed in at least two ways. R_1 and A_1 independently cue D_1 (and A_2 and R_2) or R_1 and A_1 as a unit (in conjunction) cue D_1. The exact nature of how the compound cue functions is typically not discussed.

Compound chaining offers a number of advantages. Most obviously, it addresses the intrasequence repetition problem without resorting to token representations of items. This is because, in contrast to the situation in simple chaining, the D and the second R in RADAR would now be cued by distinct cues (R + A and R + A + D + A, respectively). Furthermore, since compound chaining utilizes multiple items as cues, the probability of recovering from errors made in the production of a sequence increases. If T_1 were erroneously retrieved instead of D_1 when spelling RADAR, A_2 could potentially be retrieved next if the system were set up such that items could be retrieved on the basis of partially matching cues. That is, A_2 could be correctly retrieved if $R_1A_1T_1$ sufficiently resembled $R_1A_1D_1$ (and resembled it more than any other sequence in the lexicon). Importantly, the representational scheme may become more resilient if the lexical node, rather than simply kick-starting the process, forms a part of the multiple-item cue. In that case, the normal cue for retrieving A_2 would be [RADAR] + R_1 + A_1 + D_1. If $R_1A_1T_1$ were erroneously produced, the system might be able to recover given the complex cue [RADAR] + R_1 + A_1 + T_1. In addition, including the lexical node within the cue also allows compound chaining to use type representations to deal with the intersequence repetition problem. For example, with this feature, the D in RADAR and the T in RATIO would have distinct cues: [RADAR] + R + A and [RATIO] + R + A.

Therefore, a compound chaining theory that includes the lexical node as part of the cue is likely to be the most error resistant of the chaining approaches to serial order. We argue that the SRNs that we use to test the theory of compound chaining in spelling fall within this general class. By using them, therefore, we provide a substantial test of the theory.

In sum, at the heart of chaining theory is the elegant feature that the items themselves serve as cues. One important consequence is that the accuracy with which cues are supplied is a direct function of the accuracy with which items are retrieved. As a result, in contrast to positional theories, in chaining theories the retrieval of the wrong item negatively influences the cueing of the next item, making recovery from error a significant challenge for chaining theories.

Chaining: Internal and external cueing

A distinction can be drawn among chaining systems (simple or compound) with regard to internal versus external cueing. In the example described above and depicted in Figure 3A the item representation that is retrieved from memory (circled items) serves to drive both the next stage required for generating that item (dashed lines) and the cueing of the next item (solid lines)—an *internal-cue* system. In contrast it may not be the retrieved item but the output of the subsequent stage/s that is used as the cue (Figure 3B). For example, in spelling one may read back what one has written to cue the retrieval of the next letter in the word—an *external-cue* system. Similarly, representations of the items at later stages of processing, prior to physical production (e.g., at the letter name/shape conversion level) could be fed back, cueing the retrieval of the next item. Finally, a hybrid internal–external cue system would be one in which both internal and external cues are combined to trigger the retrieval of the next item (Figure 3C). These systems vary in their vulnerability to errors made during the *generation* of items (dashed arrows), with internal cueing systems being most vulnerable. What they share, however, is the challenge of recovering from errors made in the *retrieval* of items (solid arrows; the processes that retrieve/select an item from memory on the basis of a cue).

Evaluating chaining theories of serial order

Most of the early research on serial order was focused on exploring the behavioural implications of the item–item associations proposed in chaining theory (see Harcum, 1975, and Young, 1968, for reviews). More recent research has examined predictions of chaining theory regarding the negative impact that confusable or erroneously recalled items might have on the production of later items in a sequence. These predictions are based on the fact that in chaining systems errors should decrease the quality of the cue for subsequent items, and, similarly, if items in a sequence are confusable with each other, they will serve as a poorer cues for a subsequent item than would nonconfusable items.

Henson et al. (1996) examined these predictions in an extension of Baddeley's (1968) work that investigated the effects of phonologically confusable items on immediate serial recall. Henson et al. used sequences of six letters with one-syllable names; the names of the letters were phonologically confusable or nonconfusable with the other letters in the list. Different sequences consisted of: only confusable letters, only nonconfusable letters, and alternating nonconfusable and confusable letters. A sequence was presented visually to subjects who were then required to recall the sequence immediately by writing the letters in boxes on a sheet of paper.

Replicating Baddeley (1968), Henson et al. (1996) found that sequences containing only confusable letters were harder to recall than sequences containing only nonconfusable letters (see Figure 4). However, Henson et al. pointed out that the critical prediction for chaining theory concerns the alternating sequences. Chaining theory predicts that confusable items should serve as poorer cues than nonconfusable items to the next item in the sequence.[1] However, contrary to this prediction, nonconfusable items were retrieved just as accurately when they were cued by confusable items as when they were cued by other nonconfusable items. Henson et al. (1996) argued that

---

[1] Chaining theory also predicts that erroneously recalled items should serve as poor cues to the next item in the sequence. To isolate the effect of cue confusability, Henson et al. (1996) controlled for the effect that erroneously retrieved items had on retrieval using a conditional probability analysis. The details of this analysis are beyond the scope of this article.

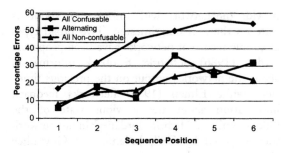

Figure 4. Error position curve for pure confusable, pure nonconfusable, and alternating sequences. In the alternating curve the peaks occur on confusable letters, and the valleys occur on nonconfusable letters. From Experiment 1 of "Unchained Memory: Error Patterns Rule Out Chaining Models of Immediate Serial Recall", by R. N. A. Henson, D. G. Norris, M. P. A. Page, and A. D. Baddeley, 1996, The Quarterly Journal of Experimental Psychology, 49A, pp. 80–115. Copyright 1996 by the Experimental Psychology Society. Adapted with permission.

this particular sawtooth pattern of performance, in which the accuracy of nonconfusable items is unaffected by the confusability of the preceding item, indicates that the serial-order mechanism of verbal working memory does not operate by chaining (but see Howard & Kahana, 2002, for a differing view). Important as they are, Henson et al.'s findings cannot, however, be automatically extended to the spelling system as it is entirely possible that different serial-order mechanisms underlie different aspects of language processing.

Investigating the serial-order mechanism of spelling: Computer simulation

There have been a handful of investigations that have used computer simulations to examine specific hypotheses regarding the organization and functioning of the spelling system (Brown & Loosemore, 1994; Brown, Loosemore, & Watson, 1993; Bullinaria, 1994, 1997; Cipolotti, Bird, Glasspool, & Shallice, 2004; Glasspool, 1998; Glasspool & Houghton, 2005; Glasspool, Houghton, & Shallice, 1995; Glasspool, Shallice, & Cipolotti, 2006; Houghton et al., 1994; Houghton, Hartley, & Glasspool, 1996; Houghton & Zorzi, 1998, 2003; Olson & Caramazza, 1994). However, only the work of Houghton and Glasspool and colleagues, has been specifically concerned with the serial-order mechanisms of spelling.

Houghton and Glasspool and colleagues have adopted largely a positional approach to the serial-order problem in spelling, using an architecture and mechanisms that they refer to as *competitive queueing*[2] (CQ; Cotelli, Abutalebi, Zorzi, & Cappa, 2003; Glasspool & Houghton, 2005; Glasspool, Shallice, & Cipolotti, 1999; Glasspool et al., 2006; Houghton et al., 1994). Very briefly, CQ specifies the position of each item in each sequence (letters in a word) by associating each item with two control-signal "counters" (the "I" and "E" nodes; see Figure 5). At each timestep, these counters simultaneously send activation to (cue) all the letters in the word, with I nodes decreasing their signal to letters as a function of the letter's distance from the start of the word and with E nodes operating in a complementary manner, with their signal decreasing as a function of a letter's distance from the end of the word. These letter units then pass their activation on to the corresponding units in the competitive filter, at which point the letters compete to be produced based on their activation strength. While the encoding of letter order makes use of a positional mechanism, the competitive part of the production process is reminiscent of the activation-based approaches of the primacy model (Page & Norris, 1998) and SOB (Farrell & Lewandowsky, 2002). After a letter is produced, the letter unit in the letter layer is inhibited (its activation is significantly decreased), a new pattern of activation is sent from the counters, and the letters compete again.

Competitive queueing networks have achieved considerable success in simulating dysgraphic performance resulting from graphemic buffer damage, including producing all of the observed error types (deletions, insertions, etc.) and exhibiting both length and serial position effects. It is beyond the

---

[2] Competitive queueing has also been proposed as a theory of verbal short-term memory (Hartley & Houghton, 1996).

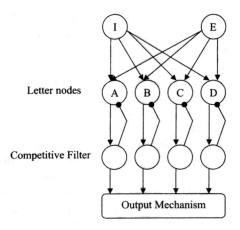

Figure 5. *A schematic depiction of the basic elements of a competitive queueing system (Houghton, Glasspool, & Shallice, 1994). A time-varying control signal, implemented as the I and E nodes, sends activation on each timestep to letter units. These units pass their activation to the next layer of letter units, which compete for selection. The letter with the highest activation is selected and produced by the output mechanism. This unit then sends inhibitory activation back to the letter units, creating a "refractory period". For clarity, a special mechanism for producing double letters has been omitted from this diagram. Reproduced with permission.*

scope of this paper to discuss specific characteristics of the CQ approach and the possible challenges it may face. However, we do return to CQ in Experiment 1, in which we argue that the SRN architecture that we have implemented differs from the CQ architecture (i.e., in Glasspool & Houghton, 2005) in just the ways a chaining system should differ from a nonchaining (positional) system.

Chaining: Simple recurrent networks

A simple recurrent network (SRN) is a type of neural network that produces its output one item at a time over a series of timesteps (Elman, 1990; Jordan, 1986). SRNs resemble standard multilayer feed-forward networks in that they have an input layer, a hidden layer, and an output layer. They differ from them, however, in that SRNs possess additional context layers, which copy the network's activation values and feed this information back to the network on the next timestep. The context layers thus serve as a sort of memory—they provide the network with information about its state on the previous timestep. Two broad types of simple recurrent networks have been proposed: Jordan (1986) networks feedback information about the network's output on the previous timestep, while Elman (1990) networks feedback information about the previous state of the hidden units. A hybrid Jordan–Elman network was proposed by Dell, Juliano, and Govindjee (1993) that made use of both of these context layers. We adopt the terminology of Dell and colleagues and term these layers the external and internal context layers, respectively (see Figure 6)

At Timestep 1, the activation on the context units is set to 0. An input representation is clamped on the input units, and activation feeds forward to the hidden units and from the hidden units to the output units, producing an output representation—the first item in a sequence. At the end of the timestep, the activation on the hidden units is copied onto the internal context units, and the activation on the output units is copied to the external context layer. At Timestep 2, the activations on the hidden units are zeroed, and activation is passed to the hidden layer from both the input layer and the context layer(s). In this way, the hidden layer thus receives information about the current input as well as about the state of the network at the previous timestep. The system then produces a pattern of activation on the output units that corresponds to the second item in the sequence. To situate ourselves within the previous discussion of serial-order theories, we can understand an SRN to basically function as follows: The context layers (and input layer) cue the retrieval of an item on the hidden layer, and this representation ultimately leads to the production of the item on the output layer.

It is generally believed that simple recurrent networks achieve serial order via a compound chaining process (e.g., Glasspool, 1998; Henson et al., 1996; Houghton & Hartley, 1995). In Elman networks, the hidden unit representation on a given timestep is a direct function of the representation on the previous timestep. Since the hidden units are capable of representing many different items, they can essentially act as a

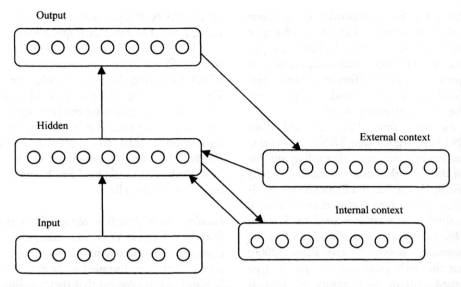

Figure 6. The basic simple recurrent network (SRN) architecture (Elman, 1990; Jordan, 1986). The network depicted here contains elements from both the Jordan and Elman architectures (the external and internal context layers, respectively) and so is a Jordan–Elman-type SRN (Dell, Juliano, & Govindjee, 1993).

buffer, maintaining a representation of the previously retrieved items. Jordan networks act in much the same way, differing from Elman networks in that they feed back to the hidden units the activation of the output layer rather than the hidden layer. If Jordan networks only fed back the activation pattern on the output layer corresponding to the most recently produced item they would be simple chaining mechanisms, cueing each item with just the previous item. They would, accordingly, be subject to all of the limitations of simple chaining. But Jordan networks do in fact operate by compound chaining: The external context layer, in addition to its connections to the hidden layer, has connections to itself.[3] This means that the activation of the context layer on timestep t is a function of the network's output on timestep t − 1 and its own activation on timestep t − 1, which includes information from the network's output on timestep t − 2. This allows the external context layer to act as a buffer, potentially encoding information from multiple previous items.

Although they all operate by compound chaining, Jordan, Elman, and Jordan–Elman networks differ in that Jordan networks are external-cue systems (Figure 3B), Elman networks are internal-cue systems (Figure 3A), while Jordan–Elman networks are a hybrid of the two (Figure 3C). Finally, the fact that both the previous state of the system and the input pattern serve as cues at each timestep would apparently place these networks into the category of compound chaining architectures that cue upcoming items with information about multiple past elements as well as information regarding the sequence (word) to be produced—for example, [RADAR] + R + A → .

It is important to note that while the architecture makes it possible for SRNs to chain, it has been argued that they do not necessarily function by chaining—simple or compound. For example, it

---

[3] Note that Jordan–Elman networks (the networks used in this study) do not contain these recurrent connections. In the Jordan–Elman networks, hidden unit activation is a function of the previously produced item (output layer activation) and the state of the hidden units on the previous timestep. It is this latter connectivity that allows the networks to function by compound chaining.

has been shown that Elman networks can develop in such a way that a subset of the hidden units function as a counter (Rodriguez, 2001). An SRN that primarily makes use of hidden unit counters may be using a representation of position to cue each item and thus should probably be considered a positional system rather than a chaining system.

Along the same lines, Botvinick and Plaut (2003, 2006) have argued that SRNs can develop different processing strategies depending on the demands of the tasks that they are trained to carry out. Specifically, Botvinick and Plaut (2006) developed an SRN architecture that performed a serial recall task similar to what was used by Henson et al. (1996) to test chaining theories of verbal working memory. Botvinick and Plaut (2006) showed that the SRN produced the specific type of sawtoothed pattern (see Figure 4) that is argued to be incompatible with a chaining mechanism of serial order. On this basis Botvinick and Plaut argued that SRNs do not necessarily chain.

Given these findings, in order to use SRNs to test whether chaining is an appropriate theory of the serial-order mechanism of spelling, we must first show that the SRNs that we have developed do, in fact, operate by chaining. We do this in Experiment 1 of the simulation studies and then go on in Experiments 2 and 3 to test the adequacy of a chaining theory of the serial-order mechanism of spelling. First, however, we present the empirical findings from two dysgraphic individuals, which form the basis of the test of the SRNs and, through them, of compound chaining itself.

CASE STUDIES

We first summarize the performance patterns of two dysgraphic individuals, which indicate that their dysgraphia originates largely, if not exclusively, at the level of the graphemic buffer—the likely locus of the serial-order mechanism for spelling (see also Houghton et al., 1994). We then describe three features of their performance that form the basis for the comparison with the SRNs in Experiments 2 and 3. The reader may refer to other reports of these individuals for more details on their performance (Buchwald & Rapp, 2006; Rapp, 2005; Rapp & Kane, 2002; Tainturier & Rapp, 2004).

B.W.N. was a 79-year-old, right-handed man who suffered two cerebrovascular accidents (CVAs) affecting the left and right parietal lobes. The earlier stroke gave rise to the dysgraphia and other language symptoms; the later one was apparently asymptomatic. R.S.B. was a 59-year-old, right-handed man who suffered a CVA that affected the anterior region of the left parietal lobe. Both individuals held PhDs and were excellent premorbid spellers.

Localization of deficits in the spelling system

Both R.S.B. and B.W.N. were administered several thousand 4–10-letter, monomorphemic words to spell to dictation. Detailed analyses (see Buchwald & Rapp, 2006) revealed that their spelling patterns corresponded in all respects to those that are expected to be observed subsequent to an impairment affecting the buffering, serial-order mechanism of the spelling system. They demonstrated length effects, no or mild effects of lexical frequency, similar performance on words and nonwords and across input and output modality, and errors that consist of substitutions, insertions, deletions, and transpositions of letters, with few phonologically plausible, semantic, or lexical substitution errors. Having established in the Introduction the relevance of these deficits for testing theories of the serial-order mechanism of spelling, we next focus on the two features of their spelling performance that serve as the basis for testing the theory of compound chaining. They are: (a) the effect of position on letter accuracy and (b) the effect of word length on letter accuracy. We analyse the effect of length in two ways, by (a) measuring the overall letter accuracy of words of different lengths and (b) measuring letter accuracy at positions common to words of different lengths (e.g., Positions 1–5 in 5- and 8-letter words).

In the section that follows, we present three analyses that quantify these effects. These analyses were performed on words drawn from the dysgraphics' spelling corpora. The word set consisted of 200 monomorphemic words that both individuals had attempted to spell; the words ranged in length from 5 letters to 8 letters, with 50 words at each length. Having selected these 200 words, a personalized word set was created for each individual such that each word set contained the same 200 word types but differed in the number of tokens of each type. For example, if B.W.N. and R.S.B. had spelled *table* 3 and 5 times, respectively, B.W.N.'s set would contain the 3 tokens of *table* that he had spelled whereas R.S.B.'s would contain his 5. An additional set of 50 nine-letter word types was selected from B.W.N.'s spelling corpus, and all tokens of those words were added to B.W.N.'s word set.[4] In total, B.W.N.'s word set contained 622 items (length 5–9; 250 word types) while R.S.B.'s contained 551 (length 5–8; 200 word types). We refer to these as *B.W.N.'s word list* and *R.S.B.'s word list*, respectively.

For the following analyses and throughout the rest of the paper, network and dysgraphic spelling was scored by a computer program (see General Methods).

Analysis 1. Effect of position on letter accuracy

In order to evaluate the effect of serial position on spelling accuracy, we combined the results of all the word lengths into a standardized space of 5 positions using a modification of the procedure used by Wing and Baddeley (1980).[5] This produced a single serial position curve for each individual. As indicated in Figure 7, both R.S.B. and B.W.N. show a bow-shaped accuracy function such that accuracy decreases towards the centre of the word and then increases again. In order to quantify both the steepness of the fall and rise as well as the symmetry of the functions, we evaluated the curves in the following way. Each participant's curve was quantified by what we will refer to as the V-metric, given in Equation 1, where $posX$ = proportion correct at position x.

$$\text{V-metric} = \frac{depth - asymmetry}{2}$$

$$= \frac{(pos1 - pos3) + (pos5 - pos3) - Abs[(pos1 - pos3) - (pos5 - pos3)]}{2}$$

(1)

The V-metric is a value ranging from -1 to $+1$ that indicates how V-shaped the curve is. It simplifies the serial position curve to a V by considering only three points of the curve: the first (pos1), middle (pos3), and last (pos5) positions. It is composed of two terms: a depth term and an asymmetry term. The depth term $(pos1 - pos3) + (pos5 - pos3)$ measures how much the simplified curve resembles an upright V. The value of this term ranges from -2 to $+2$. A serial position curve with accuracy 1,0,1 at pos1, pos3, and pos5, respectively, produces a depth value of $+2$, whereas the inverted curve (0,1,0) receives a depth value of -2. Also, note that deeper serial position curves are assigned higher values than shallower curves with the same shape (1,0,1 > 1,0.5,1).

The asymmetry term, $Abs[(pos1 - pos3) - (pos5 - pos3)]$, quantifies the asymmetry of the two sides of the V—that is, it measures their dissimilarity. The term ranges from 0 to 1, assigning a 0 to

---

[4] Given the severity of his deficit, R.S.B. had not been asked to spell many nine-letter words.
[5] In our modification, the word positions that were combined to fit the 5 standardized positions alternated symmetrically around the middle.

	1	2	3	4	5
Length 5	1	2	3	4	5
Length 6	1	2	3,4	5	6
Length 7	1	2,3	4	5,6	7
Length 8	1	2,3	4,5	6,7	8
Length 9	1	2,3	4,5,6	7,8	9

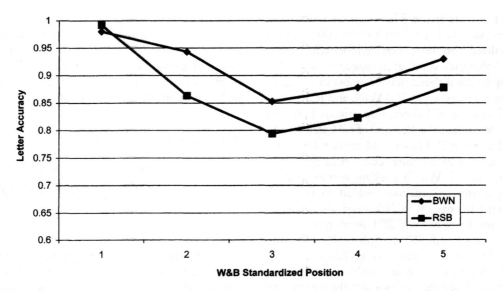

Figure 7. Letter accuracy by for B.W.N. (5–9-letter words) and R.S.B. (5–8-letter words), normalized according to a modification of the Wing and Baddeley (1980) procedure into 5 positions. Each length contributes equally.

symmetric curves and a 1 to maximally asymmetric curves. The term measures a curve's asymmetry, regardless of its orientation (curves with accuracy 1,0,1 and 0,1,0 both receive a value of 0). Taking the absolute value ensures that the term treats the two sides of the V equally.

The asymmetry term is subtracted from the depth term, in essence penalizing asymmetric curves. Symmetric curves (asymmetry = 0), receive no penalty. The resulting value is divided by 2, which forces the V-metric to range from −1 to +1. An upright V function receives a V-metric value of 1, an inverted V a value of −1, a flat function a value of 0, and a monotonically decreasing function such as 1, .5, 0 receives a value of −.5. For descriptive purposes, the depth and asymmetry terms may be thought of as the quadratic and linear trend contrasts, respectively, for three equally spaced conditions, which are then combined to produce a single value. It is important to note that the V-metric ignores performance at Positions 2 and 4, which means that it is possible in principle to have a serial position curve that scores well on the V-metric but that does not resemble a U due to the performance on these positions. This was not an issue in our studies but a modification to take these positions into account would be relatively trivial.[6]

The results of this analysis reveal that the dysgraphic individuals exhibit clear bow-shaped serial position curves (Figure 7). Both dysgraphics receive a positive V-score of .08, which one-sample t tests reveal to be significantly greater than 0: B.W.N., $t(621) = 4.40$, $p < .0001$; R.S.B., $t(550) = 4.27$, $p < .0001$. As already indicated, Wing and Baddeley (1980) and Jensen (1962) reported similar bow-shaped distributions for neurologically intact adults and children. This

---

[6] The V-score effectively measures the length of the shortest arm of the V—the V-score is positive if the short arm reverses the direction of the longer arm and negative or 0 otherwise. Because the depth and asymmetry measures are summed together, it is possible for two curves of very different shapes to receive the same V-score—a deep but asymmetric curve with a short right arm may produce the same V-score as a very shallow but perfectly symmetric curve. Since the difference between these two types of curve may hold theoretical significance, the V-score is not a good all-purpose measure of the bow shape. It does provide a rough measure of the shape, however, and is thus sufficient for our purposes. We gratefully acknowledge an anonymous reviewer for raising this issue.

reinforces the appropriateness of using dysgraphic performance, in general, and this feature, in particular, for testing theories of normal spelling. It is worth noting, however, that the source of the bow-shaped function is not well understood in either spelling or working memory.

Analysis 2a. The general effect of length on overall letter accuracy

In the spelling and working-memory literature, length effects are typically assessed by determining the number of complete sequences (e.g., words) produced correctly at each length. Measuring length effects by word accuracy, however, could potentially yield a length effect in a situation where the length of the word does not actually contribute to the probability of an error. For example, if a deficit results in a 50% chance of correctly producing a single letter regardless of the length of the word, there will be twice the likelihood of an error in eight-letter than in four-letter sequences. Simply measuring word accuracy will lead to a spurious finding of a length effect in this case.

An improvement to this traditional measure is to calculate accuracy as the number of letters spelled correctly out of the total number of letters attempted at each word length (see Buchwald & Rapp, 2008). As indicated above, both R.S.B. and B.W.N. showed significant effects of word length on letter accuracy when their entire data set was evaluated; additionally, as reported in Figure 8, similar length effects are observed with the subset of words in B.W.N.'s and R.S.B.'s word lists. In order to quantify the length effect, we calculated the slope of the linear regression line computed for letter accuracy across the different word lengths. The slope of the regression line was −0.03 for both dysgraphic participants, a value that in each case differed significantly from 0 ($p < .05$).

Analysis 2b. The specific effect of length on accuracy at shared letter positions

The previous analysis can be further refined by examining the extent to which letter accuracy at specific positions differs depending on the length of the word. For example, is the accuracy of the

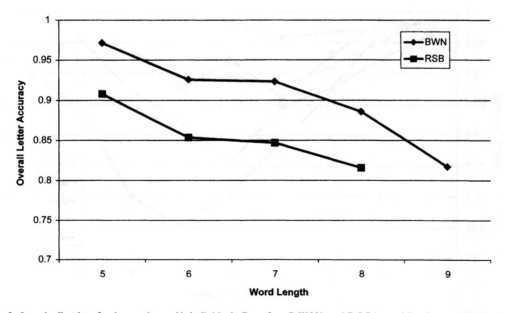

Figure 8. *Length effect data for the two dysgraphic individuals. Data from B.W.N.'s and R.S.B.'s word lists (see text for details).*

third letter in five-letter words comparable to the accuracy of the third letter in eight-letter words? Whereas the previous analysis compared the average letter accuracy of words of different lengths, the analysis detailed here compares the accuracy of specific positions across lengths, providing finer resolution. Certain serial-order mechanisms would predict that sequence length would affect item accuracy on shared positions. For example, in a limited-resource system in which the resources are fixed in "quantity", we would expect resources to be distributed more "thinly" across items as a sequence increases in length. This type of resource-limited mechanism is typically assumed to be characteristic of working-memory systems. We would expect to observe an effect of length on shared positions subsequent to damage to such a system.

The serial position data for B.W.N. and R.S.B. are graphed in Figure 9 and Figure 10. What is evident is that letter accuracy depends both on the position of the letter in the word and on the length of the word—the longer the word, the steeper the bow-shaped function. This results in different accuracies at the same position for words of different lengths and is consistent with the notion that the errors arise from disruption to a resource-limited serial-order mechanism. In order to quantify this effect, we compared accuracy at shared positions in the shortest and longest words. For R.S.B. we considered 5- and 8-letter words, and for B.W.N. we considered 5- and 9-letter words. Specifically, the probability of a correct response at each of Positions 1–5 for 8/9-letter words was subtracted from the accuracy at Positions 1–5 for 5-letter words. The differences at each position were then averaged to give a single L_{SPC} value, indicating the relationship between Positions 1–5 in the two serial position curves. If L_{SPC} is positive, Positions 1–5 differ across lengths, with an advantage to 5-letter words. If the result is negative, the reverse is true. A score of 0 indicates that the two serial position curves were identical on the shared positions. L_{SPC} can range from −1 to +1.

The results of this analysis reveal that B.W.N. has a L_{SPC} of .12, and R.S.B. has a L_{SPC} of .09, indicating that at identical positions letter accuracy

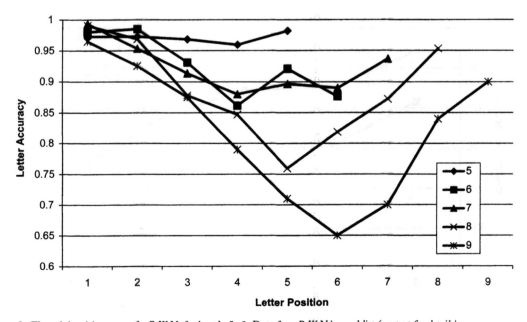

Figure 9. *The serial position curves for B.W.N. for lengths 5–9. Data from B.W.N.'s word list (see text for details).*

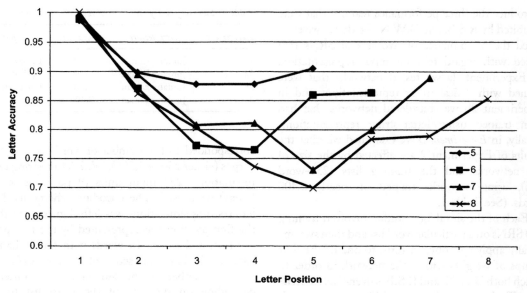

Figure 10. *The serial position curves for R.S.B. for lengths 5–8. Data from R.S.B.'s word list (see text for details).*

is lower for longer words. In order to determine whether these values were significantly different from 0, we ran Monte Carlo simulations that allowed us to determine the values the L_{SPC} would take on if there were no effect of length. The null hypothesis is that length does not matter, and so to simulate this situation, the words the patients spelled were randomly reclassified as being long or short regardless of their actual length. The L_{SPC} value was then calculated, and the procedure was repeated 10,000 times for each dysgraphic. The simulations revealed that the observed values of .12 and .09 were significantly greater than 0 (z-scores: B.W.N., 5.6; R.S.B., 3.4). The L_{SPC} values observed for B.W.N. and R.S.B. are compared to the performance of the SRNs in Experiments 2 and 3. Note that these positive L_{SPC} values are not merely a reflex of the fact that the serial position curves are bow shaped and appear to be word centred (Caramazza & Miceli, 1990). Positive L_{SPC} values would not be observed if the curves were bow shaped and word centred but overlapping at shared initial positions with the nadir of each curve positioned progressively rightward with increasing word length.

Summary

In this section we have presented evidence that two dysgraphic individuals suffer from an impairment that arguably affects the buffering/serial-order mechanism of the spelling system. We have described three reliable performance characteristics that form the basis for the simulation investigation of the hypothesis that the serial-order mechanism of spelling is based on compound chaining. In the General Discussion we discuss the possibility that not all dysgraphic individuals with deficits that presumably arise at this level of processing show all three of these characteristics.

SIMULATION STUDIES: OVERVIEW

General methods

We carried out three simulation experiments, all involving SRNs that were similarly constructed and trained. *Experiment 1* established that the SRNs are plausibly instantiating some form of compound chaining. In *Experiment 2* we examined the degree to which these SRNs, when damaged, reproduce the three performance features that were exhibited by R.S.B. and B.W.N. To do so, we evaluated the performance of two sets of SRNs that varied with regard to their input representation. In Experiment 2a we tested networks that were trained with lexical input representations and in Experiment 2b we considered networks that had been trained using letter-string representations. Finally, in *Experiment 3* we examined whether the results of Experiment 2 are affected by the size of the networks and the training lists (250-word lists), using networks trained on nearly 2,400 words. (See Table 1.)

Each of the simulation studies involved training 100 SRNs on a particular word list and then systematically applying noise, in turn, to one of the four groups of weights within the network in order to match both B.W.N. and R.S.B.'s overall letter accuracy. To be clear, the same 100 networks—with different noise values—were utilized in the simulation of both dysgraphic individuals. The general procedure was as follows (specific details are provided in subsequent sections): (a) after training, each of the 100 networks was damaged in each of the four weight locations to match the letter accuracy exhibited by B.W.N. and was then tested; (b) the weights were then restored to their trained values; (c) noise was added, in turn, to each of the four weight locations to match R.S.B.'s letter accuracy, and the 100 networks were tested again.

Simulations were run using the LENS software package (Rohde, 1999).

Architecture

The Jordan–Elman architecture was used in all three simulation studies (Figure 6; Dell et al., 1993). The input layer was fully connected to the hidden layer, which in turn was fully connected to the output layer. The internal and external context layers were also fully connected to the hidden layer. The number of input units varied depending on the type of input representation. With lexical representations, the number of input units

Table 1. *Summary of key attributes of the simulation experiments*

Experiment	Architecture	Word list	Input
1	Jordan–Elman	250	Lexical
2a	Jordan–Elman	250	Lexical
2b	Jordan–Elman	250	Letter-string
3	Jordan–Elman	2,400	Lexical

corresponded to the number of word types in the corpus (either 250 or 2,396). With letter-string representations, 234 input units (9 positions × 26 letters) were used. The encoding scheme used in letter-string simulations was left-aligned such that the first position was represented by the first pool of units, and so on. In words with fewer than 9 letters, units in the unused pools were set to 0.

The number of hidden units also differed depending on the size of the word list to be learned: 55 for the small list and 311 for the large.[7] The output layer consisted of a localist representation of each letter in the alphabet plus a start and a stop symbol, for a total of 28 units. The internal and external context layers had the same number of units as did the hidden and output layers, respectively. All units used the logistic activation function, allowing unit activation to range from 0 to +1. A bias unit with a fixed activation of +1 was connected to every noninput unit, a standard technique that makes the networks easier to train. Weights on connections could range from −1 to +1.

Word lists

It is useful to distinguish between the word set that a network was trained on and the set that it was tested on after "damage". In Experiments 1 and 2, the networks were trained on a list of 250 different words, ranging in length from 5–9 letters, 50 different words at each length (see Appendix). This training set is identical to the word types that made up B.W.N.'s word list, described in the Case Study section. When simulating B.W.N., the networks were tested using B.W.N.'s list (described in the

---

[7] These values ensured that the small and large networks carried approximately the same amount of representational load—about 40–50 characters in the training list (including start and stop symbols) per each unit in the hidden layer.

Case Study section), and when simulating R.S.B., the networks were tested on R.S.B.'s list. Recall that these two lists shared the same word types for lengths of 5–8 but differed in the number of tokens of each type. In addition, B.W.N.'s list contained an additional 50 word types of length 9. Thus, the test list for the R.S.B. simulations contained a total of 551 items (length: 5–8 letters) while the test list for the B.W.N. simulations contained a total of 622 items (length: 5–9 letters). This ensured that a very close comparison was made in our analyses between network and dysgraphic performance—the networks and dysgraphic participants spelled the same words the same number of times.

In Experiment 3, the training list contained 2,396 monomorphemic words, 3–8 letters in length and 4 phonemes long (the latter because the corpus was originally selected for another study). The list composition was as follows: length 3, 21 words; length 4, 631 words; length 5, 1,107 words; length 6, 555 words; length 7, 79 words; length 8, 3 words. The test list consisted of one token of each of the 2,396 words from the training list. Comparison on this test list was made to the errors that the dysgraphics made on their respective word lists.

Training

The networks were trained to produce the start symbol, followed by the letters in the word, followed by the stop symbol. The target vector over the output units was a value of 1 for the current letter and 0 for all other units. At the beginning of each word, the context units were set to 0, and the relevant input unit(s) were turned on. The input units remained on throughout the spelling of the word. Activation was allowed to flow to the output layers, at which point the difference between the response and the target was calculated, and a standard backpropagation algorithm (Rumelhart, Hinton, & Williams, 1986) was used to determine weight adjustment. All of the weights in the network were trained except for the weights that copied the hidden and output layers to their respective context layers—those weights were fixed at 1. The bias unit had a fixed activation of 1, and the weight of its connection to each noninput unit was adjusted in the same manner as any other connection, through backpropagation.

Batch training was used, where the network spelled 50 words before the weights were updated. Error was calculated for each batch as the summed difference on each timestep between the target output vector and the actual output vector. In Experiments 1 and 2, the networks were trained to an error criterion of 30/batch. In Experiment 3, the networks were trained to an error criterion of 25/batch. This translates to an average error of 0.002 per output unit per letter in a word. At both of these points in training, networks had achieved approximately 100% letter accuracy, and the output units were nearly binary with the selected unit at 1 and all others at 0.

In Experiments 1 and 2, the learning rate was 0.05, and momentum was 0.5. In Experiment 3, the learning rate was 0.25, and momentum was 0.5. The default LENS training option of bounded momentum descent was used in all simulations.

Simulating damage

Damage was simulated for each dysgraphic individual at four different loci in 100 different networks, for a total of 400 different damage simulations for each participant. Damaging the networks consisted of adding Gaussian noise to one of the four sets of connections: (a) the input units to the hidden units (inp → hid); (b) the hidden units to the output units (hid → out); (c) the internal context units to the hidden units (int → hid); and (d) the external context units to the hidden units (ext → hid). The effects of damage to each of the four sets of connections were evaluated because it is not known which site best corresponds to the dysgraphics' functional lesion. The mean of the noise distribution was fixed at 0, and the variance was empirically determined for each individual and for each noise locus such that, when damaged, the networks' overall letter accuracy on the test list approximated the dysgraphic's overall letter accuracy on their word list.

A fixed set of noise values was applied to the "affected" connection weights throughout the spelling of a word. That is, before a word was to be spelled, the network was in its trained, undamaged state. Noise values of the appropriate magnitude were then randomly added to the connections, and these values remained fixed until the network finished spelling the word. The noise was then removed (restoring the weights to their trained values) and was then randomly reapplied before the next word was spelled. In this manner, noise values were constant within a word but differed between words.

A computer program scored the spelling of both the dysgraphic participants and the networks. In a nutshell, the program scores a word by determining the fewest errors necessary to transform the target word into the response. The program is given a set of errors ("transformations"), which in this case consisted of substitutions, deletions, insertions, and movements. The program assigns errors to positions in the target and, using the A* pathfinding algorithm (Hart, Nilsson, & Raphael, 1968), finds the fewest necessary to produce the response. This technique does not assume any particular alignment of the target and response (e.g., left, centre, or right alignment) avoiding potential biases to the shape of the serial position curve. In cases where a response could be scored in multiple ways, an interpretation was chosen at random. On each timestep, the letter output unit with the highest activation was considered to be the one selected by the network. Since SRNs do not have a way to endogenously stop at the end of a word, the stop symbol was used as the de facto end of the word. Only the letters produced between the start and stop symbols were scored.

EXPERIMENT 1: CONFIRMING THAT THE SIMPLE RECURRENT NETWORKS OPERATE BY CHAINING

While the particular sawtooth pattern reported by Henson et al. (1996; see Figure 4 above) has been taken to be impossible for chaining systems and thus can be used as diagnostic of a nonchaining system, no one has proposed specific characteristics of a chaining system. Howard and Kahana (2002) have defined chaining systems as "those [systems] that maintain a causal relationship between one recall and the next" (p. 293). While SRNs would seem to be operating according to those principles, Botvinick and Plaut (2003, 2006) argued that SRNs are capable of functioning by means other than chaining as evidenced by their ability to reproduce the critical sawtooth pattern. Although the evidence is quite convincing, Botvinick and Plaut (2003) do not specify the formal properties of the training procedures or tasks that would or would not cause these networks to operate via a mechanism other than chaining. We thus put forward two novel analyses that may serve as diagnostics of chaining systems. While these analyses are certainly not definitive and may turn out to be neither necessary nor sufficient, they seem reasonable first steps given the fledging status of research in this area.

The proposed analyses are based on the assumption that in chaining, since each retrieved item serves as the cue to the next, any errors made in the retrieval of an item should increase the likelihood of making subsequent errors. From this assumption we developed two diagnostic tests: (a) the conditional error probability analysis and (b) the increasing representational distortion analysis. In this section, we first describe these analyses and then go on to present evidence that the SRNs we have trained to spell exhibit the characteristics predicted by these analyses. In order to show that these diagnostic criteria discriminate between systems that are presumptive chainers and nonchainers, we also apply the diagnostic tests to a set of competitive queueing (CQ) networks that have been trained to spell. We show that the performance of the CQ networks contrasts quite strikingly with that of the SRNs and that they do not clearly meet the diagnostic tests that we have proposed serve to identify serial-order mechanisms that operate via chaining.

Analysis 1: Conditional error probability

In a chaining system, the probability of making an error on position k having made one or more errors on positions 1 through $k - 1$ should be higher than the probability of making an error on position k given no previous errors. Thus a conditional probability analysis should reveal two different error rates given 0 and >0 previous errors. In contrast, nonchaining systems such as those operating by means of positional mechanisms need not show a conditional error probability effect. This is because, as discussed earlier, an error produced by a positional serial-order mechanism does not influence the functioning of the cue-supplying mechanism; as a result, errors made during element retrieval should not influence the cueing of the next element.

This is not say that the past can have no effect on the subsequent performance of a positional serial-order mechanism. For example, in a CQ system if, as a result of noise in the system, a letter was selected too early (TABLE → TL ...), its refractory period could make it incapable of being produced in the appropriate position and furthermore could potentially lead to it reappearing later in an inappropriate position. Therefore the past—early selection of the L—can change the relative standing of items in the competitive queue at later time points. However, what is critical for the comparison with a chaining system is that the letter units continue to receive the appropriate activation from the cue-supplying control signal. In chaining systems, however, since retrieved letters form part of the cue for subsequent letters, any error should increase the likelihood of a cueing error. The two classes of systems can be most directly compared in cases involving word-external letter errors (letters that are not in the target (TABLE → TO ...). Since these letters are not supposed to appear at any time in the word, their erroneous selection in a CQ system should not have a major impact on the relative status of the items in the queue. The prediction is that in a chaining system, the erroneous production of a word-external letter should increase subsequent error probabilities because the error contributes to the cueing of subsequent elements, while in a CQ system this should not be the case.

The analysis was conducted using the same networks as those that were used in Experiment 2a (see General Methods for network details) for the simulation of R.S.B.'s performance. The analysis examined the probability of making *word-external substitutions*: substitutions where the resulting letter comes from outside the word (SPRINT → SPRINK). We analysed only the errors made on 8-letter words given that, as the longest sequence in R.S.B.'s word list, it provided the greatest opportunity to observe the effects of conditional error probability.

For comparison, the same words were spelled the same number of times by the CQ network described in Glasspool and Houghton (2005). The architecture of this particular CQ network differs somewhat from the one presented in the Introduction but retains all the critical features that were discussed. For this simulation, the CV filter (consonant/vowel; see Glasspool & Houghton, 2005, for details) was turned off, and the noise level (0.38, applied to the units in the filter layer) was set so that the overall letter accuracy matched R.S.B.'s overall letter accuracy. As with the SRNs, noise was randomly reapplied after each letter.

For each network and for each letter position we calculated the proportion of responses that were either (a) incorrect and preceded by no errors or (b) incorrect and preceded by at least one error. The results are given in Figure 11.

The results clearly show that, in the SRNs, at every position, the likelihood of making an error was greater if there was an earlier error, whereas the CQ network showed no such effect.[8] Therefore, the SRNs exhibit behaviour that is consistent with what would be predicted by a chaining system, and the contrasting performance of the CQ networks serves as a confirmation of the difference between the serial-order mechanisms instantiated in these two systems.

Analysis 2: Increasing representational distortion

Given that in a chaining system an error increases the probability of a subsequent error, we should

---

[8] It is not immediately clear why the error rate for Position 2 in the competitive queueing simulation differs from the other positions. One possibility is that the data for Position 2 are drawn from a relatively small pool of errors. While Positions 3–8 each had a pool of more than 300 word-external substitution errors (with more than 5,000 errors at Position 8), only 26 word-external errors were made at Position 2. The overall pattern is clear, however.

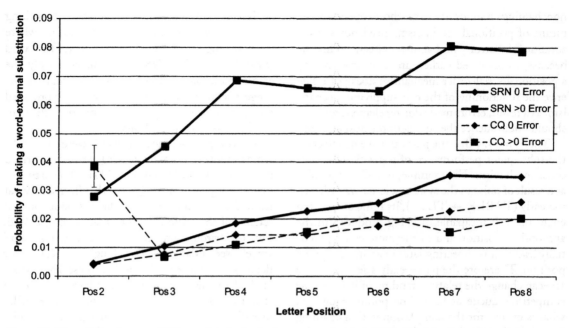

Figure 11. *The conditional error probability analysis for the simple recurrent networks (solid lines) and the competitive queueing network (dashed lines). Error bars represent one standard deviation of the mean; most error bars are too small to be graphed.*

expect this process to continue throughout a sequence, with error accumulating (snowballing) as the sequence progresses. This should influence the internal state of the system such that it should show increasing representational distortion. That is, at each subsequent retrieval step the activation state of the system should be increasingly different from its error-free state. This process should be particularly evident in a "damaged" system where the distorted representation that is generated when noise is introduced will serve as part of the cue to the next retrieval, which will in turn be subjected to further noise, resulting in greater distortion, and so on. In contrast, in a nonchaining system like CQ, noise should not have a cumulative effect. The retrieval of each item is subject to error (noise), but there should be a constant level of representational distortion at each retrieval step as the production of the elements in a sequence progresses. The fact that the cues are externally supplied should prevent representational distortion from accumulating and errors from snowballing—errors should have small and localized effects.

For this analysis, only one network was required to obtain a large enough pool of data so we randomly selected one trained SRN from the R.S.B. simulation of Experiment 2a (see General Methods for network details). First, to obtain a representation of the system in its error-free state the vectors of activation values over the hidden units were recorded while the network spelled each letter of the 50 five- and 50 eight-letter words from the training corpus. Then noise was added to the weights on the internal → hidden unit connections, and the vectors of hidden unit activation values were recorded while the network spelled the same words in a damaged state (the int → hid locus was chosen arbitrarily). The same amount of noise was applied as that in Experiment 2a (0.066; see Table 2).

To quantify the representational distortion created by the damage, the Euclidean distance between the noisy and undamaged hidden unit activation vectors was calculated for each letter position. The same procedure was carried out with the competitive queueing network, recording

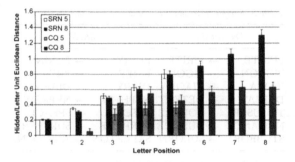

Figure 12. *The results of the representational distortion analysis for a simple recurrent network (SRN) and a competitive queueing network. Error bars represent one standard error of the mean.*

the vectors of activation values for the units in the letter layer (Figure 5; see Glasspool & Houghton, 2005, for details). Figure 12 depicts the average Euclidean distance between damaged and undamaged networks for each letter position.

The results indicate that the SRNs produced a clear and steady increase in the amount of representational distortion at each successive position in the word. This was true of both 8- and 5-letter words. The competitive queueing network, in contrast, displayed only a slight increase in distortion over time. Linear regression analyses of Positions 3–8 revealed a significant effect of position in the SRN, $t(298) = 12.36$, $p < .001$, but only a nonsignificant trend in the CQ network, $t(292) = 1.93$, $p > .05$.[9]

Discussion

In both of these analyses, the SRNs demonstrate clear signs that their functioning at a given timestep is a direct function of performance on previous timesteps. Errors increase the likelihood of making subsequent errors, and internal distortion accumulates over time. Both of these are patterns that one would expect from a system that uses its output to drive the next computation, the process that is at the heart of chaining. In contrast, the CQ networks appear to be affected very little, if at all, by previous error. This is consistent with a positional serial-order system that does not rely on previous outputs for cues for retrieval.

We have presented two diagnostic criteria that are certainly useful for identifying chaining systems. The results provide positive evidence that the SRNs are, in fact, achieving serial order through some sort of chaining mechanism. We are now in a position to examine the extent to which the SRN behaviour matches that of the dysgraphic participants.

EXPERIMENT 2: USING SIMPLE RECURRENT NETWORKS TO TEST A COMPOUND CHAINING THEORY OF THE SERIAL-ORDER MECHANISM OF SPELLING

The features of dysgraphic performance that will be used to evaluate the SRNs are: a "bow-shaped" serial position effect, an overall letter length effect, and a specific effect of length on shared letter positions.

We use two sets of SRNs that differ only in terms of their input representations—lexical and letter-string input representations (Experiments 2A and 2B, respectively). These two types of input representation were examined because they may represent quite different learning challenges for the networks. The networks with lexical input representations have a single input node that corresponds to each word. These networks must learn the letters that make up a word and their order. Since different words that share letters are not similar in terms of their input representations, this should affect the nature of the task to be learned and, as a result, the weight structure and internal network representations that develop in the course of learning. The networks with letter-string input representations face a rather different learning challenge as the individual letters that make up a word are specified by the pattern of activation on the input units. They

---

[9] Because of its architecture, the letter units in the CQ network cannot deviate from their trained values on the first timestep—this is the reason that there is no distortion on the first position. Data from Positions 3–8 were included in the analysis in order to make the two networks more comparable.

need to take the input vector that simultaneously represents the letters to be produced and learn to generate the letters one at a time, in the correct sequence. Words that are spelled similarly will have similar input representations, something that should affect the networks' solution to the problem it is faced with learning. At least superficially, the networks with letter-string representations more closely "resemble" the graphemic buffer as it has been described in the spelling literature—as a working-memory system that maintains the activation of letters while they are serially selected and passed on to subsequent production processes.

A total of 1,600 simulations were used in this experiment (100 networks × 2 input representations × 4 noise loci × 2 dysgraphic simulations). The noise values and resulting overall letter accuracies for each of the simulation sets are provided in Table 2. Each cell represents the average performance (and *SD*) of 100 networks with noise applied to a specific set of weights. B.W.N. and R.S.B.'s letter accuracy levels on this word set were: B.W.N. 90% (length 5–9) and R.S.B. 84% (length 5–8). As can be seen in Table 2, the networks with simulated damage were well matched to B.W.N. and R.S.B. in terms of letter accuracy.

As already indicated, the letter responses generated by the damaged networks were scored by a computer program. All analyses are based on letter accuracy, and errors were categorized as follows: letter substitutions, additions, deletions, and movements. We did not carry out an exhaustive analysis of error types for the networks as we did not intend to test specific predictions regarding error types and distributions. It should be noted, however, that the networks produced all of the dysgraphic error types, and sample errors are given in Table 3.

Table 3. *Sample errors made by the dysgraphics and the SRNs*

Dysgraphics		SRNs	
PIRATE	→ PIRITE	BEGIN	→ BENIN
PIGEON	→ PIGON	BRIEF	→ BRIE
VIOLA	→ VIAOLA	DIARY	→ DIARAY
DEFEAT	→ DETEAT	NEPHEW	→ NEPREW
TROUSER	→ TOUTRE	SPECIAL	→ SPEACL
NUISANCE	→ NUSSICE	SURPRISE	→ SURPRER
STUBBORN	→ SULORN	SKELETON	→ SKEOOEN

Note: SRN = simple recurrent network.

Analysis 1: Serial position analysis

The performance of 800 networks (400 of each input type) were compared to the performance of each individual. For this analysis, V-scores were calculated as described in the Case Studies section. Lengths 5–9 were evaluated for B.W.N., and lengths 5–8 were evaluated for R.S.B.

Table 4 reports the mean V-metric and range for each damage locus, for each dysgraphic participant and network type. For illustrative purposes, Figure 13 depicts the accuracy by letter position data observed for both dysgraphics as well as the average accuracy by letter position results for the

Table 2. *Network performance when simulating damage*

	B.W.N. Observed: 90%		R.S.B. Observed: 84%	
Simulations	Lexical input	Letter-string input	Lexical input	Letter-string input
inp-hid	90% (1%) [0.125]	92% (1%) [0.14]	85% (2%) [0.182]	85% (1%) [0.22]
hid-out	90% (1%) [0.4]	92% (1%) [0.5]	84% (2%) [0.5]	84% (2%) [0.65]
int-hid	89% (1%) [0.045]	91% (1%) [0.95]	83% (2%) [0.066]	83% (2%) [0.15]
ext-hid	90% (1%) [0.3]	91% (1%) [0.64]	83% (1%) [0.43]	83% (1%) [1.0]

Note: Values in each cell are the mean letter accuracy and standard deviation (in parentheses) for the 100 networks. The noise applied to the weights is given in square brackets. inp-hid = simulations where noise was applied to the weights between the input and hidden units; hid-out = between the hidden and output units; int-hid = between the internal context and hidden units; ext-hid = between the external context and hidden units. See Figure 6 for network architecture.

Table 4. Serial position effects measured by the V-metric, for both lexical-input and letter-string input networks, at each deficit locus for each dysgraphic participant

Simulations	B.W.N. (observed V-score: .08)		R.S.B. (observed V-score: .08)	
	Lexical input	Letter-string input	Lexical input	Letter-string input
inp–hid	−.23 (−.29 to −.18)	−.20 (−.27 to −.11)	−.21 (−.28 to −.13)	−.24 (−.31 to −.15)
hid–out	−.19 (−.26 to −.13)	−.13 (−.22 to −.07)	−.14 (−.19 to −.09)	−.16 (−.22 to −.09)
int–hid	−.26 (−.32 to −.21)	−.22 (−.29 to −.15)	−.24 (−.32 to −.17)	−.26 (−.34 to −.18)
ext–hid	−.24 (−.29 to −.18)	−.19 (−.26 to −.10)	−.21 (−.28 to −.14)	−.21 (−.31 to −.15)

Note: Values in each cell are the mean V-metric value and range (in parentheses) for 100 networks.

400 simulations of each input type (lexical input and letter string input).

The analysis clearly reveals that none of the 1,600 networks produced serial position curves that were as V-shaped as either B.W.N. or R.S.B.

One possible concern is that the absence of a bow-shaped serial position curve is an artefact of our training procedure. While the cause of the bow shape in dysgraphics and normal individuals is not well understood, one hypothesis is that it could be the result of an activation gradient across the letters on the output layer (M. Botvinick, personal communication, October 27, 2005). If, on each timestep, the letters are activated in proportion to their distance from the current letter (e.g., when spelling the word TABLE, the gradient on the third timestep would have B being the most active, A and L being the next most active, and T and E being the least), there would be more competition for letters in the middle of the word than for the margins, resulting in more errors in the central

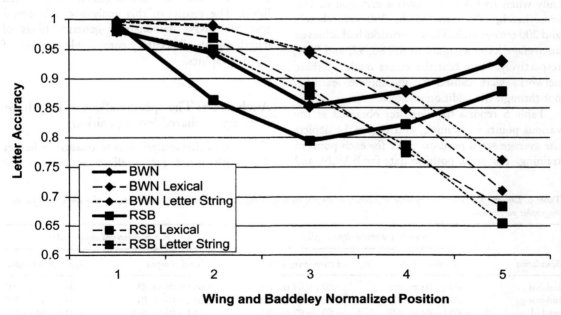

Figure 13. Serial position curve data, normalized according to a modification of Wing and Baddeley (1980). Solid lines indicate letter accuracy for each dysgraphic participant (lengths: B.W.N., 5–9; R.S.B., 5–8). Dashed lines represent the average letter accuracy for the 400 networks in each simulation (lengths: B.W.N. simulations, 5–9; R.S.B. simulations, 5–8).

Table 5. *V-metric, for lexical-input networks, at four points in training*

Error	V-score
700 (67%)	−.10 (−.21 to .01)
500 (80%)	−.09 (−.21 to .00)
300 (92%)	−.08 (−.16 to .00)
200 (97%)	−.06 (−.26 to .02)

Note: The point in training is denoted by the error/batch achieved, with the mean letter accuracy in parentheses. V-score values are the mean V-metric value for 100 networks, with the range in parentheses.

positions. Recall that in our simulations, the networks were trained until the output representations were nearly binary (with the selected unit at 1 and all other units at 0). If an activation gradient on the output units contributes to the bow shape, we could be eliminating this gradient through overtraining. If this were the case, we would expect to find bow-shaped curves earlier but not later in training. We examined the serial position curves (lengths 5–9) of the SRNs with lexical input at various points in training, specifically when they had achieved a criterion of 700 error/batch, 500 error/batch, 300 error/batch, and 200 error/batch. These networks had achieved an average letter accuracy of 67, 80, 92, and 97%, respectively. Note that the errors made by these networks were caused by incomplete learning, not through the addition of noise.

Table 5 reports the V-scores obtained at the various points in training, and Figure 14 depicts the average serial position curve for each point in training. The serial position data for B.W.N. and R.S.B. are given as reference. It is clear that bow-shaped serial position curves were not present at any point during training. This indicates that our findings do indeed reflect a systematic property of the SRNs and are not simply an artefact of our training procedure.

Analysis 2a: The general effect of length on overall letter accuracy

Letter accuracy was determined at each word length for the 800 networks (400 of each input type) used to simulate B.W.N. and the 800 used to simulate R.S.B. These 1,600 networks were analysed (as reported in the Case Studies section for B.W.N. and R.S.B.) by determining the slope of the linear regression line for the accuracy by length function.

Table 6 reports the mean slope value and range of values for each damage locus, for each dysgraphic participant and network type. Figure 15 depicts the effect of length on overall letter accuracy for the dysgraphics (solid lines) as well as the average length effect for the 400 networks involved in each simulation (dashed and dotted lines). The results of this analysis clearly reveal that the SRNs demonstrate general effects of length on overall accuracy comparable to those of the dysgraphics.

Analysis 2b: The specific effect of length on accuracy at shared letter positions

The goal of this analysis was to quantify whether the length of a sequence affects accuracy of the

Table 6. *Length effects measured by slope of accuracy by length, for lexical-input letter-string input networks, at each deficit locus for each dysgraphic participant*

Simulation	B.W.N. (observed slope: −.03)		R.S.B. (observed slope: −.03)	
	Lexical input	Letter-string input	Lexical input	Letter-string input
inp-hid	−.02 (−.03 to .01)	−.02 (−.04 to .01)	−.03 (−.06 to .01)	−.04 (−.06 to .01)
hid-out	−.03 (−.03 to .01)	−.02 (−.03 to .01)	−.03 (−.05 to .01)	−.03 (−.04 to .01)
int-hid	−.03 (−.04 to .02)	−.02 (−.03 to .01)	−.04 (−.05 to .02)	−.03 (−.04 to .00)
ext-hid	−.02 (−.04 to .02)	−.02 (−.03 to .01)	−.03 (−.04 to .01)	−.02 (−.04 to .01)

Note: Values in each cell are the mean slope for 100 networks, with range in parentheses.

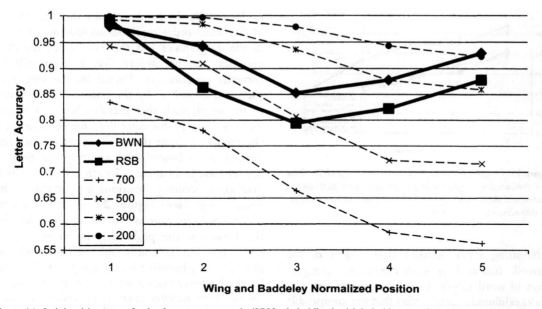

Figure 14. Serial position curves for simple recurrent networks (SRNs; dashed lines) with lexical input at four stages of training. Each line represents the average of 100 networks, and data have been normalized according to a modification of Wing and Baddeley (1980). The SRNs demonstrate monotonically decreasing curves throughout training. Dysgraphic serial position curves (solid lines) are given as reference.

elements that are in shared positions. Although both dysgraphics and networks show an overall effect of length on letter accuracy, the fact that the errors are distributed differently across position—a bow-shaped accuracy function for the dysgraphics and a decreasing function for the networks—indicates that their comparable length effects are obtained via different mechanisms. Therefore, the analysis of accuracy for comparable serial positions is of fundamental importance for understanding the basis of the error-generating mechanisms in the dysgraphics and the networks.

For this analysis, accuracy at the overlapping positions for the longest word length and the shortest word length were compared using the L_{SPC} measure. For B.W.N. this involved comparing accuracies at Positions 1–5 in 5- and 9-letter words, and for R.S.B. Positions 1–5 in 5- and 8-letter words.

Table 7 reports the mean L_{SPC} value and range for each damage locus, for each dysgraphic individual and network type. For illustrative purposes, Figure 16 depicts the accuracy by position for 5- and 8/9-letter words for the dysgraphics and also the mean values for the lexical-input and

Table 7. *Effect of length on shared positions in short and long words as evaluated by means of the L_{SPC} metric*

Simulation	B.W.N. (observed L_{SPC}: .12)		R.S.B. (observed L_{SPC}: .09)	
	Lexical input	Letter-string input	Lexical input	Letter-string input
inp-hid	−0.01 (−0.04 to 0.02)	0.00 (−0.04 to 0.04)	−0.02 (−0.08 to 0.06)	0.01 (−0.05 to 0.07)
hid-out	0.01 (−0.03 to 0.06)	0.01 (−0.02 to 0.04)	0.01 (−0.05 to 0.06)	0.02 (−0.04 to 0.08)
int-hid	0.00 (−0.04 to 0.03)	−0.02 (−0.06 to 0.03)	−0.02 (−0.06 to 0.02)	−0.02 (−0.08 to 0.02)
ext-hid	0.00 (−0.04 to 0.04)	−0.01 (−0.06 to 0.03)	−0.02 (−0.08 to 0.02)	−0.01 (−0.07 to 0.04)

Note: Values in each cell are the mean L_{SPC} value for 100 networks, with the range in parentheses.

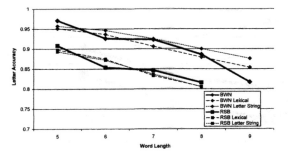

Figure 15. *Length effect data for Experiments 2a and 2b. Solid lines indicate length effect data for the dysgraphic participants. Dashed and dotted lines represent the average letter accuracy for the 400 networks in each simulation.*

letter-string input network types. Most of the networks had an L_{SPC} score near 0, indicating no effect of word length. Certainly none of the networks exhibited a length effect that was comparable to that exhibited by either B.W.N. or R.S.B.

Discussion

In summary, these three sets of analyses show that (a) virtually identical results were obtained for the different input representations; (b) virtually identical results were obtained regardless of damage locus; (c) dysgraphics and networks differed with regard to the distribution of errors across position, with dysgraphics showing a bow-shaped accuracy profile while the SRNs exhibited a simple decreasing accuracy function; (d) both dysgraphics and the SRNs exhibited a general effect of length on overall letter accuracy; and (e) only the dysgraphics exhibited a specific effect of length on letter accuracy at shared positions.

With regard to the findings that neither the nature of the input representations nor the locus of the damage did not change the outcomes, it is worth noting that in their SRN investigation of serial order in spoken production, Dell et al. (1993) utilized two input representation encodings similar to those we have used, and they too found very little difference in their performance.

The absence of an effect of length on shared positions for shorter and longer words for the SRNs reveals the fundamentally different nature of the serial-order mechanisms that are at work in the dysgraphics and the SRNs. For the dysgraphics, the probability that a letter will be correctly produced is affected by the length of the word as well as by the position of the letter in the word, such that membership in a longer word is more problematic than membership in a shorter word. Note that such an effect does not depend on a bow-shaped accuracy function as one can easily imagine a length effect in which decreasing accuracy functions are "stratified" by length (e.g., see Figure 20 in the General Discussion). In contrast to the dysgraphics, for the networks, the probability of an error in a given position is comparable across words of different lengths—that is, the length of the word in which a letter finds itself does not itself contribute to the probability of error. Therefore, the only reason that dysgraphics and networks produce comparable overall length effects (Analysis 2a) is that networks produce higher error rates on later positions than do the dysgraphics. That is, for the networks accuracy on Positions 1–5 is virtually identical for 5-letter words and 8-letter words but 8-letter words overall have lower accuracy than 5-letter words because of Positions 6–8. It is noteworthy that this absence of a length effect for shared positions is reflected in the internal representations of the SRNs. The representational distortion analysis performed in Experiment 1 found identical levels of distortion at shared positions for 5- and 8-letter words (Figure 12).

These findings are consistent with the possibility that accuracy in the dysgraphics is strongly influenced by some limited capacity or resource that is distributed more "thinly" across the elements of a longer sequence, thus increasing the probability of error on every element (except perhaps the first) in a longer sequence compared to a shorter sequence. In the SRNs, error probability is simply determined by the number of preceding elements in a sequence such that elements later in a string (regardless of sequence length) are more susceptible to error. We discuss these findings and their implications in greater detail in the General Discussion.

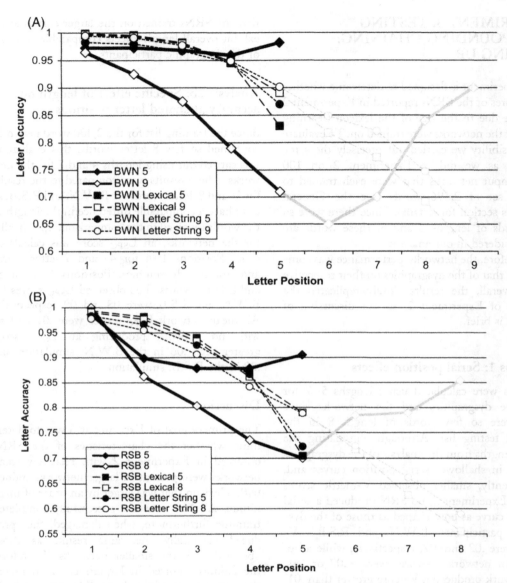

Figure 16. Serial position data relevant to the L_{SPC} calculation (B.W.N. top; R.S.B. bottom). The L_{SPC} calculation for B.W.N. and the B.W.N. simulations takes the average difference in accuracy between words of length 5 and words of length 9, at Positions 1–5. The L_{SPC} calculation for R.S.B. and the R.S.B. simulations takes the average difference in accuracy between words of length 5 and words of length 8, at Positions 1–5. This figure displays the serial position curves for the dysgraphics (solid lines), the simple recurrent network (SRN) simulations with lexical input (dashed lines), and the SRN simulations with letter-string input (dotted lines). Serial position curves for length 5 are drawn with filled dots; serial position curves for length 8/9 are drawn with open dots. Network curves are the average of 400 networks. While the dysgraphics exhibit a large difference in accuracy depending on the length of the word (length by position interaction), the networks show a very small effect, if any.

EXPERIMENT 3: TESTING COMPOUNDING CHAINING: SCALING UP

This experiment is designed to determine whether the failures of the SRNs reported in Experiment 2 could be due to the size of the lexicon (learning list) that the networks were trained on. To evaluate this possibility we carried out precisely the same analyses as we did in Experiment 2 on 100 lexical-input networks that were each trained to spell a set of 2,396 words (see the General Methods section for details). Since there were so few words of lengths 3 and 8, these words are not considered in our analyses.

As before, the networks' performance was compared to that of the dysgraphics on their respective lists. Overall, the results closely replicated the findings of Experiment 2, so our discussion of the data is brief.

Analysis 1: Serial position effects

V-scores were calculated using lengths 5–7 for both the dysgraphics and the networks since there were so few words of length 8 in the network testing list. Although eliminating the longer lengths from the analysis of the dysgraphics resulted in shallower serial position curves and, consequently, smaller observed V-metric scores than in Experiment 2, no SRN produced a serial position curve as bow-shaped as those of the dysgraphic participants. B.W.N. and R.S.B.'s V-scores were .02 and .07, respectively, while all of the mean network V-scores were −.07 or less. No network produced a V-score greater than .01.

Analysis 2a: General effect of length on overall letter accuracy

Letter accuracy at lengths 4–7 was evaluated for all of the networks, and a regression line was fitted to the data. The regression lines for B.W.N. and R.S.B. both had slope −0.03 while the mean network slopes for the different noise loci ranged from −0.04 to −0.02. This indicates that the SRNs trained on the larger corpus again exhibit overall length effects comparable to those of the dysgraphic participants.

Analysis 2b: Specific effect of length on accuracy at shared letter positions

Since the training list for the 2,400 word networks contained so few 8-letter words, this evaluation was carried out using lengths 4 and 7 for the networks. These results were compared to the results for 5- and 8-letter words for B.W.N. and R.S.B. so as to have a comparable difference in the length of the words involved in the comparison. Specifically, for the networks, an L_{SPC} score was calculated using Positions 1–4 for 4- and 7-letter words and, for the dysgraphics, Positions 1–5 for 5- and 8-letter words. The observed L_{SPC} scores for B.W.N. and R.S.B. were .08 and .09, respectively. All mean network L_{SPC} scores were .01 or less, with no network producing an L_{SPC} score greater than .06 in the B.W.N. simulation and .08 in the R.S.B. simulation.

Discussion

The primary goal of Experiment 3 was to determine whether the characteristics of the SRNs observed in Experiment 2 with relatively small networks were present in larger networks trained with a lexicon that was larger by an order of magnitude. All 100 networks successfully completed training; furthermore, when damaged, they produced essentially the same results as those observed with the smaller networks. Therefore, the failures reported in Experiment 2 to match the performance of the dysgraphic individuals do not appear to be related to the size of the lexicon that networks have acquired.

GENERAL DISCUSSION

As discussed, theories of serial order can generally be grouped into two main classes: positional theories and chaining theories. Their fundamental difference concerns the cue for the retrieval of items in a sequence. In positional theories serial order is achieved through the association of each item in a sequence to an external timing variable that cues retrieval. In contrast, in chaining theories serial order is achieved through associations between the items themselves, such that each item is a critical part of the retrieval cue for the next item. In compound chaining, the association is between multiple previous items in a sequence and the upcoming item. In the work reported in this paper we evaluated compound chaining as a theory of the serial-order mechanism of spelling. We did so by comparing the performance of simple recurrent networks (SRNs) with that of two individuals with damage to the serial-order component of the spelling system.

The SRNs were trained to spell a list of words and then damage was simulated by applying noise to different sets of connection weights. In Experiment 1 we showed that the SRNs exhibited two characteristics that we assume should be present in damaged chaining systems: (a) a significant effect of conditional error probability, such that an element in a sequence is more likely to be incorrectly produced if it is preceded by one or more errors and (b) increasing representational distortion, such that the internal representations of the system become increasingly distant from their correct state with each element that is produced. We showed that the SRNs exhibited both of these characteristics. We also showed that their performance contrasts with that of competitive queueing networks (Glasspool & Houghton, 2005) that presumably do not operate by chaining, but rather through positional encoding of serial position.

Having presented positive evidence that the SRNs are engaged in some form of chaining, we showed in Studies 2 and 3 that their performance did not match dysgraphic performance with regard to two critical characteristics: the distribution of errors across position and the effect of length on shared positions in short and long words. These failures persisted despite the use of different types of input representation (Experiment 2) and the size of the networks (Experiment 3).

Specifically, Experiments 2 and 3 clearly revealed that the performance of the SRNs was qualitatively and quantitatively different from that of the dysgraphics. While the dysgraphics exhibited bow-shaped serial position curves and lower accuracy for letters in the same positions in longer than in shorter words, the networks exhibited monotonically decreasing serial position functions and did not show this type of length effect. This last finding is particularly significant as it indicates that the similarity between the SRNs and dysgraphics with regard to an overall effect of length (Analysis 2a) is superficial and that length effects are achieved differently by the networks and dysgraphics. From these findings we conclude that SRNs and, by extension, the type of chaining they instantiate—which we assume to be some form of compound chaining—is not a correct characterization of the serial-order mechanism of spelling.

There are a number of concerns and critiques that can be raised regarding these conclusions and this approach to hypothesis testing. Some of these apply more generally to the use of simulations in testing hypotheses regarding cognitive processes and representations. We discuss some of these topics briefly in the following sections, using our work as the specific context for these broader issues.

Do the simulations allow for a sufficient test of the hypothesis?

The general question is: How can we be sure that the simulations that are used to implement and test a particular hypothesis actually implement the core features of the hypothesis? How can we know whether the successes and failures of the simulations are the consequence of these core features (and not incidental properties; see McCloskey, 1991)?

It is certainly reasonable to ask whether or not the results we have presented constitute a definitive argument against the hypothesis of compound chaining in spelling. Without advancing a formal proof, there is always room to question the strength of an empirically based argument. The simulation work may have been an inadequate test of the hypothesis because of: (a) the specific characteristics of the SRNs we implemented or (b) the possibility that SRNs—as a class—do not allow for an adequate test of the compound chaining hypothesis.

With regard to the specific implementations, our assumption is that the behaviours of interest—their failure to match the dysgraphic performance—are not the result of incidental properties of the simulations (number of hidden units, etc.) but rather a consequence of their core features. That is, we assume that the failures stem from precisely those features that implement the compound chaining mechanism. This claim is strengthened by the fact that we have presented positive evidence that the networks are performing some sort of chaining and because the same shortcomings were observed across a range of conditions and network characteristics that might have led to different behaviours. Thus, while it is true that one could vary an indefinite number of parameters, it is reasonable to conclude that our findings are likely to hold for SRNs that can be shown to be implementing some form of chaining.

Another possibility is that there is something about the specific manner in which SRNs as a class implement chaining that is responsible for the failure of the networks to match dysgraphic performance. According to this line of reasoning other approaches to the implementation of compound chaining may be more successful. While this possibility cannot be rejected out of hand, and it is most certainly an empirical question, it is not obvious to how another approach would preserve the core features of compound chaining without the limitations that our research has exposed. At the very least, our findings represent a very substantive challenge to a compound chaining theory of serial order in spelling.

Do the behavioural data constitute an appropriate "representation" of the hypothesis?

Another challenge for computational investigations of cognitive processes and representations is to identify the "key" empirical results against which the performance of the simulations should be evaluated. These behavioural results are those that are thought to be a product of the cognitive mechanism whose functions or representations are being investigated. That is, the logic is typically as follows: There is a hypothesis H about the functioning of mechanism M. Behaviours B_1-B_n are identified as being a product of (or reflecting the functioning) of mechanism M. A simulation of mechanism M is developed such that it implements hypothesis H. If the simulation then matches behaviours B_1-B_n, it is considered to be evidence in favour of hypothesis H. Clearly, if the incorrect behaviours are identified, then—whether or not the simulation matches the critical behaviours—the hypothesis may not have actually been put to a test.

Thus, in the case at hand, a critique of our conclusions could be directed at the appropriateness of the data set on which the hypothesis was tested. Are the specific length effects and serial position curve that we have reported for B.W.N. and R.S.B. a product of the functioning of the serial-order mechanism in spelling? Even if they are a product of this mechanism, are they "key"?

Two factors support our choice of measures against which to test the compound chaining hypothesis. First, there is a considerable body of work on serial-order tasks and mechanisms in other domains that has identified serial position and length effects as being central characteristics of these mechanisms. Secondly, these key features are distinct from those patterns of performance used to identify the serial-order mechanisms as the locus of impairment. Specifically, the deficits of these individuals were attributed to the serial-order mechanism on the basis of similarity of errors across output and input modalities, the types of error, and the absence of semantic and lexical effects—features that, in combination, serve as "markers" of the deficit locus. The length effect and serial position effect can be ascribed to the serial-order mechanism on that basis.

Nonetheless, the fundamental problem is that until a mechanism is well understood one cannot be sure that the critical features have been identified; of course, the research is being carried out precisely because the mechanism is not well understood.

Additional evidence, additional constraints

A clearly related issue is the status of findings that differ from those identified as the "key" results. For example, it has been argued that not all damage to the graphemic buffer results in bow-shaped serial position curves. Several cases have been reported of dysgraphic individuals with purported damage to the graphemic buffer who do not exhibit bow-shaped accuracy functions (Cipolotti et al., 2004; Katz, 1991; Kokubo, Suzuki, Yamadori, & Satou, 2001; Miceli, Benvegnù, Capasso, & Caramazza, 2004; Schiller, Greenhall, Shelton, & Caramazza, 2001; Ward & Romani, 1998). For example, Schiller et al. (2001) presented the case of P.B., a dysgraphic whose error patterns are generally consistent with damage to the graphemic buffer but who exhibits a monotonically decreasing rather than U-shaped accuracy curve (see Figure 17).

One possibility is that these data are not, in fact, generated by the serial-order mechanism of spelling or, alternatively, that the patterns that we have reported for R.S.B. and B.W.N. are not. Another is that the Schiller et al. (2001) data or ours are the result of multiple deficits, which mask the characteristics due to the damaged serial-order mechanism. Yet another possibility is the serial-order mechanism has a number of subfunctions and that damage to different subfunctions leads to different patterns of performance (Miceli & Capasso, 2006). Logically, it is even possible that some of these subfunctions operate via chaining while others do not.

However, one important thing to note about the Schiller et al. (2001) data is that while the serial position curves are clearly not bow shaped, there does appear to be an effect of length at shared positions. This can be seen in the general "stratification" of the serial position curves, which, although messier than those of R.S.B. and B.W.N., contrast strikingly with the SRNs that exhibit overlapping functions (Figure 17). In

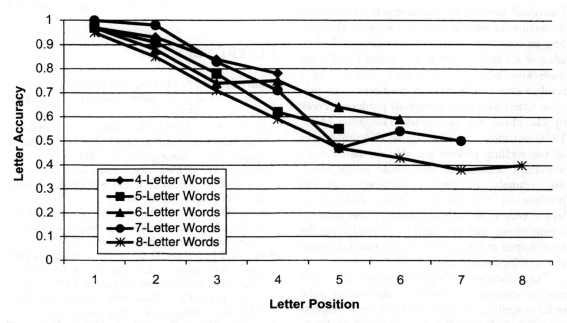

Figure 17. *Serial position curves for patient P.B. Adapted from Figure 2a of "Serial Order Effects in Spelling Errors: Evidence from Two Dysgraphic Patients", by N. O. Schiller, J. A. Greenhall, J. R. Shelton, and A. Caramazza, 2001,* Neurocase, 7, *p. 1–14.* Copyright (2001) Psychology Press.

fact, an estimate of P.B.'s L_{SPC} value for 4- versus 8-letter words yields a value of .1, quite similar to that observed for R.S.B. and B.W.N.

Are the Schiller et al. (2001) data problematic for our conclusions against the compound chaining hypothesis? Not at all. They may be comparable to findings in cognitive psychology that different experimental conditions yield different outcomes. As argued by Caramazza (1984, 1986), the damage suffered by different individuals can be compared to different experimental manipulations in different experiments with neurally intact individuals. Unless there is some reason to think that the patterns produced by R.S.B. and B.W.N. are spurious (see Miceli & Capasso, 2006, and Glasspool et al., 2006, for references), these patterns offer additional constraints on the theory. In the end, a complete account of the serial-order mechanism of spelling will provide an explanation of the multiple patterns of performance that are observed subsequent to damage.

Alternative hypotheses?

Positional theories such as competitive queueing do seem to capture important features of the spelling process. According to these theories, knowledge of a letter's position in the word is distinct from knowledge of the letter's identity. As a result, a letter can be correctly cued even when previous letters have been incorrectly produced. Work by Houghton and colleagues (Houghton et al., 1994) has shown that damage to CQ simulations of the spelling process are able to match some important features of dysgraphic performance. For example, competitive queueing networks produce all relevant error types, demonstrate length effects, preserve consonant/vowel status in substitutions, and are capable of producing the bow-shaped serial position curves (see Glasspool et al., 2006, for a review).

These successes of CQ would seem to constitute positive evidence for positional theories of serial order in spelling. Nonetheless, there are an important number of issues that have not yet been examined in detail in these systems. Thus, while competitive queueing specifically, and positional theories more generally, are quite promising, a great deal more work will be required to determine their adequacy (see Miceli & Capasso, 2006).

Computational cognitive neuropsychology

There is now a quite considerable body of research employing what Coltheart (2006) has referred to as computational cognitive neuropsychology—the use of data from neurologically injured individuals to test computer simulations instantiating specific hypotheses regarding the nature of cognitive processes and representations. Robust patterns of performance subsequent to damage have already played a central role in adjudicating between alternative hypotheses in a number of cognitive domains. The work that we have reported in this paper, along with other papers in this volume, constitutes evidence that this continues to be a powerful and fruitful approach to understanding cognition.

Manuscript received 19 March 2007
Revised manuscript received 27 September 2007
Revised manuscript accepted 8 October 2007
First published online 4 March 2008

REFERENCES

Anderson, J. R., & Matessa, M. (1997). A production system theory of serial memory. *Psychological Review, 104,* 728–748.

Baddeley, A. D. (1968). How does acoustic similarity influence short-term memory? *Quarterly Journal of Experimental Psychology, 20,* 249–263.

Badecker, W. (1996). Representational properties common to phonological and orthographic output systems. *Lingua, 99,* 55–83.

Baxter, D. M., & Warrington, E. K. (1987). Transcoding sound to spelling: Single or multiple sound unit correspondences? *Cortex, 23,* 11–28.

Botvinick, M., & Plaut, D. C. (2003). Constructive processes in immediate serial recall: A recurrent network model of the bigram frequency effect. In B. Kokinov & W. Hirst (Eds.), *Constructive memory* (pp. 129–137). Sofia, Bulgaria: New Bulgarian University.

Botvinick, M., & Plaut, D. C. (2006). Short-term memory for serial order: A recurrent neural network model. *Psychological Review, 113,* 201–233.

Brown, G. D. A., & Loosemore, R. P. W. (1994). Computational approaches to normal and impaired spelling. In G. D. A. Brown & N. C. Ellis (Eds.), *Handbook of spelling: Theory, process and intervention* (pp. 319–336). Chichester, UK: Wiley.

Brown, G. D. A., Loosemore, R. P. W., & Watson, F. L. (1993). *Normal and dyslexic spelling: A connectionist approach* (Tech. rep.). Bangor, UK: University of Wales, Bangor.

Brown, G. D. A., Preece, T., & Hulme, C. (2000). Oscillator-based memory for serial order. *Psychological Review, 107*, 127–181.

Buchwald, A., & Rapp, B. (2006). Consonants and vowels in orthographic representations. *Cognitive Neuropsychology, 23*, 308–337.

Buchwald, A., & Rapp, B. (2008). *Distinctions between long-term memory and working memory: Evidence from dysgraphia*. Manuscript submitted for publication.

Bullinaria, J. A. (1994). Connectionist modeling of spelling. In *Proceedings of the Sixteenth Annual Conference of the Cognitive Science Society* (pp. 78–83). Hillsdale, NJ: Lawrence Erlbaum Associates.

Bullinaria, J. A. (1997). Modeling reading, spelling and past tense learning with artificial neural networks. *Brain and Language, 59*, 236–266.

Burgess, N., & Hitch, G. J. (1992). Toward a network model of the articulatory loop. *Journal of Memory and Language, 31*, 429–460.

Caramazza, A. (1984). The logic of neuropsychological research and the problem of patient classification in aphasia. *Brain and Language, 21*, 9–20.

Caramazza, A. (1986). On drawing inferences about the structure of normal cognitive systems from the analysis of patterns of impaired performance: The case for single-patient studies. *Brain and Cognition, 5*, 41–66.

Caramazza, A. (1988). Some aspects of language processing revealed through the analysis of acquired aphasia: The lexical system. *Annual Review of Neuroscience, 11*, 395–421.

Caramazza, A., & Miceli, G. (1990). The structure of graphemic representations. *Cognition, 37*, 243–297.

Caramazza, A., Miceli, G., Villa, G., & Romani, C. (1987). The role of the graphemic buffer in spelling: Evidence from a case of acquired dysgraphia. *Cognition, 26*, 59–85.

Cipolotti, L., Bird, C., Glasspool, D. W., & Shallice, T. S. (2004). The impact of deep dysgraphia on graphemic output buffer disorders. *Neurocase, 10*, 405–419.

Coltheart, M. (2006). Acquired dyslexias and the computational modeling of reading. *Cognitive Neuropsychology, 23*, 96–109.

Cotelli, M., Abutalebi, J., Zorzi, M., & Cappa, S. F. (2003). Vowels in the buffer: A case study of acquired dysgraphia with selective vowel substitutions. *Cognitive Neuropsychology, 20*, 99–114.

Dell, G. S. (1986). A spreading-activation theory of retrieval in sentence production. *Psychological Review, 93*, 283–321.

Dell, G. S., Burger, L. K., & Svec, W. R. (1997). Language production and serial order: A functional analysis and a model. *Psychological Review, 104*, 123–147.

Dell, G. S., Juliano, C., & Govindjee, A. (1993). Structure and content in language production: A theory of frame constraints in phonological speech errors. *Cognitive Science, 17*, 149–195.

Ebbinghaus, H. (1885). *Über das Gedächtnis: Untersuchungen zur experimentellen Psychologie* [Memory: A contribution to experimental psychology]. Leipzig, Germany: Duncker and Humboldt.

Ellis, A. W. (1982). Spelling and writing (and reading and speaking). In A. W. Ellis (Ed.), *Normality and pathology in cognitive functions* (pp. 113–146). London: Academic Press.

Elman, J. L. (1990). Finding structure in time. *Cognitive Science, 14*, 179–211.

Farrell, S., & Lewandowsky, S. (2002). An endogenous distributed model of ordering in serial recall. *Psychonomic Bulletin & Review, 9*, 59–79.

Glasspool, D. W. (1998). *Modeling serial order in behaviour: Studies of spelling*. Unpublished doctoral dissertation, University College London, London.

Glasspool, D. W., & Houghton, G. (2005). Serial order and consonant–vowel structure in a graphemic output buffer model. *Brain and Language, 94*, 304–330.

Glasspool, D. W., Houghton, G., & Shallice, T. (1995). Interactions between knowledge sources in a dual-route connectionist model of spelling. In L. S. Smith & P. J. B. Hancock (Eds.), *Neural computation and psychology*. London: Springer-Verlag.

Glasspool, D. W., Shallice, T., & Cipolotti, L. (1999). Neuropsychologically plausible sequence generation in a multi-layer network model of spelling. In D. Heinke, G. W. Humphreys, & A. Olson (Eds.), *Connectionist models in cognitive neuroscience* (pp. 40–51). London: Springer-Verlag.

Glasspool, D. W., Shallice, T., & Cipolotti, L. (2006). Towards a unified process model for graphemic buffer disorder and deep dysgraphia. *Cognitive Neuropsychology, 23*, 479–512.

Goodman, R. A., & Caramazza, A. (1986). Aspects of the spelling process: Evidence from a case of acquired dysgraphia. *Language and Cognitive Processes, 1*, 263–296.

Harcum, E. R. (1975). *Serial learning and paralearning*. New York: Wiley.

Hart, P., Nilsson, N. J., & Raphael, B. A. (1968). A formal basis for the heuristic determination of minimum cost paths. *IEEE Transactions on Systems Science and Cybernetics SSC4, 2*, 100–107.

Hartley, T., & Houghton, G. (1996). A linguistically constrained model of short-term memory for nonwords. *Journal of Memory and Language, 35*, 1–31.

Henson, R. N. A. (1996). *Short-term memory for serial order*. Unpublished doctoral dissertation, University of Cambridge, Cambridge, UK.

Henson, R. N. A. (1998). Short-term memory for serial order: The start–end model. *Cognitive Psychology, 36*, 73–137.

Henson, R. N. A. (1999). Coding position in short-term memory. *International Journal of Psychology, 34*, 403–409.

Henson, R. N. A., Norris, D. G., Page, M. P. A., & Baddeley, A. D. (1996). Unchained memory: Error patterns rule out chaining models of immediate serial recall. *The Quarterly Journal of Experimental Psychology, 49A*, 80–115.

Hillis, A. E., & Caramazza, A. (1991). Mechanisms for accessing lexical representations for output: Evidence from a category-specific semantic deficit. *Brain and Language, 40*, 106–144.

Houghton, G. (1990). The problem of serial order: A neural network model of sequence learning and recall. In R. Dale, C. Mellish, & M. Zock (Eds.), *Current research in natural language generation*. London: Academic Press.

Houghton, G., Glasspool, D. W., & Shallice, T. (1994). Spelling and serial recall: Insights from a competitive queueing model. In G. D. A. Brown & N. C. Ellis (Eds.), *Handbook of spelling: Theory, process and intervention* (pp. 365–404). Chichester, UK: John Wiley & Sons.

Houghton, G., & Hartley, T. (1995). Parallel models of serial behavior: Lashley revisited. *Psyche, 2*, 1–25.

Houghton, G., Hartley, T., & Glasspool, D. W. (1996). The representation of words and nonwords in short-term memory: Serial order and syllable structure. In S. E. Gathercole (Ed.), *Models of short-term memory* (pp. 101–127). Hove, UK: Psychology Press.

Houghton, G., & Zorzi, M. (1998). A model of the sound–spelling mapping in English and its role in word and nonword spelling. In M. A. Gernsbacher (Ed.), *Proceedings of the Twentieth Annual Conference of the Cognitive Science Society* (pp. 490–501). Mahwah, NJ: Lawrence Erlbaum Associates.

Houghton, G., & Zorzi, M. (2003). Normal and impaired spelling in a connectionist dual-route architecture. *Cognitive Neuropsychology, 20*, 115–162.

Howard, M. W., & Kahana, M. J. (2002). A distributed representation of temporal context. *Journal of Mathematical Psychology, 43*, 269–299.

Jensen, A. R. (1962). Spelling errors and the serial-position effect. *Journal of Educational Psychology, 53*, 105–109.

Jones, D. M., Beaman, P., & Macken, W. J. (1996). The object-oriented episodic record model. In S. E. Gathercole (Ed.), *Models of short-term memory* (pp. 209–238). Hove, UK: Psychology Press.

Jordan, M. (1986). Attractor dynamics and parallelism in a connectionist sequential machine. In *Proceedings of the 8th Annual Conference of the Cognitive Science Society* (pp. 531–546). Hillsdale, NJ: Lawrence Erlbaum Associates.

Katz, R. B. (1991). Limited retention of information in the graphemic buffer. *Cortex, 27*, 111–119.

Kokubo, K., Suzuki, K., Yamadori, A., & Satou, K. (2001). Pure kana agraphia as a manifestation of graphemic buffer impairment. *Cortex, 37*, 187–195.

Kremin, H. (1987). Is there more than ah-oh-oh? Alternative strategies for writing and repeating lexically. In M. Coltheart, G. Sartori, & R. Job (Eds.), *The cognitive neuropsychology of language* (pp. 295–335). Hove, UK: Lawrence Erlbaum Associates.

Ladd, G. T., & Woodworth, R. S. (1911). *Elements of physiological psychology*. New York: Charles Scribner's Sons.

Lashley, K. S. (1951). The problem of serial order in behavior. In J. A. Jeffress (Ed.), *Cerebral mechanisms in behavior* (pp. 113–146). New York: John Wiley & Sons.

Lee, C. L., & Estes, W. K. (1981). Item and order information in short-term memory: Evidence for multilevel perturbation processes. *Journal of Experimental Psychology: Human Learning and Memory, 7*, 149–169.

Lewandowsky, S., & Murdock, B. B. (1989). Memory for serial order. *Psychological Review, 96*, 25–57.

MacKay, D. G. (1982). The problem of flexibility, fluency and speed–accuracy trade-off in skilled behavior. *Psychological Review, 89*, 483–506.

MacKay, D. G. (1987). *The organization of perception and action: A theory for language and other cognitive skills*. Berlin, Germany: Springer-Verlag.

McCloskey, M. (1991). Networks and theories: The place of connectionism in cognitive science. *Psychological Science, 2*, 387–395.

McCloskey, M., Badecker, W., Goodman-Schulman, R. A., & Aliminosa, D. (1994). The structure of graphemic representations in spelling: Evidence from a case of acquired dysgraphia. *Cognitive Neuropsychology, 11*, 341–392.

Miceli, G., Benvegnù, B., Capasso, R., & Caramazza, A. (2004). The categorical distinction of consonant and vowel representations: Evidence from dysgraphia. *Neurocase, 10*, 109–121.

Miceli, G., & Capasso, R. (2006). Spelling and dysgraphia. *Cognitive Neuropsychology, 23*, 110–134.

Olson, A., & Caramazza, A. (1994). Representation and connectionist models: The NETspell experience. In G. D. A. Brown & N. C. Ellis (Eds.), *Handbook of spelling: Theory, process and intervention*. Chichester, UK: John Wiley & Sons.

Page, M. P. A., & Norris, D. (1998). The primacy model: A new model of immediate serial recall. *Psychological Review, 105*, 761–781.

Patterson, K. (1986). Lexical but nonsemantic spelling? *Cognitive Neuropsychology, 3*, 341–367.

Rapp, B. (2002). Uncovering the cognitive architecture of spelling. In A. Hillis (Ed.), *Handbook on adult language disorders: Integrating cognitive neuropsychology, neurology and rehabilitation*. Philadelphia: Psychology Press.

Rapp, B. (2005). The relationship between treatment outcomes and the underlying cognitive deficit: Evidence from the remediation of acquired dysgraphia. *Aphasiology, 19*, 994–1008.

Rapp, B., Epstein, C., & Tainturier, M.-J. (2002). The integration of information across lexical and sublexical processes in spelling. *Cognitive Neuropsychology, 19*, 1–29.

Rapp, B., & Kane, A. (2002). Remediation of deficits affecting different components of the spelling process. *Aphasiology, 16*, 439–454.

Richman, H. B., & Simon, H. A. (1994). *EPAM simulations of short-term memory (Complex Information Processing Working Paper #514)*. Carnegie-Mellon University, Department of Psychology, Pittsburgh, PA, USA.

Rodriguez, P. (2001). Simple recurrent networks learn context-free and context-sensitive languages by counting. *Neural Computation, 13*, 2093–2118.

Rohde, D. L. T. (1999). *Lens: The light, efficient, network simulator* (Tech. Rep. No. CMU-CS-99-164). Pittsburgh, PA: Carnegie Mellon University, Department of Computer Science. Retrieved September, 2004, from http://tedlab.mit.edu/~dr/Lens/

Rumelhart, D. E., Hinton, G., & Williams, R. J. (1986). Learning internal representations by error propagation. In D. E. Rumelhart & J. L. McClelland (Eds.), *Parallel distributed processing: Explorations in the microstructure of cognition* (Vol. 1, pp. 318–362). Cambridge, MA: MIT Press.

Schiller, N. O., Greenhall, J. A., Shelton, J. R., & Caramazza, A. (2001). Serial order effects in spelling errors: Evidence from two dysgraphic patients. *Neurocase, 7*, 1–14.

Shattuck-Hufnagel, S. (1979). Speech errors as evidence for a serial-order mechanism in sentence production. In W. E. Cooper & E. C. T. Walker (Eds.), *Sentence processing: Psycholinguistic studies presented to Merrill Garrett* (pp. 295–342). Hillsdale, NJ: Lawrence Erlbaum Associates.

Tainturier, M.-J., & Rapp, B. C. (2004). Complex graphemes as functional spelling units: Evidence from acquired dysgraphia. *Neurocase, 10*, 122–131.

Ward, J., & Romani, C. (1998). Serial position effects and lexical activation in spelling: Evidence from a single case study. *Neurocase, 4*, 189–206.

Wickelgren, W. A. (1965). Short-term memory for phonemically similar lists. *American Journal of Experimental Psychology, 78*, 567–574.

Wickelgren, W. A. (1969). Context-sensitive coding, associative memory, and serial order in (speech) behavior. *Psychological Review, 76*, 1–15.

Wing, A. M., & Baddeley, A. D. (1980). Spelling errors in handwriting: A corpus and a distributional analysis. In U. Frith (Ed.), *Cognitive processes in spelling* (pp. 251–279). London: Academic Press.

Young, R. K. (1968). Serial learning. In T. R. Dion & D. L. Hornton (Eds.), *Verbal behavior and general behavior theory*. Englewood Cliffs, NJ: Prentice-Hall.

APPENDIX

The 250-word set

R.S.B.'s word list consisted of tokens of length 5–8 words. B.W.N.'s word list consisted of tokens of length 5–9 words. This 250-word set made up the simple recurrent network (SRN) training list for Experiments 2 and 3.

Length 5	Length 6	Length 7	Length 8	Length 9
ACRID	AVENUE	ABSENCE	ALPHABET	ADVANTAGE
ALLOW	BASKET	ANGUISH	ANCESTOR	ADVENTURE
BEGIN	BISQUE	ATHLETE	APPROACH	ALLIGATOR
BRIEF	BLIGHT	AWKWARD	AQUARIUM	AMPHIBIAN
CABIN	CANVAS	BAPTIST	ARGUMENT	APATHETIC
CABLE	CATTLE	BRACKET	AUDIENCE	ARCHITECT
CHEER	CENTER	BREADTH	BEQUEATH	ASCERTAIN
CHILD	CHALET	BREATHE	BEVERAGE	AUTHENTIC
CIGAR	CHANGE	BROTHER	BOUTIQUE	AUTHORITY
CLOWN	CONVEY	BRUSQUE	COMPLETE	BIOGRAPHY
CRAWL	CREATE	CABARET	CONSTRUE	BOOMERANG
CRIME	DEFEAT	CAUTION	COQUETTE	BURLESQUE
DIARY	DONKEY	COLLEGE	CRITIQUE	CACOPHONY
DRAMA	DRAWER	COMMENT	DAUGHTER	CALCULATE
DRAWL	EXCESS	CONDUCT	DEMOCRAT	CALIBRATE
EAGLE	EXTEND	CROCHET	DEMOLISH	CANDIDATE
FABLE	FUMBLE	CROUTON	DISTANCE	CATHEDRAL
FLOAT	FUTURE	CURTAIN	ESCARGOT	CELEBRATE
FLOOR	GERBIL	CUSHION	ETHIOPIA	CHOCOLATE
GLOVE	HEIGHT	DELIGHT	EXCHANGE	CIGARETTE
GREAT	HOLLOW	FACTORY	FESTIVAL	COMPLAINT
GRIEF	KNIGHT	FREIGHT	FRAGMENT	CORIANDER
GRUNT	LIQUOR	GOURMET	FREQUENT	CROCODILE
HOUSE	MARBLE	HARVEST	IMBECILE	DORMITORY
HUMAN	MEDLEY	HAUGHTY	INSTINCT	ECCENTRIC
ISSUE	MILIEU	INSIGHT	LANGUAGE	FASCINATE
KNIFE	MOSQUE	INSTANT	LIMERICK	GERIATRIC
LEAST	NAUSEA	JEALOUS	MOUNTAIN	GRIEVANCE
MACHO	NEPHEW	LEOPARD	MYSTIQUE	GROTESQUE
MARSH	OPAQUE	MACHINE	NEIGHBOR	HEURISTIC
NASAL	PARADE	MARQUIS	NUISANCE	HOSTILITY
NOISE	PIGEON	MILLION	ORIGINAL	IMMIGRANT
PAGAN	PIRATE	NUCLEAR	PRACTICE	IMPLEMENT
PLUSH	PLEASE	OBLIQUE	PRESSURE	INTERPRET
PORCH	SALAMI	PHANTOM	PROVINCE	KNOWLEDGE
SCREW	SANITY	PICTURE	PURCHASE	MASTICATE
SEDAN	SAVAGE	PRIVATE	QUESTION	METHODIST
SHEEP	SEARCH	PROVIDE	SCHEDULE	MOUSTACHE
SHOVE	SHADOW	REFLECT	SCRAMBLE	PARAGRAPH
SIGHT	SHREWD	RETREAT	SENTENCE	PATHOLOGY
SPEAK	SPREAD	ROOSTER	SHOULDER	PURGATORY
STRUM	SQUAWK	SINCERE	SKELETON	RESIDENCE
TIARA	TACKLE	SPECIAL	SPACIOUS	RIGHTEOUS
TORCH	TENNIS	SPLOTCH	STUBBORN	SCOUNDREL
TOWER	THOUGH	SURFACE	SURPRISE	SOPHOMORE
TREAT	TRAVEL	SUSPEND	SYMPATHY	SYNTHESIS

ULCER	UNIQUE	SWALLOW	THOROUGH	TELEPATHY
VIOLA	URCHIN	TABLOID	THOUSAND	TURQUOISE
WATER	WEIGHT	TROUBLE	TOMORROW	VENTRICLE
WORLD	YELLOW	TROUSER	TWILIGHT	YESTERDAY

The many places of frequency: Evidence for a novel locus of the lexical frequency effect in word production

Mark Knobel
Cognitive Neuropsychology Laboratory, Harvard University, Cambridge, MA, USA

Matthew Finkbeiner
Macquarie Centre for Cognitive Science, Macquarie University, Sydney, Australia

Alfonso Caramazza
Cognitive Neuropsychology Laboratory, Harvard University, Cambridge, MA, USA, and Center for Mind/Brain Sciences, University of Trento, Trento, Italy

The effect of lexical frequency on language-processing tasks is exceptionally reliable. For example, pictures with higher frequency names are named faster and more accurately than those with lower frequency names. Experiments with normal participants and patients strongly suggest that this production effect arises at the level of lexical access. Further work has suggested that within lexical access this effect arises at the level of lexical representations. Here we present patient E.C. who shows an effect of lexical frequency on his nonword error rate. The best explanation of his performance is that there is an additional locus of frequency at the interface of lexical and segmental representational levels. We confirm this hypothesis by showing that only computational models with frequency at this new locus can produce a similar error pattern to that of patient E.C. Finally, in an analysis of a large group of Italian patients, we show that there exist patients who replicate E.C.'s pattern of results and others who show the complementary pattern of frequency effects on semantic error rates. Our results combined with previous findings suggest that frequency plays a role throughout the process of lexical access.

Perhaps the most robust effect in all of psychology is the effect of frequency. Frequency effects have been observed in a wide range of behaviour, from complex sequence prediction (e.g., Stadler, 1992) to face recognition (e.g., Lewis, 1999). Essentially, the more often one encounters a stimulus the more quickly and easily one is able to process it. With respect to the cognitive system, frequency effects are presumed to reflect the increase in processing fluency that comes with greater practice or learning.

Within the domain of lexical access, the more frequently a particular lexical item occurs in spoken and written language (measured by how often a word occurs in a large corpus of written text and/or speech), the more quickly and accurately that item is able to be processed. This so called "lexical frequency effect" has been observed in a wide variety of tasks, including picture naming (e.g., Gilhooly & Gilhooly, 1979; Oldfield & Wingfield, 1965), written picture naming (e.g., Bonin & Fayol, 2002), word naming (e.g., Ellis & Morrison, 1998; Forster & Chambers, 1973; Gerhand & Barry, 1999a), and lexical decision (e.g., Brysbaert, Lange, & Van Wijnendaele, 2000; Gerhand & Barry, 1999b; Morrison & Ellis, 1995). In this article, we focus on the lexical frequency effect in speech production tasks and, specifically, in picture naming.

Many of the above studies and others have also looked at the contribution of age of acquisition (AoA), a variable correlated with frequency, to performance on various lexical tasks. It remains an open question, particularly in picture naming, whether the lexical frequency effect is really an AoA effect, or whether both factors contribute to performance on these tasks (see Johnston & Barry, 2006, for a recent review). We do not wish to prejudge the issue and use the term frequency only to reflect the fact that we have used frequency norms in our study.

Evidence for frequency effects in picture naming has come from the contrasting response latencies observed in picture naming and picture recognition tasks. While picture naming regularly produces frequency effects, no effects of lexical frequency are found when participants simply need to recognize the pictures (Jescheniak & Levelt, 1994; Wingfield, 1967, 1968; but see Bartram, 1976; Kroll & Potter, 1984). These results have been interpreted as showing that frequency effects arise in word production processes subsequent to picture recognition processes.

The effects of word frequency are perhaps most pronounced in the performance of neuropsychological patients, including Alzheimer's disease patients (e.g., Sailor, Antoine, Diaz, Kuslansky, & Kluger, 2004; Silveri, Cappa, Mariotti, & Puopolo, 2002; Thompson-Schill, Gabrieli, & Fleischman, 1999), semantic dementia patients (e.g., Bird, Lambon Ralph, Patterson, & Hodges, 2000), and aphasic patients. With respect to this latter group, it has been widely demonstrated that patients name pictures with high-frequency names more accurately than they name pictures with low-frequency names (e.g., Cuetos, Aguado, Izura, & Ellis, 2002; Feyereisen, Van der Borght, & Seron, 1988; Gordon, 2002; Howard, Patterson, Franklin, Morton, & Orchard-Lisle, 1984; Nickels & Howard, 1994, 1995; Schwartz, Wilshire, Gagnon, & Polansky, 2004; Wilshire, 2002).

Given the ubiquity of the frequency effect in lexical access, it is not surprising that models of lexical access have been developed to explain first and foremost the frequency effect. For example, the search model (Forster, 1976), which assumes localist representations, stipulates that lexical representations are positioned within the search space on the basis of frequency, with high-frequency (HF) words at the beginning of the search and low-frequency (LF) words at the end. In contrast, activation models that assume localist representations implement frequency either by varying selection thresholds, with HF nodes having a lower selection threshold than LF nodes, or by increasing resting activations for HF nodes relative to LF nodes. Distributed connectionist (henceforth connectionist) models, on the other hand, which do not posit localist lexical representations, implement frequency effects through the strengthening of connections between semantic, phonological, and intermediary (i.e., hidden) nodes. As an emergent property of their learning rules, connectionist models come to represent lexical frequency through training (Monsell, 1991). Although the search model and connectionist models have enjoyed some success in the word recognition literature, most models of speech production, while based on the activation framework like connectionist models, assume localist lexical representations and are not trained. Since frequency is not the guiding principle in this modelling framework, as it is in the search model, for example, there are more options for how frequency can be implemented in models of speech production. Before we discuss implementing lexical frequency in these models, we briefly introduce their basic architecture.

The current models of lexical access in speech production (e.g., Caramazza, 1997; Dell, 1986; Levelt, Roelofs, & Meyer, 1999) agree on three stages in word production: semantic, lexical, and segmental. The semantic stage encompasses selecting the concepts that one wishes to express verbally. The lexical stage includes selecting the lexical nodes that correspond to the selected concepts. Finally, the segmental stage involves selecting the phonological segments (i.e., phonemes) specified by the lexical node. The output from this final stage is eventually translated into the movements of the articulators. This depiction is, of course, a simplification that ignores the many differences between these models, including differences in processing dynamics and in the number of lexical stages. We return to these issues and the specifics of each model in our General Discussion.

Word frequency effects can be implemented in this simple three-stage model at five possible loci. These are: (a) semantics, (b) the interface between semantics and the lexical level, (c) the lexical level, (d) the interface between the lexical and segmental levels, and (e) the segmental level (see Figure 1). Placing lexical frequency effects at the level of semantics (Option 1), though logically possible, is unlikely since words are not represented at this level. If lexical frequency effects are found to originate from the level of semantics, it would most likely indicate that a semantic variable that is correlated with lexical frequency, such as familiarity, concreteness, or imageability, underlies these effects (e.g., Bates et al., 2003). Likewise, placing lexical frequency at the segmental level (Option 5) also seems unlikely, given that only sublexical phonological

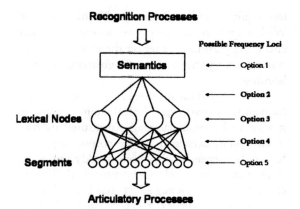

Figure 1. *A basic model of word production. The five logically possible loci for the frequency effect are shown, with the three likely loci highlighted.*

information is represented at this level. Here again, factors correlated with lexical frequency, such as number of phonemes or syllables, phoneme or syllable frequency, or transitional probabilities between phonemes, would be the more likely cause, not lexical frequency (e.g., Vitevitch, 2002). By process of elimination, it seems reasonable to suggest that lexical frequency effects arise either as a function of the connections that interface with the lexical level (Options 2 and 4) or as a function of the lexical representations themselves (Option 3).

We point out that these three possible loci of the lexical frequency effect do not necessarily constitute mutually exclusive hypotheses. It is not only logically possible that frequency may affect processing at several stages of lexical access, but we suggest that this should be taken as the default assumption. Since lexical frequency effects in speech production are said to reflect the frequency with which different lexical items are retrieved from memory and encoded phonologically for production, it would be surprising if the advantage for higher frequency words were not reflected in all stages of lexical access.

Previous work on isolating the locus of the frequency effect in speech production has led to the conclusion that frequency effects arise at the lexical level. For example, Dell (1990) found that neurologically intact participants produced fewer errors on high-frequency word pairs (e.g., "vote pass") than on low-frequency word pairs (e.g., "vogue pang") in a phonological error elicitation task. Dell successfully simulated these effects by representing lexical frequency in the resting activation levels of lexical nodes in a localist spreading-activation network. Though modelling frequency in this way led to results that were consistent with the results of the behavioural experiments, implementing frequency at other loci may have led to similarly successful results.

In another line of work with normal individuals, Jescheniak and Levelt (1994) determined that lexical frequency effects arise at the lexical level by ruling out the semantic and postlexical levels as possible loci. They reasoned that if frequency occurred at the level of lexical selection, then the time difference between accessing HF and LF words would disappear with a delay that was long enough to allow for the access of even the slowest LF words. On the other hand, if frequency effects arose at postlexical levels in production, then frequency effects should still be present after a delay. Jescheniak and Levelt had participants name pictures and found that the frequency effects obtained in picture naming disappeared in a delayed cued-naming paradigm. Thus, Jescheniak and Levelt interpreted the disappearance of frequency effects after a delay as indicating that the frequency effects were not coming from postlexical processes.

Furthermore, Jescheniak and Levelt (1994) also found that the frequency effects observed in picture naming disappeared in a word–picture matching task. Since participants were still required to recognize the picture in order to reply if it matched the previously presented word, Jescheniak and Levelt argued that frequency effects could not be coming from recognition processes. Having eliminated both pre- and postlexical loci for frequency effects, Jescheniak and Levelt concluded that the frequency effects observed in the no-delay condition arose from the lexical level of word production. Their modelling proposal was quite similar to that of Dell (1990).[1] They suggested that these effects could be modelled as a difference in resting activation levels between HF and LF words, with HF words having a higher resting activation. This increase in resting activation would allow HF words to be available for lexical selection (and, hence, produced) more quickly than LF words in localist spreading-activation type models (see also Levelt et al., 1999).

A particularly clear demonstration of the lexical locus of the frequency effect comes from the study by Finocchiaro and Caramazza (2006). They found that production latencies of pronominal clitics (i.e., pronouns) were sensitive to the lexical frequency of the replaced noun. They ruled out the possibility that participants were covertly producing the noun's phonology by showing that phonologically related distractor words did not produce facilitation, an effect that is typically observed when participants are asked to name the pictures (e.g., Damian & Martin, 1999; Meyer & Schriefers, 1991). Combined, these two findings suggest that the lexical frequency effect that they observed arose at a level of processing that preceded access to the segmental information. Finocchiaro and Caramazza (2006) concluded that the lexical frequency effect arose at the point of lexical selection.

While the studies that we have reviewed here have concluded that lexical selection is the locus of the frequency effect, frequency effects, as we pointed out above, could also arise in the interface between semantics and the lexicon and/or in the interface between the lexicon and phonology (for this latter possibility see Barry, Morrison, & Ellis, 1997; Brown & Watson, 1987; Caramazza & Miozzo, 1997; MacKay, 1987). In the present study, we pursue these possibilities by

---

[1] At a finer grain, Dell (1990) and Jescheniak and Levelt (1994) came to different conclusions about the locus of frequency effects within word production. Dell put the frequency effect at the lemma, or syntactic form, level, while Jescheniak and Levelt put it at the lexeme, or phonological form, level. These distinctions within the lexical level are not universally accepted (see Caramazza, 1997; Caramazza & Miozzo, 1997). We discuss the issue of multiple lexical levels in our General Discussion.

investigating the distributions of specific error types as a function of target lexical frequency in an aphasic patient. For example, we ask whether or not semantic errors (e.g., patient responds "tiger" when presented with a picture of a giraffe) or phonological nonword errors (e.g., "piaffe" as an approximation of "giraffe") occur more often when the to-be-named picture has a low-frequency name than when it has a high-frequency name. On the assumption that the origin of specific error types (e.g., semantic, phonological) can be isolated in the speech production system, this strategy allows for the opportunity to determine which levels of processing are sensitive to lexical frequency. Below we discuss the rationale used to determine the source of specific error types within the speech production system.

Semantic errors can have either a lexical/phonological source or a semantic source. In the case of a semantic source, semantic errors may be due to a damaged semantic system not sending enough activation down to the lexical level to guarantee the selection of the target lexical representation. Alternatively, damage at the semantic level may be so severe that the wrong concept is selected, and lexical access continues accurately, just for the wrong target. In the case of a lexical or phonological source, semantic errors may arise as a result of an impairment in selecting the correct lexical representation or in selecting its corresponding phonology. For example, if the lexical selection mechanism is damaged, it may be difficult to select the target word from its semantically related neighbours that are also highly activated (e.g., Caramazza & Hillis, 1990; Nickels, 1995). Alternatively, if the target's phonology is unavailable, the patient may reselect a related (semantically or possibly phonologically) lexical item and proceed with producing this new item to show that they understand the task. This latter possibility differs from the other explanations in that it is a conscious strategy on the part of the patient and requires an additional selection step.

Fortunately, it is possible to distinguish patients who make semantic errors as a result of semantic level damage from those with lexical/phonological level damage. Individuals with semantic level damage typically have deficits in a wide variety of tasks, including those that require the patient to retrieve factual information about the target item (e.g., "Does a bird have four legs?"). In the case of patients who make semantic errors as a result of lexical/phonological (but not semantic) level damage, these patients perform normally in semantic judgement or sentence comprehension tasks.

Phonological errors (both word and nonword) arise during lexical access, or at a later postlexical stage (Kay & Ellis, 1987; Nickels, 1995). The explanation for the former case is that there is not enough activation coming from the lexical level to select all the constituent phonemes correctly, leading to phonological errors. Additionally, phonological word errors may arise by misselection of a word phonologically related to the target (Dell, Schwartz, Martin, Saffran, & Gagnon, 1997; Gagnon, Schwartz, Martin, Dell, & Saffran, 1997). In the postlexical case, there are problems with peripheral output mechanisms, such as articulatory control.

Once again, it is generally possible to distinguish patients who make phonological errors as a result of lexical level damage from those who make errors as a result of postlexical level damage. Patients with postlexical level damage have similar problems across all production tasks, including naming, reading, and repetition. In contrast, patients with lexical damage should perform worse in naming than in reading and repetition, since these latter tasks can be accomplished using nonlexical processes (Goldrick & Rapp, 2007).

Given that different error types occur as a result of damage to different stages of processing, we can look at the effect of lexical frequency on each error type to determine the range of processing stages that are sensitive to lexical frequency. If lexical frequency, and not a related variable, affects the likelihood of observing a particular error type, then we have support for the notion that lexical frequency is represented at the level of the system from which those errors arise. If we find that semantic errors are affected by frequency and, importantly, that these errors are not due to semantic level damage, then it is reasonable to consider that lexical frequency is represented either in the interface between semantics and the lexicon or at the point of lexical selection. If we find that lexical frequency affects the likelihood of observing phonological approximations of target names, then we have evidence for lexical frequency being represented in the interface between the lexicon and segmental representations.

Several studies have looked at frequency effects on semantic errors (Caramazza & Hillis, 1990; Nickels & Howard, 1994), phonological errors (Gagnon et al., 1997; Goldrick & Rapp, 2007; Schwartz et al., 2004; Wilshire & Fisher, 2004), or both (Cuetos et al., 2002; Feyereisen et al., 1988; Nickels, 1995). For example, two group studies report frequency effects on semantic errors in picture naming. In the first study, an investigation of operativity (i.e., how manipulable an object is) on aphasic errors, Feyereisen et al. (1988) report an effect of frequency on semantic errors, such that there were fewer semantic errors on higher frequency targets. In the second study, Cuetos et al. (2002) also found a similar pattern, whereby semantic errors decreased as target AoA decreased. Taken together, these findings suggest that frequency may affect semantic error rates; this is especially true for the Cuetos et al. study, which took into account other correlated factors such as imageability and word length. Unfortunately, these studies do not report the nature of the patients' deficits, and so it is unclear whether the lexical frequency effect should be attributed to prelexical, lexical, or postlexical levels of processing.

The few studies that have investigated the level of damage seem to agree that lexical frequency affects the rate of semantic errors, but only when errors arise as a result of lexical-level damage. For example, Caramazza and Hillis (1990) reported two patients who produced mostly semantic errors but who had intact semantics. Interestingly, though both patients showed frequency effects on their overall reading performance, only one, R.G.B., showed a frequency effect on his rate of semantic errors in picture naming and reading (more errors on categories with lower frequency words than on those with higher frequency words). Though this pattern of performance has rarely been reported in the literature (see also Hirsh & Ellis, 1994; Zingeser & Berndt, 1988, for potentially similar cases), the case of R.G.B. demonstrates that lexical frequency can have an effect on semantic error rates. In contrast to patient R.G.B., Nickels and Howard (1994) looked at familiarity effects on semantic errors for 8 patients, whom they determined had semantic damage, and found no effect of familiarity (as a proxy for frequency) on their semantic errors (see also Hillis, Rapp, Romani, & Caramazza, 1990).

Studies that have looked at phonological errors have also found that the likelihood of observing these types of error is sometimes sensitive to lexical frequency. In their group of patients, Cuetos et al. (2002) found that phonological errors decreased with target AoA overall. Feyereisen et al. (1988) also found that phonological errors decreased as a function of lexical frequency. Schwartz et al. (2004) also looked at lexical frequency effects on phonological errors in their sample of 18 patients. For their analysis, they split the phonological errors (based on a very liberal criterion) into proximate errors (those that preserved >50% of the target's phonemes) and remote errors (those with <50% of the target's phonemes). They found that log frequency only had a significant effect on proximate errors, not on remote errors. This frequency effect was in the intuitive direction—higher frequency targets led to fewer proximate phonological errors. Again, the findings reported in all three studies suggest that target lexical frequency may affect the likelihood of observing a phonological error. These findings could be taken as initial support for the hypothesis that frequency effects arise at the interface between lexical and segmental levels, but there are two difficulties that prevent making a strong conclusion about the level at which this effect arises: (a) heterogeneous groups of patients were used without specification of the individual deficits, and (b) word and nonword errors were collapsed into one category.

The study by Gagnon et al. (1997) overcomes our second objection by looking only at the phonological word errors of a group of 9 patients. They found that the frequency of such errors was higher than a conservative chance estimate of such a frequency, suggesting that frequency plays a role in such errors. Based on this and several other findings, they argued that at least some phonological word errors arise at the level of lexical selection. However, by looking only at phonological word errors, they cannot strongly constrain where to place frequency in the lexical system, especially if one believes their arguments for feedback of activation between levels of the lexical system.

Nickels (1995) also found effects of familiarity (as a proxy of frequency) on phonological error rates in her patients. A total of 3 out of the 15 patients showed familiarity effects individually. For all three patients a reduction in phonological errors led to a reduction in overall error. These were the same three patients who showed an overall familiarity effect upon naming; however, none of these patients or any of the others showed a significant effect of familiarity on semantic errors, though this is not surprising given that none of the other patients exhibited a familiarity effect on their *correct* responses. This study goes beyond the previous studies in showing that familiarity (as a proxy of frequency) affects phonological error rates in individual patients.

Similarly, in a study of the effect of phonological neighbourhood size on aphasic speech production, Gordon (2002) reports an effect of lexical frequency on patients' phonological error rates in picture naming and picture description tasks. The frequency effect held for 27 out of 32 individual patients in naming and 26 out of 34 in picture description. Overall, patients found it easier to name words with higher frequency and more dense neighbourhoods.

Mirroring the findings for semantic errors, a recent study by Goldrick and Rapp (2007) found that frequency affects phonological errors (word and nonword) only when such errors arise from a lexical deficit. They contrasted two patients, one with a lexical phonological deficit, and the other with a postlexical phonological deficit. Though both made similar kinds of errors, only the one with a lexical deficit showed any effect of frequency on response accuracy.

Taken together, these studies show that target lexical frequency affects the likelihood of patients making semantic and phonological errors, so long as their deficit is lexical in nature. Though these studies have revealed a robust effect of frequency on individual error types, they have not revealed the locus of this frequency effect. To do so, it is important to include an in-depth analysis of a patient's deficits and a systematic analysis of all error types as a function of target frequency. One purpose of the present article is to provide such an analysis.

The rest of this article is organized into three sections. In the first section, we present E.C., an aphasic patient who produces many different types of errors and whose overall picture-naming performance is affected by lexical frequency. These features make him an ideal candidate for localizing the effect of lexical frequency. To anticipate our results, we found that target lexical frequency did not modulate the likelihood of E.C. making a semantic error but did modulate his phonological nonword error rate. We take these findings to suggest that one locus of the lexical frequency effect is in the connections between the lexicon and segmental phonology.

In the second section of the paper we test the lexical-segmental hypothesis of lexical frequency by implementing frequency into a range of computational word production models. We directly compare models in which lexical frequency is implemented in the lexical-segmental connections with models in which frequency is implemented in the semantic-lexical connections and in the lexical nodes themselves. To anticipate our findings once again, placing frequency in the lexical-segmental connections led to the best fit of E.C.'s pattern among the three alternative hypotheses. Thus, the modelling work provides support for the suggestion that lexical frequency may be represented in the lexical-segmental connections.

In the third section of the article, we reanalyse the picture-naming data of a group of Italian aphasic patients both to look for a confirmation of E.C.'s pattern of performance and to see whether this technique of analysing specific error types as a function of lexical frequency might not reveal complementary patterns of performance. In this section of the paper, we report both patients like E.C., who show an effect of lexical frequency on phonological nonword errors, and those who, unlike E.C., exhibit an effect of lexical frequency on semantic errors. Taken together, these patterns of performance challenge the idea of a single locus of the lexical frequency effect in speech production. This work has strong implications for how we should think about lexical frequency and for how lexical frequency should be implemented in computational models of speech production.

PATIENT E.C.

Case history

E.C. is a 52-year-old, right-handed man with a bachelor's degree. He worked with computers before having a left-hemisphere stroke that resulted in language and attention difficulties. A magnetic resonance imaging (MRI) scan revealed a large perisylvian infarction, which included the superior temporal gyrus, extending into the supramarginal gyrus, the frontal operculum and inferior frontal gyrus, and part of the insula. E.C.'s language deficit is best classified as conduction aphasia. We started testing the patient 5 years and 8 months after the cerebral vascular accident (CVA). E.C. continues to use his dominant right hand after his stroke.

Nonlanguage testing

E.C. showed no evidence of bucco-facial apraxia. He showed a reduced digit span of 4 forwards and 2 backwards. His performance on Raven's progressive matrices was 52/60 (86.7%), which places him in the 98th percentile for his age. E.C. also correctly copied several pictures that we presented him, including a clock, a vase with flower, and the "Ogden scene" (a house with a fence and two trees). He could easily discern the difference between real and chimeric pictures (e.g., a picture of half of a penguin joined to half of a traffic light), scoring 20/20 (100%), though he had difficulties naming some of the objects involved.

Language evaluation

E.C. made frequent hesitations in his spontaneous speech, had word-finding difficulties, and made several semantic errors and phonological nonword errors—phonological approximations of the target. On single-word production tasks, he performed poorly across the board. His oral reading was impaired for words (55/75, 73%) and nonwords (7/10, 70%), showing problems with both verbs and nouns. His written spelling was also impaired, when elicited both by a picture (5/10, 50%) and from dictation (3/10, 30%); his oral spelling was similarly impaired (1/5, 20%). Across all spelling tasks, his responses would often share letters with the target, but they were rarely phonologically plausible. E.C. was also markedly impaired in simple repetition tasks for words (21/35, 60%) and nonwords (2/5, 40%). There was a clear length effect on his error rate—logistic regression, $\chi^2(1) = 6.43$, $p = .011$, Nagelkerke $R^2 = .277$—for word repetition, and errors tended to be phonologically or morphologically related to the target. Picture naming was the most impaired (3/20, 15%), with errors being mostly semantic and phonological in nature.

In contrast to his single-word production, E.C. did quite well in auditory word–picture matching (49/50, 98%), lexical discrimination (40/40, 100%), lexical decision (18/20, 90%), and auditory-visual word matching (19/20, 95%). Together these findings suggest that audition and comprehension for single words was relatively intact.

In sentence processing, E.C. showed a similar disparity between his comprehension and production. His auditory sentence to picture matching was mildly impaired (31/36 correct, 86%). E.C. performed worse on passive (12/16 correct, 75%) than on active sentences (19/20 correct, 95%). He did not make a single mistake (12/12 correct, 100%) in comprehending plural morphology in sentences (e.g., "The horse was followed by the dogs"). E.C.'s grammaticality judgements were also fairly good (9/10 correct, 90%). His only mistake was in accepting "the boy was followed the girl" as grammatical.

On the production side, E.C. seemed capable of producing short adjective–noun phrases (8/10 correct, 80%). However, his production in unconstrained (1/3 correct, 33%) and constrained sentences (0/3 correct, 0%) was quite low, which matched his performance for picture descriptions. E.C.'s sentence completion was also quite impaired (11/21, 52%; chance = 33%). Similarly, he also had trouble with sentence repetition (2/5 correct, 40%). His difficulty was proportional to the complexity of the sentences.

Further investigation of E.C.'s reading suggested damage to both his sublexical and lexical routes. Evidence of damage to his sublexical route was seen in his impaired nonword reading (34/80; 43%), while evidence for lexical-route damage came from significant effects of frequency and imageability on his word-reading performance (155/240; 65%).[2] He was better at reading more frequent and more imageable words. The imageability effect suggested problems with semantic processing, while the frequency effect provided evidence of lexical damage. The same list of words was also read to E.C. for a repetition task. His performance was slightly better than the reading (173/240; 72%). Word length was the only factor that affected his repetition performance. E.C. was better at reading and repeating shorter words. This effect indicated damage to accessing the segments and/or damage to postlexical processes. The fact that E.C. made similar errors (mostly substitution, addition, deletion, and transposition errors[3]) in reading words and nonwords and in repeating words suggested that there is a common locus of damage where the lexical and sublexical streams meet, in segmen processing, or in later postlexical stages.

To investigate further the extent of E.C.'s semantic deficit, we used a revised version of the original central attributes test (Caramazza & Shelton, 1998); this revised version of the test consisted of 305 "true/false" statements probing particular attributes of common living and nonliving objects, such as "A shirt is made of cloth" and "A squirrel eats nuts". E.C.'s performance on this task was better than chance (50%), but impaired (219/305 correct, 72%). There was no difference between his knowledge of visual and nonvisual attributes. His attribute knowledge was best for fruits and vegetables (21/24 correct, 88%), followed by animate living things (115/154 correct, 71%), with inanimate objects being worst (83/127 correct, 65%). The fact that that E.C. had trouble with this task indicated that his semantic system is also damaged.

Experimental investigation

We were particularly interested in E.C.'s picture-naming ability because E.C.'s functional deficit appears to span all three levels of the speech production system: semantic, lexical, and postlexical. We reasoned that this particular case afforded a unique opportunity to asses the effects of frequency on a variety of different error types within a single patient.

Over the course of a year E.C. was asked to name all 260 items from the Snodgrass and Vanderwart (1980) picture set twice. E.C. also named all 175 items of the Philadelphia Naming Test (Roach, Schwartz, Martin, Grewal, & Brecher, 1996) once. The stimuli were printed out on separate sheets of paper and were presented one at a time to E.C., who had unlimited time to name them.

---

[2] A logistic regression was conducted with log frequency, length in letters, imageability, and noun–verb status. The overall model was significant, $\chi^2(4) = 37.55, p < .001$, Nagelkerke $R^2 = .199$. Log frequency (Wald = 7.27, $p = .007$), length in letters (Wald = 13.84, $p < .001$), and imageability (Wald = 6.85, $p = .009$) were the significant individual factors. His repetition data were analysed using a logistic regression with the same four factors. This time the overall model was also significant, $\chi^2(4) = 9.54, p = .049$, Nagelkerke $R^2 = .056$. The only significant factor was length in letters (Wald = 6.28, $p = .012$).

[3] Regularization errors (e.g., [hɛrθ] for "hearth") and morphological errors were also common in word reading, while lexicalization errors were common in nonword reading.

The results from both tests were scored according to the criteria in Dell et al. (1997). We scored the first whole response. The major error categories were semantic, phonological (or formal), mixed, unrelated, or nonword and were classified according to the following rules:

Correct. The response must contain all the phonemes of the target. The only exceptions were for plural/singular morphology and for synonyms.

Phonological (formal). Unlike the general category of phonological errors that we discussed in the Introduction, this category here (and in all further usage) refers to only phonological *word* errors; phonological nonword errors are included in the nonword category. The criteria were designed to be fairly broad (Dell et al., 1997). In order to qualify, an error had to share a single phoneme with the target at the beginning, end, or any other position when both were lined up left to right. Errors that also shared two phonemes (excluding unstressed vowels and plural morphemes) with the target in any position were also counted as phonological errors.

Mixed. An error that meets the criteria for both semantic and phonological errors (see above).

Unrelated. All single-word errors that are not related to the target (see *Other* errors).

Nonword. Any response that is not in the English lexicon. Both phonologically related and unrelated responses were scored as nonwords, including those with a potential semantic relationship to the target.

Other. This is the category of errors that are not explained by the original model and includes: no responses, definitions and circumlocutions, parts of a picture, single morphemes, and visually related responses with no clear semantic relationship.

Analyses

We were most interested in the possible effect of lexical frequency on each of E.C.'s error types. To investigate this possibility we used several binary logistic regressions on the same dataset, one for correct responses and one each of the following error types: semantic, phonological (formal), mixed, and nonword. "Other" errors were not analysed since this was a heterogeneous category and since errors of this type have not been considered in previous modelling work (Dell et al., 1997). We also did not analyse unrelated errors since E.C. produced so few of them.

Each binary logistic regression analysis included log frequency as an independent variable: $\log 10(\text{frequency} + 1)$, where frequency is the CELEX lemma frequency; Baayen, Piepenbrock, & van Rijn, 1993. Independent variables also included imageability (MRC Psycholinguistic Database; Wilson, 1988), number of phonemes and number of phonological neighbours. Phonological neighbours were calculated using those words that appeared in both the Carnegie Mellon Pronouncing Dictionary (Version 0.6; Weide, 1994) and the CELEX lemma frequency dictionary (for a total of 25,815 words). Neighbours were considered to be all words in the intersection dictionary that were a single phoneme addition, deletion, or substitution away from the target word (following Vitevitch, 2002). We ran a second set of analyses without imageability to confirm the other factors since we could not obtain imageability ratings for all our items. Compound, plural, and multiple word targets were not included in the dataset.

Results

Out of the 589 items that we analysed, E.C. made 200 errors (66.0% correct). The breakdown of the errors by types is as follows: 82 semantic (13.9%), 14 phonological (2.4%), 15 mixed (2.5%), 3 unrelated (0.5%), 37 nonword (6.3%), and 49 other (8.3%) errors. Most of E.C.'s nonword errors were clear phonological approximations of the target (e.g., "strew" for the target picture of a screw and "toa, toach, tosh . . ." for the target picture of a toaster). When looking at the error distribution by frequency, we found a clear pattern for both semantic and nonword errors, the two main categories of E.C. errors. Semantic errors were not affected by frequency, while nonword errors decreased as target frequency increased (see Figure 2). Since we conducted five analyses on the same dataset (the correct response analysis and the analyses of semantic, phonological, mixed, and nonword errors), we adjusted our critical α level to .01 using Bonferroni correction. We report significant, $\alpha \leq .01$, and marginal values, $.01 < \alpha \leq .05$. Confirmatory analyses of the other factors using the larger dataset without imageability ratings were held to the same critical alpha level.

For the overall analysis of errors, there were 589 cases, of which 200 were errors. The overall model was significant, $\chi^2(3) = 31.68$, $p < .001$, Nagelkerke $R^2 = .072$, and the factors of log frequency (Wald = 10.79, $p < .001$) and number of phonemes (Wald = 7.11, $p = .008$) were significant. When the analysis was repeated with imageability, 481 cases were included, of which 157 were errors. The overall model was again significant, $\chi^2(4) = 56.7$, $p < .001$, with a Nagelkerke R^2 of .155. The only significant factor was imageability (Wald = 31.67, $p < .001$), while log frequency (Wald = 5.24, $p = .022$) and number of phonemes (Wald = 5.43, $p = .020$) were marginal. Errors tended to occur on less frequent, longer, and less imageable items.

In the analysis of semantic errors relative to the other error types (including correct responses), the overall model was not significant, $\chi^2(4) = 8.2$, $p = .085$, Nagelkerke $R^2 = .030$. However, the individual factor imageability was significant (Wald = 7.18, $p = .007$). Semantic errors were potentially more likely for low-imageability words. When the analysis was repeated without imageability, the model was again not significant, $\chi^2(3) = 3.13$, ns, Nagelkerke $R^2 = .010$. None of the factors frequency, length, or number of phonological neighbours was significant in this analysis (all $ps > .1$).

The analysis of nonword errors was significant overall, $\chi^2(4) = 44.24$, $p < .001$, Nagelkerke $R^2 = .250$, with log frequency being significant (Wald = 11.64, $p = .001$) and length in phonemes being marginal (Wald = 9.66, $p = .02$). Both these factors were significant in the analysis without imageability (Wald = 12.15, $p < .001$, for frequency; Wald = 14.06, $p < .001$, for phonemes), as was the overall analysis, $\chi^2(3) = 46.73$, $p < .001$, Nagelkerke $R^2 = .204$. Longer and lower frequency targets were more likely to lead to nonword errors.

Though E.C. made few phonological and mixed errors, the analyses of these errors were both significant: phonological, $\chi^2(4) = 16.14$, $p = .003$, Nagelkerke $R^2 = .234$; mixed, $\chi^2(4) = 16.32$, $p = .003$, Nagelkerke $R^2 = .170$. Imageability (Wald = 14.02, $p < .001$) was the only significant factor, while number of phonological neighbours (Wald = 3.86, $p = .049$) was marginal. Phonological errors were more likely to occur on targets that were lower in imageability and had more phonological neighbours. The analysis without imageability was marginal, $\chi^2(3) = 9.77$, $p = .021$, Nagelkerke $R^2 = .082$, and showed number of phonological neighbours also to be marginal (Wald = 4.65, $p = .031$). In this analysis,

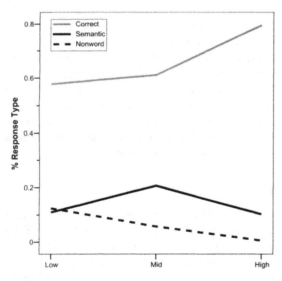

Figure 2. *A breakdown of E.C.'s major response types by target frequency. Only correct response and semantic and nonword errors are shown. Low-frequency items (n = 201) had a frequency $\leq$ 12. Mid-frequency items (N = 193) had a frequency > 12 and $\leq$40. High-frequency items (N = 195) had a frequency >40.*

number of phonemes turned out to be significant (Wald = 11.35, $p = .001$). In the case of mixed errors, lower frequency targets (Wald = 8.48, $p = .004$) and possibly targets in more dense phonological neighbourhoods (Wald = 5.59, $p = .018$) led to more such errors. When the analyses of mixed errors were repeated without imageability, frequency was again a significant factor (Wald = 6.96, $p = .008$), and phonological neighbourhood size was marginal (Wald = 5.35, $p = .023$). The overall model was marginal, $\chi^2(3) = 10.70$, $p = .013$, Nagelkerke $R^2 = .085$.

Discussion

The results of the overall naming performance support the idea that E.C. has several impairments spanning the production system. The fact that he produced fewer errors when naming pictures with names that have been rated as being more imageable (just as he did in the reading task) and that this imageability effect was mostly carried by his semantic errors supports the idea that he has damage to the semantic system. The effect of frequency supports the idea that his difficulty in production tasks is also partly due to damage to the lexical system. His similar performance on naming, reading, and repetition suggests that he may additionally have damage to his postlexical system. This is further supported by his difficulties in reading words and nonwords and with the similar kinds of errors that he produced in all production tasks.

The particularly intriguing aspect of E.C.'s performance comes from the analysis of his specific error types and the effect of lexical frequency on the distributions of those errors. Though there were fewer errors overall as a function of frequency, the effect of lexical frequency on the individual error types varied greatly. The striking finding is that phonological nonword errors were strongly affected by lexical frequency, while semantic errors were not.[4] Crucially, the effect of frequency on E.C.'s performance held even after the effects of imageability, length, and number of phonological neighbours were factored out. Thus, the effect of lexical frequency on E.C.'s phonological nonword errors cannot be reduced to a combination of variables that are correlated with lexical frequency. Of the three likely implementations of lexical frequency in the basic model (see Figure 1), only a locus at the lexical-segmental interface can readily account for how lexical frequency could affect the likelihood of observing a phonological nonword error.

In the next section, we use a computational modelling approach to test the hypothesis that E.C.'s picture naming and, specifically, the interaction between lexical frequency and phonological nonword error rates, are best accounted for by a model in which lexical frequency is implemented in the lexical-segmental connections. This work reveals that only by implementing lexical frequency in the lexical-segmental connections is one able to successfully model E.C.'s pattern of performance.

FREQUENCY MODELLING

Several studies have attempted to simulate patterns of errors produced by aphasic patients in a simple picture-naming task (Dell et al., 1997; Foygel & Dell, 2000; Ruml & Caramazza, 2000; Ruml, Caramazza, Capasso, & Miceli, 2005; Ruml, Caramazza, Shelton, & Chialant, 2000; Schwartz, Dell, Martin, Gahl, & Sobel, 2006). The architecture and dynamics of the underlying (normal) model of production in all these studies have been similar. In modelling the frequency pattern exhibited by patient E.C., we started with the same basic architecture (Dell et al., 1997) and varied several core assumptions. We then implemented lexical frequency in three different loci: (a) the interface between semantic and

---

[4] Frequency was also found to affect mixed errors, but not phonological (word) errors. Since there were few errors in each of these categories (2.4% for phonological; 2.5% for mixed) we do not discuss these findings further.

lexical levels, (b) the lexical level, and (c) the interface between lexical and segmental levels. Our goal was not only to find the best fit to E.C.'s pattern, but also to see how robust our findings would be across several core assumptions. We describe the basic model, our variations, and our extensions of the model to incorporate frequency in turn.

Architecture and dynamics
The architecture of the general lexical model (see Introduction) consists of three levels of representations: semantic, lexical, and segmental. Semantic nodes represent conceptual features, lexical nodes represent abstract word forms, and segmental nodes represent abstract phonemes. The following equations govern the spread of activation for a node m at any level of the system for the next time step ($t + 1$):

$$a_{t+1}(m) = old + incoming + noise$$
$$old = (1 - decay) \times a_t(m) + decay \times resting(m)$$
$$incoming = \sum_{n \in N} max[0, connection(n, m) \times a_t(n)]$$

where $a(m)$ represents the activation of node m at a certain time step (either at the current time step or the previous). N is the set of all other nodes that are connected to node m. This architecture and these dynamics are general to a localist connectionist implementation of the general model of lexical access. *Decay*, *resting*, and *connection* are parameters of the model. The *connection* and *resting* parameters are especially important for our modelling work. *Connection*(n,m) refers to the strength of the connection from node n to node m. These parameters may be all set to the same value, or may vary by levels in the system (depending on the implementation of damage, see below). They may also vary by individual items (specifically for the target), an aspect we utilize for our frequency modelling (see below). The *resting* parameter reflects resting activation, which is an implicit part of this modelling approach (Dell, 1990), but has been set to zero for the above studies. This parameter is included in the equations because we utilize it for one of our frequency manipulations (see below).

In addition to these general assumptions, Dell et al. (1997) add several additional assumptions and specified additional parameters. A major assumption that they include is interactivity in the system. In other words, all connections between nodes are bidirectional, so activation flows forwards and backwards in the system. The other major assumption of Dell et al. (1997) is that of distributed semantic representations—that is, semantic features are represented without unitary concept nodes (see Rapp & Goldrick, 2000, for a modified architecture that includes such nodes). Another added assumption is that all connections are excitatory (not inhibitory) and that there are no connections between nodes at the same level. A related assumption that is also included is that while negative activations can exist at nodes (due to noise), they are not propagated.

The following parameters are also part of Dell et al.'s (1997) implementation: original activation of target's semantic nodes, time steps until lexical selection, jolt activation to winning node of lexical selection, and time steps until selection of segments. Lexical access is simulated in the model by setting the activation level of the semantic representations associated with the target word to the predetermined value (fixed at 10 units). The activation levels of all representations in the network are then updated for the specified number of time steps (fixed at 8 steps). After this time, the activation level of the most active lexical representation is raised to a predefined high level (a level of 100 units was used), corresponding to the notion of lexical selection. Activations are further propagated for another specified number of time steps (also 8 steps), after which the most active onset, vowel, and coda phonemes are chosen as the output of the model. The fixed number of time steps does not allow the model to predict reaction times in a straightforward manner. Through the addition of the lexical jolt, the Dell et al. implementation incorporates the idea of two separate selection steps: one lexical, and one phonological.

Without noise, the general model cannot make an error. In order to produce errors, noise is included in the first equation. The Dell et al. (1997) implementation specifies two types of noise, calculated by the following equation:

$$noise = R(intrinsic) + R(activation) \times a_t(m)$$

where $R(x)$ represents a random sample drawn from a normal distribution with a mean of zero and a standard deviation of x^5. *Intrinsic* and *activation* are parameters in the Dell et al. implementation (fixed to 0.01 and 0.16, respectively). There is both an intrinsic noise component in each node and a noise component that depends on how highly activated the node is. Because of the contribution of noise to the activation levels, the selected lexical representation does not necessarily correspond to the target word, and even if it does, the selected segmental representations are not necessarily those associated with the selected lexical node. Along with correct responses, the model can produce the following errors: semantically related, phonologically related (formal), mixed (both semantically and phonologically related), unrelated, and nonword. By simulating many trials, one can accumulate an estimate of the probabilities of the various categories of responses and determine whether the model represents a mechanism sufficient to generate a distribution measured from a human experimental participant.

Our own work uses the Dell et al. (1997) model, but tries to generalize across two key assumptions that have been questioned in the literature: neighbourhood and level of interactivity. We discuss these assumptions and the steps that we took to generalize across them in our own modelling.

Neighbourhood
The lexicon used by Dell et al. (1997) includes only a few word nodes. While many magnitudes smaller than a typical speaker's lexicon, the relationships between these nodes were nevertheless designed to reflect the neighbourhood of the average word that is used in picture-naming experiments. The original neighbourhood was constructed to reflect random error opportunities in the English language. It consists of a target word (e.g., "cat"), a semantic neighbour (e.g., "dog"), two formal neighbours (e.g., "hat" and "mat"), and two unrelated neighbours (actually phonological neighbours of the semantic neighbour of the target; e.g., "log" & "fog"). There is also a slightly modified version of the network that replaces one formal neighbour (e.g., hat) with a mixed (i.e., semantically and phonologically related) neighbour (e.g., "rat"). Runs from these two neighbourhoods are sampled 90% and 10% of the time, respectively, to produce a final distribution of errors. All words in this neighbourhood (and those described below) were of the form consonant–vowel–consonant.

Rapp and Goldrick (2000) have criticized the above neighbourhood. They determined that words that are semantically related have a slightly higher chance of also being phonologically related. They pointed out that semantically related items in the original neighbourhood were slightly less phonologically related to the target. To remedy this they created a larger, 29-word lexicon for modelling, which takes this phonological overlap into account. This neighbourhood has the added advantage of producing all possible error types using a single neighbourhood (as compared to sampling from two neighbourhoods, which artificially limits the maximum number of mixed errors).

We used both these neighbourhoods in our modelling work to be confident that our results would not be tied to idiosyncratic elements of a single neighbourhood. To further confirm the reliability of our models, we also ran our simulations with a third neighbourhood[6] that was

---

[5] Our implementation of Dell et al.'s (1997) model uses George Marsaglia and Wai Wan Tsang's (2000) ziggurat algorithm for generating normally distributed random numbers. We thank them for making their code publicly available.

[6] We would like to thank Wheeler Ruml for providing us with this neighbourhood and for creating the algorithm by which it was constructed.

created using an automated search algorithm to better fit both the criteria of random error opportunity (Dell et al., 1997) and greater phonological opportunity (Rapp & Goldrick, 2000). The details of the automated search procedure can be found in Ruml et al. (2005, Appendix B). Throughout the rest of this paper, we refer to these neighbourhoods by the number of lexical nodes (N) that they contain: 6 N for Dell et al.'s (1997) original neighbourhood, 20 N for our new neighbourhood, and 29 N for Rapp and Goldrick's (2000) neighbourhood.

Interactivity

As we describe above, Dell et al.'s (1997) original model is highly interactive. That is, there is feedback from the segmental level to the lexical level and from the lexical level to the semantic level. There has been disagreement for quite some time over whether the production system is interactive and, if so, to what extent (e.g., Goldrick & Rapp, 2002; Rapp & Goldrick, 2000; Ruml et al., 2005).

Even though originally conceived as being an interactive model, the implementation of the Dell model easily allows for modification of the interactivity assumption. In the current work, we included models with full interactivity, like the original model, with restricted interactivity, where there was only feedback from the segmental level to the lexical level (Goldrick & Rapp, 2002; Rapp & Goldrick, 2000), and with no interactivity, a simple cascaded model. We were interested in seeing how our frequency manipulations would be affected by changes in the interactivity of the system. Combing the three types of neighbourhood with the three types of interactivity produced nine models. When discussing these models we use the following abbreviations to refer to their level of interactivity: "H" for high interactivity, "R" for restricted interactivity, or "C" for cascaded.

Implementations of brain damage

What we have described so far is the normal production model underlying our work. In order to model E.C.'s condition we must make further assumptions about how the normal system is damaged. In our current work we considered two implementations of brain damage: weight-decay and semantic-phonological connection strength (henceforth semantic-phonological). Weight-decay instantiates the global damage (or globality) hypothesis of brain damage (Dell et al., 1997), while semantic-phonological instantiates the levels of damage hypothesis of brain damage[7] (Foygel & Dell, 2000; see also Ruml & Caramazza, 2000).

The global damage hypothesis assumes that aphasic performance can be captured by diffuse damage to the entire model. The weight-decay implementation simulates global damage to the system by changing the global connection strength of the model and/or the rate of activation decay (in the equations presented above, these would be the *connection* and *decay* parameters, respectively). The levels of damage hypothesis, contrary to the global damage hypothesis, claim that there are independent levels in the system where damage can occur. In word production, these levels have been taken to be the semantic and phonological levels. In the semantic-phonological implementation this damage is simulated by changing the connection weights between the semantic and lexical nodes and between the lexical and segmental nodes independently. Thus semantic and phonological deficits can be more intuitively modelled in the system. There is mounting evidence suggesting that this is the preferred method for modelling patients (Foygel & Dell, 2000; Ruml & Caramazza, 2000; Ruml et al., 2000; Schwartz et al., 2006), but we include an implementation of the global damage hypothesis for the sake of completeness (cf. Dell, Lawler, Harris, & Gordon, 2004; Schwartz et al., 2006). Combining the 9 models from the previous

---

[7] We wish to stress the difference between theory and implementation, since it is possible to implement the same theory in different ways. For example, see Rapp and Goldrick (2000) for other implementations of the global damage and levels of damage hypotheses.

section with these two implementations of brain damage produced a total of 18 models. In discussing our models, we use the following abbreviations to refer to the type of brain damage implementation: Global for the global damage implementation and Levels for the levels of damage implementation.

Fitting patients

Before modelling E.C.'s errors as a function of frequency, it was necessary to determine the correct damage settings for each type of model (i.e., each combination of neighbourhood type, interactivity type, and damage implementation). Fitting such models to patients has been considerably researched (e.g., Dell et al., 2004; Foygel & Dell, 2000; Ruml & Caramazza, 2000) and consists of mapping out the parameter space of the damage theory to a certain grain. At each combination of parameters, the model is run extensively (10,000 trials) to get an estimate of the distribution at those settings. With such a map, fitting a patient consists of finding the point on the map with a distribution most similar to that of the patient, using χ^2 as the measure of fit (e.g., Dell et al., 2004; Foygel & Dell, 2000). We fit our models to E.C. using a method quite similar to that of Foygel & Dell (2000).[8] The parameter settings of this fit for each model were used as the "average" frequency point in the data obtained from our manipulations of frequency in the models.

We fitted E.C. based on his overall performance on the first and second administrations of the Snodgrass and Vanderwart (1980) picture set and on a single administration of the Philadelphia Naming Test. The same items as those that were used in the patient analyses (see "Patient E.C." section above) were used for the fitting procedure. E.C.'s performance across the three administrations did not differ reliably: $\chi^2(5) = 4.60$, $p = .467$, for the first and second administrations of the Snodgrass and Vanderwart pictures; $\chi^2(5) = 4.79$, $p = .442$, for the first administration of the Snodgrass and Vanderwart pictures and the Philadelphia Naming Test; $\chi^2(5) = 2.41$, $p = .790$ for the second administration of the Snodgrass and Vanderwart pictures and the Philadelphia Naming Test.

Frequency implementation

The architecture of the general model of lexical access lends itself to three loci for frequency: the interface between semantic and lexical levels, the lexical level, and the interface between lexical and segmental levels. Lexical frequency can be implemented as either of the connection strengths between representational levels or the resting activation level of the lexical nodes, respectively (e.g., Dell, 1990; Stemberger, 1985).[9] Specifically, we allowed the frequency of the target to vary, keeping the rest of the network resting activations or connections as they were.

The first step was to fit each model to E.C.'s performance. Taking this fitted model, we then applied each of the above frequency manipulations in turn. We allowed target resting activation to vary from −0.10 to +0.10 (inclusive) in 0.01-unit steps. For connection strength (either semantic-lexical or lexical-segmental), we allowed the target connection strength to vary from 0.00 to +0.20 (inclusive) in 0.01-unit steps. At each point we ran the model 10,000

---

[8] Both our mapping procedure and that of Foygel and Dell (2000) used a smart procedure to only add points to the parameter map if they were significantly different from their surrounding neighbours (based on a χ^2 criterion). The slight difference between our procedure and theirs is that in ours the decision to add each new point is done on a point-by-point basis and not for groups of five points. Our maps allowed connection strength to vary from 0.001 to 0.1 and decay to vary from 0.5 to 1.0. The maximum level of expansion (i.e., grain) that we allowed was 1/128. We created a map for each of the nine models (i.e., three levels of interactivity crossed with three neighbourhoods) with each of the two implementations of damage, for a total of 18 maps. In testing our procedure, we obtained fits for their patients that were comparable to published results.

[9] Another possible locus of frequency within the model is in the jolt strength. Higher frequency lexical nodes can receive a higher jolt of activation after they are selected. The results of such an implementation should be quite similar to the lexical-segmental connection locus that we do implement, since both have frequency effects occurring mostly after lexical selection. Please see our General Discussion for our reasons for not manipulating jolt strength in the model.

times to obtain a distribution of errors. Distributions for settings greater than the "average" point would reflect modelled performance on increasingly higher frequency words, and likewise points smaller than the "average" point would reflect performance on lower frequency words. We deliberately tried to capture a wide range of the model's performance over our frequency manipulations—most likely greater than the frequency difference that could be obtained in an experimental setting.

Analysis
While it is important to look at the qualitative patterns produced by the different frequency implementations to see how well they capture E.C.'s data, it is equally important to be able to quantify their goodness of fit, especially since we wish to directly compare the three frequency implementations. In our approach, we split E.C.'s data into low-, medium-, and high-frequency groups and compare within each of our 18 models how well each implementation can match E.C.'s low- and high-frequency error distributions. We discuss the details of this process and the analysis of the results below.

We looked at how well the three frequency implementations could capture E.C.'s performance. This was done in the following way. For each model we found the point that minimized the χ^2 difference between the model's error distribution and E.C.'s low-frequency error distribution. Then, we also found the point with the best χ^2 fit to E.C.'s high-frequency error distribution. We restricted the range of the search for the best low-frequency point to be below the "average" frequency point. Likewise, the range of the search for the best high-frequency point was restricted to be above the average frequency point. We did not search for the best χ^2 fit of E.C.'s medium frequency distribution, since theoretically the "average" point was most appropriate to match this distribution.

We ran a single repeated measures analysis of variance (ANOVA) on the high and low χ^2 fits of the models. The within-models factors were frequency implementation (i.e., semantic-lexical connections, lexical resting activations, or lexical-segmental connections) and frequency distribution (i.e., high or low). Any significant differences observed in this analysis must have their source in the frequency implementations since the same underlying models were used each time. Based on our account of E.C.'s performance, we predicted that implementing frequency in the lexical-segmental connection strengths would give the best fits for E.C.'s performance. We did not include the fits to E.C. medium-frequency distribution, since these were exactly the same across the three frequency implementations for each model.

Results

A total of 54 model runs were produced by crossing the factors interactivity (H, R, or C), neighbourhood (6N, 20N, or 29N), damage implementation (global, levels), and frequency implementation (semantic-lexical connections, lexical resting activations, and lexical-segmental connections). Some models were a better χ^2 fit to E.C.'s overall error distribution than others. The actual fits are summarized for each of the models in Table 1. Using our fitting procedure, the original model from Dell et al. (1997; i.e., global 6N-H) accounted best for patient E.C.'s overall performance, before frequency was implemented. Below we present the qualitative results of the individual runs and the quantitative analysis comparing the three frequency implementations.

Qualitative results
In discussing our qualitative results, we focus on the frequency range in our modelling output that corresponds to E.C.'s performance range as we ascertained through our fitting procedures. While space here permits us to provide only several representative graphs of the semantic and nonword error trends, all modelling graphs (with all error types in colour) can be found online at: http://www.wjh.harvard.edu/~caram/frequency_modeling/index.html

Semantic–lexical connections. We found that implementing frequency in the semantic–lexical connections produced error distributions that were different from E.C.'s pattern. Not surprisingly, implementing lexical frequency at this level in the model produced an effect of frequency on the semantic error rate whereas E.C.'s semantic error rate was not modulated by target lexical frequency. All 18 models showed this trend, along with a decrease of phonological, mixed, and unrelated errors as frequency increased, though different models predicted different rates of decrease for these errors.

With regard to nonword errors, there were two distinct patterns produced by our models. The six high-interactivity models showed nonword errors decreasing as a function of frequency, though at a slower rate than semantic errors, while all restricted interaction and cascading models showed no effect of frequency on nonword errors. See Figure 3 for representative graphs of these two dominant patterns from the Levels 6N-H and Levels 6N-C models.

Lexical resting activations. Implementing lexical frequency in the resting activation levels of the lexical nodes led to a similar patterning of semantic, phonological, mixed, and unrelated errors across all 18 models. See Figure 4 for a representative graph from the Levels 6 N-H model. Just as when frequency was implemented in the semantic–lexical connections, all models produced fewer semantic errors as frequency increased. In contrast, these models showed little or no change in the rate of nonword error rates in the range of E.C.'s performance.

Lexical–segmental connections. When implementing lexical frequency in the lexical–segmental connections, all 18 models produced the same pattern

Table 1. *All models fitted to E.C.'s performance to the combined data from two administrations of the Snodgrass and Vanderwart picture set and one administration of the Philadelphia Naming Test*

Model	Correct	Semantic	Phonological	Mixed	Unrelated	Nonword	Sem|Weight	Phon|Decay	RMSD	χ-squared
EC	0.7204	0.1519	0.0259	0.0278	0.0056	0.0685				
Global 6N-H	0.7306	0.1336	0.0345	0.0350	0.0059	0.0604	0.0969	0.8516	0.010	3.79
Global 20N-H	0.6630	0.0756	0.0266	0.1122	0.0101	0.1125	0.0474	0.6836	0.055	83.92
Global 29N-H	0.7360	0.0890	0.0264	0.0788	0.0171	0.0527	0.0296	0.6172	0.035	46.16
Global 6N-R	0.7128	0.0789	0.0608	0.0081	0.0312	0.1082	0.0196	0.5820	0.039	84.25
Global 20N-R	0.6837	0.0474	0.0637	0.0495	0.0459	0.1098	0.0288	0.6016	0.054	150.93
Global 29N-R	0.7515	0.0684	0.0384	0.0456	0.0243	0.0718	0.0103	0.5195	0.038	63.30
Global 6N-C	0.7743	0.0742	0.0397	0.0090	0.0242	0.0786	0.1000	0.6602	0.041	70.40
Global 20N-C	0.7451	0.0467	0.0393	0.0404	0.0369	0.0916	0.0899	0.6484	0.047	130.88
Global 29N-C	0.7455	0.0751	0.0355	0.0445	0.0274	0.0720	0.0869	0.6445	0.035	52.64
Levels 6N-H	0.7520	0.0853	0.0557	0.0131	0.0299	0.0640	0.0211	0.0250	0.035	53.38
Levels 20N-H	0.7849	0.0521	0.0292	0.0555	0.0221	0.0562	0.0250	0.0281	0.051	107.27
Levels 29N-H	0.7194	0.0845	0.0341	0.0699	0.0198	0.0723	0.0250	0.0242	0.033	46.41
Levels 6N-R	0.7176	0.0910	0.0781	0.0109	0.0486	0.0538	0.0211	0.0296	0.038	73.55
Levels 20N-R	0.6867	0.0501	0.0702	0.0553	0.0574	0.0803	0.0265	0.0304	0.053	144.77
Levels 29N-R	0.7144	0.0661	0.0592	0.0583	0.0304	0.0716	0.0312	0.0281	0.041	82.67
Levels 6N-C	0.7403	0.0889	0.0544	0.0103	0.0401	0.0660	0.0250	0.0335	0.033	60.14
Levels 20N-C	0.7334	0.0545	0.0461	0.0507	0.0617	0.0536	0.0296	0.0420	0.048	121.36
Levels 29N-C	0.7874	0.0781	0.0317	0.0382	0.0215	0.0431	0.0366	0.0428	0.043	52.75

Note: Picture set: Snodgrass & Vanderwart, 1980. Philadelphia Naming Test: Roach et al., 1996. These were the fits of each model to the overall data before frequency implementations were tested. H = high interactivity; R = restricted interactivity; C = cascaded. N = number of lexical nodes. RMSD = root mean square deviation.

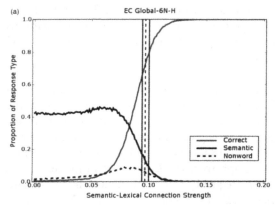

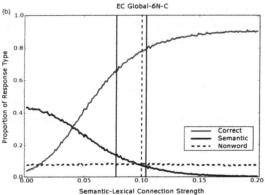

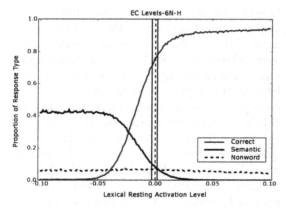

Figure 4. *Example graph of implementing frequency as the resting activation of the lexical nodes. The model shown is Levels 6N-H. The vertical dotted line shows the settings of the model that was fitted to E.C. before frequency manipulations and represents the average frequency word. The vertical solid lines to the left and right of the average line show the best model fits to E.C.'s low and high distributions, respectively.*

Figure 3. *Example graphs of implementing frequency as the connection strength between semantic and lexical nodes. Panel a shows model Levels 6N-H, while Panel b shows model Levels 6N-C. The vertical dotted line shows the settings of the model that was fitted to E.C. before frequency manipulations and represents the average frequency word. The vertical solid lines to the left and right of the average line show the best model fits to E.C.'s low and high distributions, respectively.*

of sharply decreasing nonword errors as target frequency increased. This decrease was larger than that observed in the two previous frequency implementations. Phonological and unrelated errors were also generally seen to decrease as frequency increased, but to a lesser degree than nonword errors.

The high and restricted interaction models produced fewer semantic and mixed errors as frequency increased, though this frequency effect was attenuated relative to the effect of frequency on the nonword errors. In contrast, the cascading models did not exhibit an effect of frequency on the semantic and mixed error rates. See Figure 5 for representative graphs of these two main patterns from Levels 6N-R and Levels 6N-C.

Quantitative results

In order to analyse the effects of frequency implementation, we included model ($N = 18$) as a random factor in a 3 × 2 repeated measures ANOVA. Only the main effect of frequency implementation, $MSE = 2,145.1$, $F(1.18, 20.02) = 99.05$, $p < .001$,[10] was significant. The lexical-segmental connection weights implementation of frequency produced better χ^2 fits (mean = 21.72, $SD = 12.99$) than did either the semantic-lexical connection weights (mean = 31.57, $SD = 13.21$) or lexical resting activation levels implementations (mean = 32.34, $SD = 13.36$). The main effect of

---

[10] The Huynh–Feldt correction was applied because the sphericity assumption was not met.

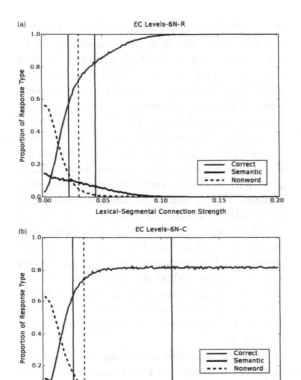

Figure 5. Example graphs of implementing frequency as the connection strength between lexical and segmental nodes. Panel a shows model Levels 6N-R, while Panel b shows model Levels 6N-C. The vertical dotted line shows the settings of the model that was fitted to E.C. before frequency manipulations and represents the average frequency word. The vertical solid lines to the left and right of the average line show the best model fits to E.C.'s low and high distributions, respectively.

frequency distribution, $MSE = 712.7$, $F(1, 17) = 1.53$, $p = .233$, was not significant. Fits to high- and low-frequency distributions were comparable. More importantly, the interaction between the two main factors was also not significant, $MSE = 75.14$, $F(1.07, 18.18) = 1.11$, $p = .311$.[11] The overall fits of the three frequency manipulations to E.C.'s error distributions, collapsed across low and high distributions, are shown in Figure 6.

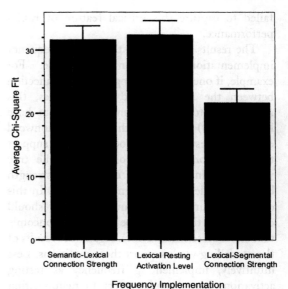

Figure 6. Average χ^2 fits between each of the three frequency implementations and E.C.'s low- and high-frequency error distributions. Low- and high-frequency fits are combined for each frequency manipulation.

Discussion

The purpose of this modelling work was to determine which implementation of lexical frequency would best fit E.C.'s pattern of performance. Remember, the key feature of E.C.'s performance was that his nonword error rate was modulated by lexical frequency, while his rate of semantic errors was not. The implementation of lexical frequency that best captured this feature of E.C.'s performance was the lexical-segmental connection strength implementation. Placing lexical frequency between the lexical and segmental layers gave the best fit for E.C.'s performance for both high- and low-target-frequency items; this was true for models incorporating different assumptions of interactivity and lexical neighbourhood sizes. In contrast, implementing lexical frequency in the semantic-lexical connections or in the activation levels of the lexical nodes themselves

---

[11] The Huynh–Feldt correction was applied because the sphericity assumption was not met.

failed to capture this critical feature of E.C.'s performance.

The results obtained for these three frequency implementations make intuitive sense. For example, if one were to strengthen the connection between the semantic and lexical nodes, this should lead to fewer semantic errors, but have little (if any) effect on the rate of nonword errors. The results of the modelling work support these intuitions. The opposite should be true when one increases the connection strength between the lexical and segmental nodes. In this case, the number of nonword errors should decrease, and there should be little to no concomitant effect on semantic errors. Again, the results of the modelling work support these intuitions. Less intuitively, implementing frequency as resting activations has a similar effect to manipulating semantic-to-lexical connections. Here the target's higher resting activation reduces competing word response, especially semantic errors, while having less of an effect on the nonword errors, since the jolt of activation that comes from lexical selection washes away most of the resting activation differences.

It may be surprising that the best fitting model for patient E.C. was the Global 6N-H, given the evidence that we have cited favouring the levels of damage hypothesis. This model was particularly successful in producing a high rate of semantic errors. We believe this is due to the combination of a high decay rate with full interactivity, which has been shown to lead to increases in such errors (see Dell et al., 1997; Foygel & Dell, 2000; Ruml & Caramazza, 2000). Our implementation of the levels of damage hypothesis does not allow for manipulation of the decay parameter of the models. However, the success of this particular model does not mean that it is correctly simulating E.C.'s semantic errors. We concluded earlier that a good part of E.C.'s semantic errors were of a semantic origin, while the semantic errors that the model produces are only postsemantic or lexical in origin. This fact highlights an inherent limitation of all our models—namely, that they cannot produce semantic errors of a strictly semantic origin. While this limitation does not affect our investigation of the frequency effect, it is necessary to fully model E.C.'s word production deficits. We return to this point in the General Discussion.

The upshot of this modelling work is that it supports the hypothesis that at least one locus of the frequency effect should be in the connections between the lexical and segmental levels. This is the only apparent way to model E.C.'s performance successfully.[12] In the following section we review the data of a large set of Italian aphasic patients to determine how target lexical frequency modulates specific error types in a large population

---

[12] A potential challenge to this conclusion comes from a proposal by Dell (1990). He proposed, but never implemented, the hypothesis that lexical frequency effects in production could be explained as semantic and/or phonological neighbourhood effects. This hypothesis challenges an underlying assumption of our work, which is that the semantic and phonological neighbourhoods of a higher frequency word are the same as those neighbourhoods of a lower frequency word. This assumption is probably incorrect, at least for phonological neighbourhoods, given the significant correlation ($r = -.49, p < .01$) between frequency and phonological neighbourhood size in our own data (see also Gordon, 2002). Nevertheless, while phonological neighbourhood size affects E.C.'s rates of phonological and mixed errors, significant effects of lexical frequency persist in regression analyses of E.C.'s performance, despite the inclusion of phonological neighbourhood size and other semantic and phonological measures as cofactors. Putting these analyses aside, we explored the possibility further by trying to simulate E.C.'s lexical frequency effects through modifying semantic and phonological neighbourhoods in the largest neighbourhood (that of Rapp & Goldrick, 2000). Adding more semantic neighbours led to the models (H, R, and C) producing more semantic and nonword errors, with a much larger increase in semantic errors. Overall accuracy also decreased. This pattern was quite unlike E.C.'s. In the case of adding more phonological neighbours, models produced slightly fewer nonword and semantic errors, but instead of leading to fewer errors as a function of frequency (as in E.C.'s case), this decrease led to a corresponding increase in phonological errors (see also Dell & Gordon, 2003). It is clear from these investigations that semantic and phonological neighbourhoods cannot explain the lexical frequency effects that we observe in E.C.'s performance.

of patients. This review reveals that E.C.'s pattern of performance is not an isolated pattern. This review also reveals a patient whose performance is best explained by implementing lexical frequency in the semantic-to-lexical connections.

ITALIAN PATIENTS

In the first section of this article, we reported patient E.C., who showed a clear effect of frequency on his overall naming performance. This effect was carried by a decrease in his nonword errors as target frequency increased; his rate of semantic errors, in contrast, was not modulated by lexical frequency. In the present section, we investigate a large group of aphasic patients to see whether E.C.'s pattern of errors replicates in other patients. Furthermore, we investigate the possibility that some patients might exhibit other patterns that lend themselves to clear interpretation with regard to understanding frequency. To this end, we reanalysed the picture naming data from 48 out of the 50[13] aphasic participants reported in Ruml et al. (2005) with regards to frequency.

Participants
The 48 aphasic patients in this study were 33 males and 17 females, of whom 46 are right-handed, and 2 are left-handed postmorbidly. A total of 40 suffered from CVAs, 3 from primary progressive aphasia (PPA), and 5 from herpes virus encephalitis (HVE). Detailed information about each participant is provided in Appendix A of Ruml et al. (2005).

Picture naming
Pictures ($N = 128$) consisting of 11 semantic categories (animals, body parts, fruits and vegetables, food, professions, kitchenware, clothing, tools, furniture, means of transportation, and musical instruments) were used to assess naming performance. Participant F.D.I. completed three administrations of this list, while participants P.G.E., E.M.A., G.M.A., and S.F. also named additional stimuli.

Scoring was again in line with Dell et al. (1997) and similar to the system used for E.C., with the following exceptions for correct and phonological (word) error classification. In classifying correct responses, changes in inflectional morphology were still considered correct. In the case of phonological errors, using the loose criteria that Dell et al. use to classify these errors in English would lead to an inordinate amount of errors being classified as phonological in Italian. This is due to two main differences between the languages: (a) Italian words tend to be longer and do not contain any unstressed vowels like the English schwa (~), and (b) most words in Italian end in one of four possible vowels (a, e, i, o). Ruml et al. (2005) made the following modified criteria to obtain a more reasonable measure of phonological overlap in Italian: The target and response must share: (a) one third of the phonemes irrespective of sequence, (b) two initial phonemes, (c) two phonemes from the first syllable in any sequence, or (d) three phonemes in the same sequence in any position. In all cases the inflectional (final) vowel was not counted.

Analyses
We analysed the Italian participants in a manner similar to that of E.C. The following analyses were done for each participant individually. We performed an overall binary logistic regression on correct responses versus errors with frequency (Bortolini, Tagliavini, & Zampolli, 1972) and letter length.[14] We also ran separate binary logistic regressions for each error type. Thus there was a separate analysis for semantic, phonological, mixed, unrelated, and nonword errors. As in our analyses of E.C.'s performance, we again did not include "other" errors in these analyses, since this was a heterogeneous category and not able to be simulated in current instantiations of speech production models. The independent variables were again log frequency

---

[13] We were unable to obtain enough items with frequency ratings for patients A.S. and C.L.B.
[14] Given Italian's shallow orthography, letter length is very close to the phoneme length.

and letter length.[15] Since we conducted five analyses on the same dataset (the overall analysis and analyses of semantic, phonological, mixed, and nonword errors), we adjusted our critical α level to .01 using Bonferroni correction. We report significant, $\alpha \leq .01$, and marginal values, $.01 < \alpha \leq .05$. Confirmatory analyses of the other factors using the larger dataset without imageability ratings were held to the same critical alpha level.

Results

A total of 11 of the patients (out of 48) showed a significant effect of log frequency on overall naming; 6 more showed a marginal effect. For each of these patients, error rates decreased as target lexical frequency increased. A total of 3 also showed a significant or marginal length effect; 3 other patients showed significant or marginal effects of length, but not of frequency. All patients showing frequency effects made fewer errors as frequency was increased, and likewise, all patients showing length effects made fewer errors as length decreased.

Looking now at specific error types, starting with semantic errors, we found 5 patients (A.C.O., G.I.M., E.M.A., G.M.A., and S.F.) who showed significant log frequency effects on semantic errors and another (W.M.A.) who showed a marginal effect. In all cases, the rate of semantic errors increased as target frequency decreased. There was also a patient (M.I.O.) who showed a significant length effect, where longer words led to more semantic errors.

When looking at nonword errors, patients G.N.I. and I.F.A. exhibited a marginal frequency effect. For these patients lower frequency targets led to more nonword errors. A total of 3 other patients (D.R.U., F.S., and S.F.) showed marginal length effects on nonword errors. Longer words led to more nonword errors for all patients.

Patients made very few phonological, mixed, and unrelated errors. For each of these error types, patients did not exhibit any effects of either frequency or length.

Discussion

The results of these analyses revealed 2 patients, who, similar to E.C., showed frequency effects on nonword errors. Neither showed a frequency effect on semantic errors, also like E.C. However, this finding is not surprising, since G.N.I. and I.F.A. did not make many semantic errors.

In contrast to E.C. and the above 2 patients, we also found 6 patients who showed frequency effects on semantic errors, and none of these patients showed a frequency effect on their nonword errors. Again, this was to be expected for 5 of them, since they did not make many nonword errors. However, W.M.A., who made 68 nonword errors, also did not exhibit a frequency effect on these errors. Thus, patient W.M.A. shows the opposite pattern to that of patient E.C. (see Figure 7).

As we discussed in the Introduction, nonword errors can stem from two loci: either in segmental processing in the lexical access stage, or at any postaccess stage, such as articulation. W.M.A. had severe difficulties with reading and repeating both words and nonwords (see Miceli, Benvegnu, Capasso, & Caramazza, 1997, for a full case description of W.M.A.). Furthermore, W.M.A. also had similar difficulties in picture naming, though his performance was better than in reading and repetition. In this regard W.M.A.'s profile is similar to E.C.'s. The important difference between these patients is that W.M.A. has "severe dysarthria" (p. 52), while E.C. does not. Such a peripheral disorder easily explains both why W.M.A. produced so many nonword errors and why there was no frequency effect on their production.

There is a similar explanation for why W.M.A. shows a frequency effect on his semantic errors,

---

[15] Unfortunately we were unable to get norms for enough of our items on semantic or other phonological factors to merit an analysis including them. Since we did not include imageability and phonological neighbourhood size into our analyses of the Italian patients, any frequency effects that we describe here could potentially be effects of imageability and/or phonological neighbourhood size, even though those factors were not responsible for the frequency effects observed in patient E.C.

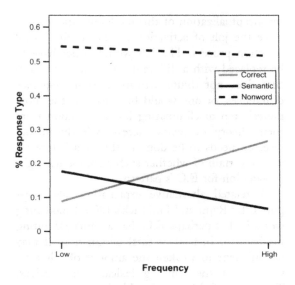

Figure 7. W.M.A.'s response types by frequency. Low-frequency (N = 68) items have a frequency ≤ 3, and high-frequency items (N = 60) have a frequency > 3.

but E.C. does not. Semantic errors, like nonword errors, may also have several sources. We have already argued that E.C.'s semantic errors mainly come from his damaged semantic system and thus do not exhibit a lexical frequency effect. On the other hand, while W.M.A. clearly has semantic damage, he may also have a further deficit in the lexicon and/or in the connections between semantics and the lexicon. Either of these deficits is consistent with the frequency effects observed on W.M.A.'s semantic errors.

In explaining W.M.A.'s pattern of performance, we are led to consider a different locus of frequency in the production system in order to explain the frequency effect observed on his semantic errors. His pattern resembles the patterns exhibited by our models in which frequency was implemented in either the semantic-lexical connections (see Figures 3a and 3b) or at the lexical resting activations (see Figure 4). In fact, W.M.A.'s pattern, together with those of several other Italian patients and of other patients reported in the literature (e.g., Caramazza & Hillis, 1990), provides support for placing an additional locus of the frequency effect in either the connections between semantics and the lexical level or at the lexical level itself.

GENERAL DISCUSSION

We have reported results from three separate lines of research. First, we reported findings from an in depth investigation of a single patient's (E.C.) error types in a picture-naming task as a function of lexical frequency. The principal finding of E.C.'s performance was that his nonword errors (generally phonological approximations of the targets) exhibited a very strong effect of lexical frequency whereas his semantic errors did not. Second, we reported findings from a computational modelling approach in which we contrasted several different implementations of lexical frequency to determine which implementation best captured E.C.'s performance. The principal finding of this work was that implementing lexical frequency in the lexical-segmental connections (but not the semantic-lexical connections or the resting activation levels of lexical representations) best captured E.C.'s performance. To determine the generality of E.C.'s pattern of findings, we analysed the specific error types of 48 different aphasic patients in a picture-naming task. This analysis revealed that 2 of the 48 patients exhibited a similar pattern to that of E.C., suggesting that it is not unusual to find an influence of lexical frequency on nonword error rates.

The finding that an individual's likelihood of making a nonword error is modulated by the frequency of the to-be-named item is striking and has important implications for how we conceptualize the dynamical properties of the speech production system. To the extent that nonword error rates are modulated by the target's lexical frequency, then it must be that these errors arise at a level of processing in which lexical frequency is represented. Because it is very unlikely that lexical frequency is represented in phonological segments, the most reasonable way to account for this finding is to place lexical frequency in the lexical-segmental connections. As we mentioned above, the modelling work confirmed this conclusion.

Of course, lexical frequency is highly correlated with other variables, such as length (in this case, number of phonemes) and number of neighbours (phonological), and it may be that these correlated variables, not frequency, modulate nonword error rates. To test for this possibility, we included each of these variables as predictors of E.C.'s nonword errors in a simultaneous regression analysis. We found that, though each variable contributed to E.C.'s nonword error rate, lexical frequency explained 2.5% of the variance independently of length (1.6% variance independently) and neighbourhood size (0.2% variance independently). As such, we are confident that, while variables correlated with lexical frequency undoubtedly contribute to the likelihood of observing a nonword error, the effect of lexical frequency on this error type is reliable and independent of these correlated variables.

Alternative accounts to the lexical-segmental hypothesis

We have argued that the most straightforward way to account for E.C.'s performance (and the performance of the three patients who showed a similar profile) is to implement lexical frequency in the lexical-segmental connections. But is this the only way to capture E.C.'s performance? As we have noted in our modelling discussion, the lexical jolt assumed by our modelling work (Dell et al., 1997) washes out frequency differences when frequency is implemented as lexical resting activations or semantic-lexical connections strengths. Removing this jolt of activation would allow such implementations to also strongly affect nonword errors through cascading (as they already do to a much smaller extent). When they reduced the strength of the jolt in their simulations, Rapp and Goldrick (2000) found a corresponding increase in nonword errors.

The gain from removing the jolting mechanism might be a single locus account of frequency effects on both semantic and phonological nonword error rates. However, removing the lexical jolt of activation would require a sizeable reconceptualization of this modelling framework, since the jolt of activation represents the lexical selection process. The jolt would either have to be replaced with a different selection mechanism that does not dilute activation from frequency differences, or one would have to take the more radical step of eliminating lexical selection from their theory of lexical access. Clearly further research needs to be done in this area before we can be certain of whether such a step is the right explanation for E.C.'s pattern.

A related alternative explanation, also supported by Rapp and Goldrick's (2000) modelling work, is that perhaps E.C. has a damaged jolting mechanism. Instead of total elimination, it may be sufficient to weaken the amount of jolt activation that the winning lexical item receives. This type of damage should also lead to more nonword errors for higher frequency words, even if the locus of frequency is in the lexical nodes or the semantic-lexical connections. Such an account needs only to assume a single locus of frequency to explain our results.

While such an account may seem appealing, using the jolting mechanism of the model as a theoretical explanation at this time is premature for several reasons. Currently, the jolting mechanism is used to add seriality to the model by enhancing the winner of lexical selection, but it is not the only possible implementation of seriality. As Rapp and Goldrick point out (2000, Footnote 9, p. 480) a competitive output mechanism can serve the same purpose.

Furthermore, it is unclear what theory of damage is instantiated by damaging the jolting mechanism. The jolt for lexical selection has been viewed as a signal from the syntactic frame to produce a particular word in an utterance (Dell et al., 1997), so most likely, damage to the jolting mechanism would thus reflect a theory of syntactic damage. It is possible that E.C.'s syntactic system is damaged in some way and is leading to his word production deficits. However, we cannot produce any finer grained predictions for his syntactic performance from the model, since the syntactic system of the theory has never been implemented. We are only left with the prediction about rates of nonword errors, but this is just a small part of the predictions that a syntactic theory of damage would make about performance. Without the rest of these predictions for comparison, it is impossible to truly evaluate whether damaging the jolting mechanism is the proper way to model E.C.'s syntactic damage. Such difficulties make it premature to consider damaging the jolting mechanism as an alternative account to the one that we have proposed.

One locus or several?
We have suggested that our findings support a lexical-segmental locus of the frequency effect, but we should be clear that we do not think that this is the only place that lexical frequency exerts its effects. For example, in the sample of 48 patients, one (W.M.A.) exhibited a pattern of performance that is best explained by implementing frequency in the semantic-lexical connections. We do not take this finding to be contradictory to our suggestion of a lexical-segmental locus for frequency. Rather, we suggest that lexical frequency is probably represented throughout all of the levels and connections that participate in the lexical access process. This notion of a "distributed" lexical frequency follows naturally from the activation framework upon which models of speech production are constructed. Word production involves the translation of one's intentions to speak into motor movements. Thus, to the extent that each unique utterance involves processes to be carried out over unique representations and connections, it follows that the frequency with which one translates a particular intention into articulated speech (e.g., "dog" or "eagle") should have a bearing on all processes essential to the translation of those intentions.

Implications for extant models of word production
Our results have serious implications for how frequency effects should be modelled in lexical production. Models such as those by Levelt et al. (1999) and Dell (1990) split the lexical level into two stages to account for morphological processes. Dell claimed that the locus of the frequency effect is at the whole-word or lemma stage, while Levelt et al. have argued for placing the frequency effect at the subsequent morpheme or lexeme stage. We claim that neither of these accounts can accommodate our findings.

We have explicitly shown that the model by Dell and colleagues (1997) does not explain frequency effects on nonword errors with frequency only at the lexical level, but this version of the model has only a single lexical level, while the version used by Dell (1990) had two lexical levels. Nevertheless, the addition of another lexical layer should not change the finding that implementing frequency at either lexical level cannot explain frequency effects on nonword errors as long as there is some seriality mechanism between the lexical selection(s) and the selection of segments.

It is very difficult to extrapolate our modelling results to the model by Levelt and colleagues (1999), given not only the differences in number of lexical levels, but also in the general processing dynamics. Furthermore, their model also has two lexical levels and does not lend itself to modelling patient errors. Nevertheless, their current assumptions with regard to frequency seem incapable of theoretically explaining frequency effects on sublexical processes. We direct our criticisms to specific features of their own modelling architecture. The first alternative for implementing frequency in their modelling framework, proposed by Jescheniak and Levelt (1994), represents frequency as the selection threshold for lexeme (i.e., morpheme) representations. Higher frequency lexemes have lower selection thresholds than lower frequency lexemes. Frequency, implemented in this way, would not affect the amount of activation reaching a word's segments and should not affect their chance or rate of selection. The second alternative, proposed by Roelofs (1997), implements frequency in the process of verifying that the correct lexeme has been selected, with higher frequency lexemes being verified faster than lower frequency lexemes. This implementation also seems to fail in explaining a frequency effect on nonword errors, since the verification process does not affect the amount of activation flowing to a word's segments based on its frequency.

The model by Dell and colleagues (1997) can be extended to cover our results by adding a frequency locus in the connections between lexical nodes and their segments. However to still explain the frequency effects on semantic errors by patients and the work on frequency effects in normals, this new locus must be in addition to the current locus of frequency that these models currently posit. The model by Levelt and colleagues (1999) may be modified in a similar manner to obtain frequency effects, but since it allows cascading from the lexeme node to its segments without a jolt of activation interceding, a simpler modification is possible. Frequency could be implemented as lexeme resting activation levels, instead of the current proposals of activation threshold or the verification time. Higher frequency words would have higher resting level activations and thus more activation would flow to their segments, making their selection more likely. Such a modification would straightforwardly explain frequency effects on nonword errors, but it would seem necessary to include an additional locus of frequency in the model to explain frequency effects on semantic levels, perhaps at the level of the abstract word form (lemma), since there is no cascading of information from the lemma level to the lexeme level. While our proposed modifications to these models do not go against their major architectural assumptions, these modified models must be thoroughly tested to see whether they perform as well as the original models, specifically with regard to frequency effects, but also with regard to other effects when frequency is concurrently modelled.

Our results may also be indicative of how frequency is represented in general by cognitive systems. Having several loci of frequency in a system is fundamentally problematic for models that can only accommodate a single locus of frequency. Specifically, our findings should be seen as problematic for the class of search models that have been proposed in the domain of word recognition (e.g., Forster, 1976). These models implement lexical frequency effects as an ordered search through the lexicon. Higher frequency words are checked against the input before lower frequency words. While such a search can explain frequency effects at a single level quite well (Murray & Forster, 2004), extending it to explain effects at two or more levels becomes difficult. It is easiest to explain this difficulty with respect to a hypothetical search model of production. Such a model would easily explain frequency effects on reaction times and, with minor extensions, on errors as well. However, the errors that it would be able to explain are word errors, not nonword errors. Another mechanism would be necessary to explain nonword errors. However, the problem is that such a model would predict no difference in the rate of nonword errors as a function of the lexical frequency of the target. Since frequency is represented in the order of the items, once an item is selected, there is no residual effect (e.g., activation) that remains to influence access to its segments. Though the search model currently attempts to only explain frequency affects in word recognition, our results question its ability to generalize to other domains in explaining frequency effects.

Future directions

A question that our research does not resolve is whether the other locus of frequency is best modelled as connection strength between the semantic and lexical system or as the resting activation level of lexical nodes. Our own simulations show these two loci produce very similar qualitative results. Both predict a stronger effect of frequency on semantic errors than nonword errors such that relative to the total error distribution semantic errors decrease while nonword errors increase. Future work will have to take a more fine-grained approach to differentiating between these two accounts and the third possibility that both are involved in representing frequency.

While we have modelled the frequency effects observed in our patients' performance to a large extent, another limitation of our work is that our model cannot capture our patients' word production disorders in their entirety. Our model is restricted to the lexical system, but we have argued that E.C. and several of our Italian patients have both prelexical semantic damage and postlexical phonological damage in addition to lexical damage. In order to model these latter types of damage it is necessary to extend our model with a semantic system (see Rapp & Goldrick, 2000, for an implementation of such a system) and a system for sublexical phonology. Such an extended model would have the additional benefit of allowing us to simultaneously model several loci of frequency at the same time, since we would have sources of errors that would not be affected by any lexical loci of frequency.

CONCLUSION

We have reported patient E.C., who made predominately semantic and phonological nonword errors in picture naming. In an analysis of his error types as a function of the lexical frequency of the to-be-named picture, we found that E.C.'s nonword errors exhibited an effect of frequency (high-frequency targets elicited fewer nonword errors) and that his semantic errors did not. We suggested that the best way to account for this finding is to place lexical frequency in the lexical-segmental connections. Support for this conclusion was provided through a computational modelling approach in which we contrasted several different implementations of lexical frequency and in which we found that implementing lexical frequency in the lexical-segmental connections (but not the semantic-lexical connections or the resting activation levels of lexical representations) best captured E.C.'s performance. Finally, we reported an investigation of 48 additional aphasic patients, which revealed that two of the 48 patients exhibited a similar pattern to that of E.C., suggesting that it is not unusual to find an influence of lexical frequency on nonword error rates.

It is important to reiterate that while we take these findings to suggest that lexical frequency should be located in the lexical-segmental connections, we have not argued that this is the only possible locus of lexical frequency. In contrast, we have suggested that lexical frequency may be distributed throughout the lexical access system and that lexical-segmental connections constitute just one possible locus. If this conclusion is correct, this would have important implications for extant models of word production in capturing the dynamical properties of lexical access.

Manuscript received 17 January 2007
Revised manuscript received 4 June 2007
Revised manuscript accepted 11 June 2007
First published online 9 September 2007

REFERENCES

Baayen, R. H., Piepenbrock, R., & van Rijn, H. (1993). The CELEX Lexical Database [CD-ROM]. Philadelphia: University of Pennsylvania, Linguistic Data Consortium.

Barry, C., Morrison, C. M., & Ellis, A. W. (1997). Naming the Snodgrass and Vanderwart pictures: Effects of age of acquisition, frequency and name agreement. *Quarterly Journal of Experimental Psychology, 50A*, 560–585.

Bartram, D. J. (1976). Levels of coding in picture–picture comparison tasks. *Memory & Cognition, 4*, 593–602.

Bates, E., D'Amico, S., Jacobsen, T., Szekely, A., Andonova, E., Devescovi, A., et al. (2003). Timed picture naming in seven languages. *Psychonomic Bulletin & Review, 10*, 344–380.

Bird, H., Lambon Ralph, M. A., Patterson, K., & Hodges, J. R. (2000). The rise and fall of frequency and imageability: Noun and verb production in semantic dementia. *Brain & Language, 73*, 17–49.

Bonin, P., & Fayol, M. (2002). Frequency effects in the written and spoken production of homophonic picture names. *European Journal of Cognitive Psychology, 14*, 289–314.

Bortolini, U., Tagliavini, C., & Zampolli, A. (1972). *Lessico di frequenza della lingua italiana contemporanea* [Frequency dictionary of the contemporary Italian Language]. Milan: Garzanti.

Brown, G. D., & Watson, F. L. (1987). First in, first out: Word learning age and spoken word frequency as predictors of word familiarity and word naming latency. *Memory & Cognition, 15,* 208–216.

Brysbaert, M., Lange, M., & Van Wijnendaele, I. (2000). The effects of age-of-acquisition and frequency-of-occurrence in visual word recognition: Further evidence from the Dutch language. *European Journal of Cognitive Psychology, 12,* 65–85.

Caramazza, A. (1997). How many levels of processing are there in lexical access? *Cognitive Neuropsychology, 14,* 177–208.

Caramazza, A., & Hillis, A. E. (1990). Where do semantic errors come from? *Cortex, 26,* 95–122.

Caramazza, A., & Miozzo, M. (1997). The relation between syntactic and phonological knowledge in lexical access: Evidence from the "tip-of-the-tongue" phenomenon. *Cognition, 64,* 309–343.

Caramazza, A., & Shelton, J. R. (1998). Domain-specific knowledge systems in the brain: The animate–inanimate distinction. *Journal of Cognitive Neuroscience, 10,* 1–34.

Cuetos, F., Aguado, G., Izura, C., & Ellis, A. W. (2002). Aphasic naming in Spanish: Predictors and errors. *Brain & Language, 82,* 344–365.

Damian, M. F., & Martin, R. C. (1999). Semantic and phonological codes interact in single word production. *Journal of Experimental Psychology: Learning, Memory, and Cognition, 25,* 345–361.

Dell, G. S. (1986). A spreading-activation theory of retrieval in sentence production. *Psychological Review, 93,* 283–321.

Dell, G. S. (1990). Effects of frequency and vocabulary type on phonological speech errors. *Language & Cognitive Processes, 5,* 313–349.

Dell, G. S., & Gordon, J. K. (2003). Neighbors in the lexicon: Friends or foes? In N. O. Schiller & A. S. Meyer (Eds.), *Phonetics and phonology in language comprehension and production: Differences and similarities.* New York: Mouton.

Dell, G. S., Lawler, E. N., Harris, H. D., & Gordon, J. K. (2004). Models of errors of omission in aphasic naming. *Cognitive Neuropsychology, 21,* 125–145.

Dell, G. S., Schwartz, M. F., Martin, N., Saffran, E. M., & Gagnon, D. A. (1997). Lexical access in aphasic and nonaphasic speakers. *Psychological Review, 104,* 801–838.

Ellis, A. W., & Morrison, C. M. (1998). Real age-of-acquisition effects in lexical retrieval. *Journal of Experimental Psychology: Learning, Memory, and Cognition, 24,* 515–523.

Feyereisen, P., Van der Borght, F., & Seron, X. (1988). The operativity effect in naming: A re-analysis. *Neuropsychologia, 26,* 401–415.

Finocchiaro, C., & Caramazza, A. (2006). The production of pronominal clitics: Implications for theories of lexical access. *Language & Cognitive Processes, 21,* 141–180.

Forster, K. I. (1976). Accessing the mental lexicon. In R. J. Wales & E. Walker (Eds.), *New approaches to language mechanisms* (pp. 27–85). Amsterdam: North Holland.

Forster, K. I., & Chambers, S. M. (1973). Lexical access and naming time. *Journal of Verbal Learning & Verbal Behavior, 12,* 627–635.

Foygel, D., & Dell, G. S. (2000). Models of impaired lexical access in speech production. *Journal of Memory & Language, 43,* 182–216.

Gagnon, D. A., Schwartz, M. F., Martin, N., Dell, G. S., & Saffran, E. M. (1997). The origins of formal paraphasias in aphasics' picture naming. *Brain and Language, 59,* 450–472.

Gerhand, S., & Barry, C. (1999a). Age-of-acquisition and frequency effects in speeded word naming. *Cognition, 73,* B27–B36.

Gerhand, S., & Barry, C. (1999b). Age of acquisition, word frequency, and the role of phonology in the lexical decision task. *Memory & Cognition, 27,* 592–602.

Gilhooly, K. J., & Gilhooly, M. (1979). Age-of-acquisition effects in lexical and episodic memory tasks. *Memory & Cognition, 7,* 214–223.

Goldrick, M., & Rapp, B. (2002). A restricted interaction account (RIA) of spoken word production: The best of both worlds. *Aphasiology, 16,* 20–55.

Goldrick, M., & Rapp, B. (2007). Lexical and post-lexical phonological representations in spoken production. *Cognition, 102,* 219–260.

Gordon, J. K. (2002). Phonological neighborhood effects in aphasic speech errors: Spontaneous and structured contexts. *Brain & Language, 82,* 113–145.

Hillis, A. E., Rapp, B. C., Romani, C., & Caramazza, A. (1990). Selective impairment of semantics in lexical processing. *Cognitive Neuropsychology, 7,* 191–243.

Hirsh, K. W., & Ellis, A. W. (1994). Age of acquisition and lexical processing in aphasia: A case study. *Cognitive Neuropsychology, 11,* 435–458.

Howard, D., Patterson, K., Franklin, S., Morton, J., & Orchard-Lisle, V. M. (1984). Variability and consistency in picture naming by aphasic patients. *Progress* in aphasiology. In F. C. Rose (Ed.), *Advances in neurology* (Vol. 42). New York: Raven Press.

Jescheniak, J. D., & Levelt, W. J. M. (1994). Word-frequency effects in speech production—retrieval of syntactic information and of phonological form. *Journal of Experimental Psychology: Learning, Memory, and Cognition, 20*, 824–843.

Johnston, R. A., & Barry, C. (2006). Age of acquisition and lexical processing. *Visual Cognition, 13*, 789–845.

Kay, J., & Ellis, A. (1987). A cognitive neuropsychological case study of anomia. Implications for psychological models of word retrieval. *Brain, 110*, 613–629.

Kroll, J. F., & Potter, M. C. (1984). Recognizing words, pictures, and concepts: A comparison of lexical, object, and reality decisions. *Journal of Verbal Learning & Verbal Behavior, 23*, 39–66.

Levelt, W. J. M., Roelofs, A., & Meyer, A. S. (1999). A theory of lexical access in speech production. *Behavioral and Brain Sciences, 22*, 1–37.

Lewis, M. B. (1999). Age of acquisition in face categorisation: Is there an instance-based account? *Cognition, 71*, B23.

MacKay, D. G. (1987). *The organization of perception and action. A theory for language and other cognitive skills*. New York: Springer Verlag.

Marsaglia, G., & Tsang, W. W. (2000). The ziggurat method for generating random variables. *Journal of Statistical Software, 5*, 1–7.

Meyer, A. S., & Schriefers, H. (1991). Phonological facilitation in picture–word interference experiments: Effects of stimulus onset asynchrony and types of interfering stimuli. *Journal of Experimental Psychology: Learning, Memory, and Cognition, 17*, 1146.

Miceli, G., Benvegnu, B., Capasso, R., & Caramazza, A. (1997). The independence of phonological and orthographic lexical forms: Evidence from aphasia. *Cognitive Neuropsychology, 14*, 35–69.

Monsell, S. (1991). The nature and locus of word frequency effects in reading. In D. Besner & G. W. Humphreys (Eds.), *Basic processes in reading: Visual word recognition* (pp. 148–197). Hillsdale, NJ: Lawrence Erlbaum Associates, Inc.

Morrison, C. M., & Ellis, A. W. (1995). Roles of word frequency and age of acquisition in word naming and lexical decision. *Journal of Experimental Psychology: Learning, Memory, and Cognition, 21*, 116–133.

Murray, W., & Forster, K. (2004). Serial mechanisms in lexical access: The rank hypothesis. *Psychological Review, 111*, 721–756.

Nickels, L. (1995). Getting it right? Using aphasic naming errors to evaluate theoretical models of spoken word production. *Language & Cognitive Processes, 10*, 13–45.

Nickels, L., & Howard, D. (1994). A frequent occurrence? Factors affecting the production of semantic errors in aphasic naming. *Cognitive Neuropsychology, 11*, 289–320.

Nickels, L., & Howard, D. (1995). Aphasic naming: What matters? *Neuropsychologia, 33*, 1281–1303.

Oldfield, R., & Wingfield, A. (1965). Response latencies in naming objects. *Quarterly Journal of Experimental Psychology, 17A*, 273–281.

Rapp, B., & Goldrick, M. (2000). Discreteness and interactivity in spoken word production. *Psychological Review, 107*, 460–499.

Roach, A., Schwartz, M. F., Martin, N., Grewal, R. S., & Brecher, A. (1996). The Philadelphia naming test: Scoring and rationale. *Clinical Aphasiology, 24*, 121–133.

Roelofs, A. (1997). The weaver model of word-form encoding in speech production. *Cognition, 64*, 249–284.

Ruml, W., & Caramazza, A. (2000). An evaluation of a computational model of lexical access: Comment on Dell et al. (1997). *Psychological Review, 107*, 609–634.

Ruml, W., Caramazza, A., Capasso, R., & Miceli, G. (2005). Interactivity and continuity in normal and aphasic language production. *Cognitive Neuropsychology, 22*, 131–168.

Ruml, W., Caramazza, A., Shelton, J. R., & Chialant, D. (2000). Testing assumptions in computational theories of aphasia. *Journal of Memory and Language, 43*, 217–248.

Sailor, K., Antoine, M., Diaz, M., Kuslansky, G., & Kluger, A. (2004). The effects of Alzheimer's disease on item output in verbal fluency tasks. *Neuropsychology, 18*, 306–314.

Schwartz, M. F., Dell, G. S., Martin, N., Gahl, S., & Sobel, P. (2006). A case-series test of the interactive two-step model of lexical access: Evidence from picture naming. *Journal of Memory and Language, 54*, 228–264.

Schwartz, M. F., Wilshire, C. E., Gagnon, D. A., & Polansky, M. (2004). Origins of nonword phonological errors in aphasic picture naming. *Cognitive Neuropsychology, 21*, 159–186.

Silveri, M. C., Cappa, A., Mariotti, P., & Puopolo, M. (2002). Naming in patients with Alzheimer's disease: Influence of age of acquisition and categorical effects. *Journal of Clinical & Experimental Neuropsychology, 24*, 755–764.

Snodgrass, J. G., & Vanderwart, M. (1980). A standardized set of 260 pictures: Norms for name agreement, image agreement, familiarity, and visual complexity. *Journal of Experimental Psychology: Human Learning & Memory, 6*, 174–215.

Stadler, M. A. (1992). Statistical structure and implicit serial learning. *Journal of Experimental Psychology: Learning, Memory, and Cognition, 18*, 318.

Stemberger, J. P. (1985). An interactive activation model of language production. In A. W. Ellis (Ed.), *Progress in the psychology of language production* (Vol. 1). London: Lawrence Erlbaum Associates.

Thompson-Schill, S. L., Gabrieli, J. D. E., & Fleischman, D. A. (1999). Effects of structural similarity and name frequency on picture naming in Alzheimer's disease. *Journal of the International Neuropsychological Society, 5*, 659–667.

Vitevitch, M. S. (2002). The influence of phonological similarity neighborhoods on speech production. *Journal of Experimental Psychology: Learning, Memory, and Cognition, 28*, 735–747.

Weide, R. L. (1994). *CMU pronouncing dictionary*. From speech at Carnegie Mellon University. Retrieved 7 February 2005, from http://www.speech.cs.cmu.edu/cgi-bin/cmudict

Wilshire, C. E. (2002). Where do aphasic phonological errors come from? Evidence from phoneme movement errors in picture naming. *Aphasiology, 16*, 169–197.

Wilshire, C. E., & Fisher, C. A. (2004). "Phonological" dysphasia: A cross-modal phonological impairment affecting repetition, production, and comprehension. *Cognitive Neuropsychology, 21*, 187–210.

Wilson, M. (1988). MRC psycholinguistic database: Machine-usable dictionary, Version 2.00. *Behavior Research Methods, Instruments & Computers, 20*, 6–10.

Wingfield, A. (1967). Perceptual and response hierarchies in object identification. *Acta Psychologica, 26*, 216–226.

Wingfield, A. (1968). Effects of frequency on identification and naming of objects. *American Journal of Psychology, 81*, 226–234.

Zingeser, L. B., & Berndt, R. S. (1988). Grammatical class and context effects in a case of pure anomia: Implications for models of language production. *Cognitive Neuropsychology, 5*, 473–516.

Does like attract like? Exploring the relationship between errors and representational structure in connectionist networks

Matthew Goldrick
Department of Linguistics, Northwestern Institute on Complex Systems, Northwestern University, Evanston, IL, USA

Many cognitive psychological studies assume that error probabilities reflect the structure of cognitive representations (e.g., if the representations of two lexical items overlap, they are more likely to interact in a word exchange error than are two lexical items with nonoverlapping representations). However, since errors directly reflect the properties of neurobiological structures and processes, this assumption rests on the correspondence between cognitive and neurobiological elements. Analytical and simulation studies of connectionist networks are used to examine the consequences of different cognitive-neurobiological relationships (e.g., localist vs. distributed representations) for effects of representational structure on error probabilities. The results reveal that such effects are influenced by the nature of the relationship between network and cognitive representations. While errors on localist network representations always reflect the degree to which cognitive representations overlap, distributed representations only do so under specific conditions. Furthermore, the effects of cognitive representational structure on error probabilities are shown to be stronger under localist than under distributed representations.

Cognitive psychological investigations of both neurologically intact and impaired individuals relies on behavioural data to inform theories of cognition. Critical to such investigations is the assumption that a well-defined relationship exists between the physical states that realize cognitive processes and the abstract entities that make up theories of cognition. The important role of such correspondences in cognitive neuropsychological inference has been highlighted by Caramazza's (1984, 1986) *transparency assumption*. If "local" modifications to the cognitive system can be induced by brain damage, it must be the case that neurological components correspond in a specific way to components of the cognitive system.

For example, consider the (in)famous logic of double dissociations. This refers to the observation of at least two individuals with complementary dissociations in task accuracy—that is, one individual is impaired on Task A but not B, while the other is impaired on Task B but not A. From this pattern of performance, the "standard" double-dissociation inference is that Tasks A and B are performed by distinct cognitive functions (Dunn & Kirsner, 2003). At least two

---

Correspondence should be addressed to Matthew Goldrick, Department of Linguistics, Northwestern University, 2016 Sheridan Rd., Evanston, IL 60208, USA (E-mail: Matt-Goldrick@northwestern.edu).

I thank Robert Daland for extremely helpful discussions of this research.

assumptions underlie this inference. First, there must be two distinct cognitive functions or processes that are necessary and sufficient for behaviour on the two distinct tasks. For example, in "dual-route" theories of morphological processing, inflecting morphological irregular forms (e.g., is–was) requires a lexical memory system, whereas inflecting novel words (e.g., plip–plipped) requires a grammatical combinatorial system (Pinker & Ulman, 2002). This work focuses on the import of the second critical assumption—namely, that the neural mechanisms realizing these processes are sufficiently distinct so as to permit damage to selectively disrupt each process (see, e.g., Pinker & Ulman, 2002, for such a morphological processing proposal). Since behavioural deficits directly reflect the disruption of particular neurobiological structures, the implications of such patterns for cognitive theories rest on the link between these neurobiological structures and particular cognitive components.

As reviewed in more detail below, connectionist research has cast some doubt on whether the specific correspondences underlying the double dissociation inference are necessary properties of the mind/brain. Simulation results suggest that behavioural distinctions can be observed in the absence of cognitive distinctions (e.g., in the context of morphology, see Joanisse & Seidenberg, 1999). Analyses of connectionist architectures suggest that in certain circumstances cognitive distinctions may not be reflected behaviourally (Smolensky, 2006c). In light of this work the research reported here considers an important assumption of many cognitive psychological studies.

(C0) *Error probabilities reflect the degree of overlap between mental representations.* If at some level of mental representation/processing M, the representations of X and Y have a higher degree of overlap than X and Z, all else being equal errors on target X arising at level M are more likely to result in Y than Z.

For example, in the study of spontaneous speech errors, many studies have observed that word exchanges frequently involve words from the same grammatical category (e.g., This *spring* has a *seat* in it; Garrett, 1980). This (along with other observations) led researchers to claim that at a level of mental representation operating over roughly word-sized elements, grammatical category is represented (Garrett, 1976, et seq.). This representational assumption, accompanied by (C0), allows these theories to account for the speech error patterns. At this level of processing, the representations of two words that are from the same grammatical category overlap—they both include the same representational element (e.g., NOUN).[1] In contrast, the representation of a matched word from a different grammatical category will possess a different representational element (e.g., VERB). Following (C0), then, errors are more likely to involve words from the same than from different grammatical categories.

Many similar examples can also be found in the cognitive neuropsychological literature. For example, Rapp and Caramazza (1997) analysed the letter substitution errors of dysgraphic individuals with deficits to allographic conversion processes. They found that such substitutions were more likely to involve letters that shared component strokes than visuospatial components. Based on this pattern of performance, Rapp and Caramazza concluded that at this level of mental representation orthographic word forms are represented in terms of stroke, not visuospatial, components. Similar to the example above, the logic utilized in this study is that because at the level of allographic conversion procedures letters are represented in terms of component strokes, all else being equal errors will be more likely to result in letters that share than differ in stroke components.

---

[1] Note that this logic relies on the overlap of representational elements, rather than a broader notion of representational similarity. As shown by a wide body of research, "similarity" is a complex concept (both empirically and theoretically), which is much broader than simple representational overlap (see, e.g., Medin, Goldstone, & Gentner, 1993, for discussion).

Since errors, like all behaviour, reflect the properties of neurobiological structures and processes, the inferences made in these studies critically rely on the assumption that some aspect of representational structure at the neural level corresponds to that at the cognitive level. Is this necessarily the case? In primary sensory systems, where neural representations are closely related to specific properties of stimulus features (e.g., location in the visual field in primary visual cortex; Hubel & Wiesel, 1962), the structure of neurobiological representations is clear. However, in higher cognitive domains it is possible that neural representations are quite highly distributed, perhaps across multiple brain areas (e.g., Mesulam, 1990). Consequently, it is less clear how overlap between neurobiological representations does or does not reflect the degree to which cognitive representations overlap.

To help clarify the validity of this assumption, this work uses connectionist networks as an approximation of brain systems. Mathematical and simulation analyses examine two different frameworks for relating cognitive and network level representations: localist, where network components directly correspond to elements of cognitive theories (Page, 2000); and distributed, where each network component realizes multiple cognitive elements (e.g., Hinton, McClelland, & Rumelhart, 1986). The analysis then examines the extent to which error probabilities reflect the degree to which cognitive representations overlap with one another. The results reveal that the precise nature of the relationship between cognitive and network structures exerts a sizeable influence on the effect of representational overlap on error probabilities.

The nature of cognitive-neural correspondences: Connectionist evidence

The double dissociation logic outlined above—relying on differential patterns of task accuracy to diagnose the presence of two distinct cognitive processes—has been extensively criticized in connectionist research (for recent reviews, see Kello, Sibley, & Plaut, 2005; Plunkett & Bandelow, 2006; and the discussion in *Cortex* accompanying Dunn & Kirsner, 2003). Plaut (1995) examined this in the context of reading via meaning. An attractor network was trained to map from distributed representations of orthography to phonology via semantics: for example, LOCK to (small metallic security device) to /lɑk/. Critically, the same set of network mechanisms were used to compute the mapping for both concrete (e.g., MILK) and abstract (e.g., JUSTICE) words. Following training, the network was subjected to damage by removing a certain proportion of randomly selected connections in various subparts of the network. In some cases this damage resulted in relatively robust double dissociations in reading accuracy on concrete versus abstract words.

This pattern of performance supports the claim that distinctions in neural processes—as reflected by double dissociations—may not correspond to completely distinct or modular cognitive processes. However, the results do not rule out the existence of well-defined relationships between neural elements and other types of cognitive structures. For example, Plaut (1995) claims that these dissociations occur due to functional distinctions between different types of representations. Concrete words—with rich, more interrelated semantic representations—develop stronger semantic attractors, making them more reliant on attractor processing. Abstract words, in contrast, have weak attractors, making them more reliant on other processes within the network. The neural-processing distinctions revealed by dissociations may therefore correspond to some distinction within the cognitive system, albeit not the one assumed by traditional double dissociation logic.

Consistent with this analysis, other systems with a clear absence of functional specialization do not exhibit double dissociations. Plaut, McClelland, Seidenberg, and Patterson (1996) analysed a set of connectionist simulations of the direct (nonsemantically mediated) orthography to phonology mapping in reading (i.e., mapping LOCK to /lɑk/, without accessing representations corresponding to meaning). Their extensive analysis reveals no evidence of significant functional divisions within networks computing this function. In particular, damage to these networks did not result in double dissociations between word classes (e.g., regular words such as LOCK vs. exceptional words such as YACHT). In order to produce dissociations of empirically adequate magnitudes, the authors were forced to rely on damage to distinct processing systems: the nonsemantically mediated versus semantically mediated reading pathways (see also Plaut, 1997). These results suggest that networks such as those studied by Plaut (1995) are able to account for dissociations because of the presence of a neural-processing distinction that corresponds to a critical cognitive distinction.

However, in more recent work, Smolensky (2006c) has argued that certain constructed connectionist systems demonstrably violate correspondences between components of cognitive and neural processes. He considers the specific example of processing compositional symbolic representations. In a purely serial symbolic theory, processing of such representations requires the independent processing of their components. For example, to interpret the sentence "Dog bites man", a serial symbolic sentence-processing mechanism must independently process the structural components of the sentence—for example, subject (dog), predicate (bites man); only after these interpretations were completed could the processor combine the interpretations to yield a parse for the full sentence. Smolensky details how it is possible to construct a connectionist architecture that allows for simultaneous parallel processing of all constituents. A single weight matrix can simultaneously calculate the interpretations for each constituent—(man) (bites dog)—and combines them to provide a unitary interpretation for the entire sentence. This architecture therefore lacks a one-to-one correspondence between cognitive and neural processes; multiple symbolic processing steps at the cognitive level correspond to a single parallel process at the neural level.

Critically, this design has implications for the patterns of performance that can be observed following damage. Smolensky (2006c, pp. 575–576) details how in such an architecture processing of a compositional representation can be spared even if the individual components are themselves disrupted. For example, suppose processing of the constituent (man) is disrupted by damaging connection weights, yielding a distorted output. We can construct a specific disruption of the connection weights involved in the processing of the other constituent (bites dog) in such a way as to exactly cancel out the distortions on (man). Then, when the whole structure is processed in a parallel fashion, the two forms of damage cancel one another out. This interaction across two constituents allows the whole structure—(man) (bites dog)—to be processed correctly, even though the constituents themselves are not. If there was a one-to-one relationship between cognitive and neural processes, this would be impossible; as detailed above, in serial symbolic processing systems processing the parts of componential representation is a necessary step in processing the whole.

Note that this result is not a necessary outcome of damage to the parallel-processing architecture. It may be highly improbable that two forms of damage would happen to exactly cancel one another out. The critical point is that this outcome is completely impossible in a serial symbolic processing system.

Taken together, these studies suggest that the relationship between cognitive and neural processes may not necessarily be one to one—and that such failures can have a critical impact on the interpretation of behavioural results. However, note that the connectionist work reviewed above has primarily focused on double dissociations in task accuracy. The direct impact of such findings is correspondingly limited to studies that rely exclusively on this type of inference. As noted by McCloskey (1993, 2001, 2003), a great deal of cognitive neuropsychological research relies on much more nuanced analysis of the fine-grained structure of performance data. Therefore, it is not clear whether these criticisms extend more broadly to other assumptions and methods in cognitive (neuro)psychology.

Overview of the current study

With this in mind, the work reported here examines the assumption that error probabilities reflect the overlap of cognitive representations (where more probable implies greater overlap). Since this has been a powerful inference tool in many studies, it is critical to analyse its validity—particularly with respect to processing systems that assume nontransparent relationships between processing units and cognitive representations (e.g., distributed representations).

Two techniques are applied to this issue. First, the behaviour of simple two-layer linear networks is analysed. Since they share core properties with the nonlinear networks with hidden units typically utilized in connectionist studies of cognitive processes, considering their behaviour has proven to be a useful technique for understanding the cognitive implications of connectionist computation (see, e.g., Plaut et al., 1996; Smolensky, 1986; Stone, 1986). This is due to the fact that (unlike nonlinear networks with hidden units) these two-layer simplified networks are amenable to closed-form analysis. This allows their behaviour to be characterized directly and precisely without relying on the intercession of simulations. Using such an analysis, the relationship of error probabilities to the degree of overlap of cognitive representations is considered for both localist and distributed representations under damage to either processing units or connection weights. These reveal that error probabilities can reflect cognitive representational overlap under both forms of representation and types of damage. However, the particular form of the relationship between cognitive and network representations has important influences on the effects of representational structure. In the final section, simulation analyses are performed to examine the potential impact of some of the formal analyses' simplifying assumptions on the conclusions of the closed-form analysis.

ANALYSIS: DAMAGE TO REPRESENTATIONAL UNITS

The consequences of disruption to the processing units are considered first. This has been utilized in a number of simulation studies. For example, Hinton and Shallice (1991) simulated damage by randomly removing a proportion of internal (hidden and cleanup) processing units from their attractor network. Rapp and Goldrick (2000) simulated damage to particular representational levels in the speech production system by increasing the amount of activation-dependent noise on particular units (see also Dell, Schwartz, Martin, Saffran, & Gagnon, 1997). Note that the former damage technique has often been considered to be constant across an entire simulation, whereas the latter is assumed to vary from trial to trial. For the purposes of this discussion we abstract away from these differences and consider damage to be a stochastic process distributed over some set of independent network events (either simulations or trials).

Input unit damage as linear transformation

The simplest feed-forward connectionist network consists of two representational layers (an input layer of N units and an output layer of M units), which are connected by a set of weights. The activation of each output unit i (o_i) is simply a linear sum of the activation of each input unit (t_j) times the weight of its connection to that output unit (w_{ji}). (Note that absent weights can be represented by the value 0.)

$$o_i = \sum_j t_j w_{ji} \qquad (1)$$

Using linear algebra, we can characterize this computation as the multiplication of an N dimensional input vector $\mathbf{t}$ by an N × M weight matrix $\mathbf{W}$ (whose elements j, i correspond to the weight from input j to output unit i). This yields an M dimensional output vector $\mathbf{o}$.

$$\mathbf{o} = \mathbf{t}\mathbf{W} \qquad (2)$$

If an input unit is damaged, the activation it sends to the output units will be altered. For example, suppose an input unit is "ablated" by completely removing it from the network. The output units it is connected to will now receive 0 units of activation from the ablated input unit.

This can be represented in the output unit activation equation (Equation 1) by multiplying each input unit's activation by a "damage value" d_j, which is equal to 0 for units that have been ablated and 1 for units that are intact:

$$o_i = \sum_j t_j d_j w_{ji} \qquad (3)$$

As noted above, some studies have assumed that damage corresponds to activation-dependent noise on units. This can be represented by allowing d_j to take on values other than 0 or 1. For example, to represent damage that reduces the activation of particular units by 50%, d_j would be set to .5.

In linear algebra terms, this can be represented by matrix multiplication.

$$o = tDW \qquad (4)$$

where D is a $N \times N$ diagonal "damage matrix," whose diagonal elements correspond to d_j. In this form, this type of damage clearly corresponds to linear transformation of input vectors (Smolensky, 1986).

Input unit damage: Errors over localist representations and cognitive representational structure

Preliminary definitions

This section uses this linear transformation formalism to consider the relationship between cognitive structure and errors induced on localist input representations. Note that t denotes the *t*arget representation; c the representation *c*loser to the target, and f the representation *f*urther away from the target.

(C1) *Error probabilities following unit damage with localist representations reflect the degree of overlap of cognitive representations*. Let there be a feedforward connectionist network with two layers of processing units corresponding to mental representational levels I (the input to some cognitive process P) and O (the output of process P). Suppose at representational level I the cognitive representations of t and c have a higher degree of overlap than t and f (and c and f are otherwise matched). Subsequent to damage to network processing units at the network level corresponding to I, errors arising on localist network representations of target t are more likely to result in c than f.

The definitions below spell out the terms of (C1) in more detail. The cognitive level definitions are specified first.

(D1) *Cognitive representation*. At a particular level of mental representation I, cognitive representations have available a set of N structural positions, indexed by 1...N. A cognitive representation t consists of a binding of a representational element to each of these structural positions (where t_i denotes the element bound to position i).

For example, suppose the (cognitive) phonological representation of consonant–vowel–consonant words (e.g., "cat") consists of three structural positions: onset—the initial portion of the syllable; vowel—the nucleus of the syllable; coda—postnuclear position. The (cognitive) phonological representation of CAT is then a binding of the segments (/k/, /æ/, /t/) to each of these positions. The relevant degree of overlap of such representations is defined below.

(D2) *Matched cognitive representations of varying degrees of overlap*. Let c and f be two *matched* nontarget cognitive representations where c is *closer* to the target t than is f.

- *closer*: there is at least one structural position a such that $t_a = c_a \neq f_a$
- *matched*: for all structural positions b where $t_b \neq c_b$, $c_b = f_b$

Turning to the network level, (C1) requires us to define localist representations and the nature of damage to the network.

(D3) *Localist network representations*. A cognitive representation is realized locally if the elements in each structural position are realized by a unique set of network units.

For example, if segments in onset, vowel, or coda position are realized by activating distinct units (e.g., onset /k/ corresponds to one unit and coda /k/ another), phonological representations are realized locally (e.g., the phonological representations of Dell, 1986; Dell et al., 1997).

Note that this definition is somewhat broader than that adopted by some theorists. Although (D3) includes cases where each cognitive representation corresponds to a *single* network unit (e.g., a unique onset /k/ unit), it is not limited to them. Under (D3), it is also possible to have a localist representation where network units within a structural position are not transparently semantically interpretable (as in "microfeature" representations; see, e.g., Hinton et al., 1986). Here, localist simply refers to a representation in which each structural position is realized by a distinct, independent set of network units. The structure of representations within the position may be distributed over several units or confined to a single unit.

As noted above the analysis here considers damage as a stochastic process disrupting a deterministic network (this process could vary randomly over separate simulations, or across individual trials within a single simulation). The critical assumption here is that damage is more likely to lead to small rather than large disruptions to processing.

(D4) *Probability distribution of network behaviour following input unit damage.*
Let $\bar{\mathbf{D}}$ be a random variable over diagonal matrices distributed according to some strictly decreasing function f.

$$\Pr(\bar{\mathbf{D}} = \mathbf{D}^a) = f(\|diag(\mathbf{D}^a) - \mathbf{1}^n\|)$$

where $\mathbf{1}^n$ is an N-dimensional vector of 1s (i.e., the intact network state), and $\| \; \|$ denotes the Euclidean norm.

Substitution errors and representational overlap
With the various terms in (C1) clarified, consider the conditions under which substitution errors arise. Let $\mathbf{i}^t$ and $\mathbf{o}^t$ be localist network representations corresponding to the cognitive representations of the input and output for target t. Let $\mathbf{i}^s$ and $\mathbf{o}^s$ be the corresponding representations for a nontarget item s. To define the probability that an error t $\rightarrow$ s will be produced, let $\bar{\mathbf{o}}$ be a random variable characterizing the network's output following damage (where $\bar{\mathbf{D}}$ is defined above):

(D5) $\Pr(\bar{\mathbf{o}} = \mathbf{o}^s) = \Pr(\mathbf{i}^t \bar{\mathbf{D}} \mathbf{W} = \mathbf{o}^s)$

Assume the network has been trained such that (without damage) it will correctly compute the input–output mappings for both t and s. Define $\mathbf{D}^s$ to be the diagonal damage matrix satisfying Equation 5.[2]

$$\mathbf{i}^s = \mathbf{i}^t \mathbf{D}^s \qquad (5)$$

Since the network has been trained to perform the input–output mapping for s, $\mathbf{o}^s = \mathbf{i}^s \mathbf{W}$. Therefore, $\mathbf{D}^s$ will induce the substitution error t $\rightarrow$ s.

$$\mathbf{o}^s = \mathbf{i}^t \mathbf{D}^s \mathbf{W} \qquad (6)$$

We can therefore write the probability of the substitution error t $\rightarrow$ s as the probability that the damage matrix will be equal to $\mathbf{D}^s$.

$$\Pr(\bar{\mathbf{o}} = \mathbf{o}^s) = \Pr(\mathbf{i}^t \bar{\mathbf{D}} \mathbf{W} = \mathbf{o}^s) = \Pr(\bar{\mathbf{D}} = \mathbf{D}^s) \quad (7)$$

To produce a substitution, then, a damage matrix must warp the input vector of the target so as to produce the input vector corresponding to the error. The connection to representational overlap is readily apparent; mapping the input vector to a representation that shares elements in the same structural positions will require less

---

[2] Such a mapping will exist between all pairs of input and output network representations so long as no vectors have elements with value 0.

warping than will mapping to a vector that does not share representational elements.

Combined with the probability distribution defined for network damage (D4), this observation provides the desired result. As shown in more detail in Appendix A, for network units where warping is required, the diagonal elements of the damage matrix must not be equal to 1 (if they were, the vector would not be warped). Therefore, the more warping that is required, the greater the number of diagonal elements that must not be equal to 1. Since, following (D4), probability is inversely related to the number of such diagonal elements, damage requiring more warping is less probable than damage requiring less warping. Since errors with greater overlap require less warping, they are therefore more probable than errors with less overlap.

Input unit damage: Errors over distributed representations and cognitive representational structure

Preliminary definitions
This section applies the linear transformation formalism for network damage to distributed input representations.

(C2) *Error probabilities following unit damage with appropriately structured distributed representations reflect the degree of overlap of cognitive representations.* Suppose at some level of mental representation I, the cognitive representations of t and c have a higher degree of overlap than t and f (and c and f are otherwise matched). Subsequent to damage to network processing units at the network level corresponding to I, errors arising on appropriately structured distributed representations of target t are more likely to result in c than f.

Fully distributed representations contrast with localist representations in violating the one-to-one correspondence of network structures and cognitive structures.

(D6) *Fully distributed representations.* A cognitive representation is realized in a fully distributed fashion if the elements in each structural position are realized by overlapping sets of network units.

For example, in simulations exploring their connectionist theory of nonsemantic word reading, Plaut et al. (1996) found that the representations the network developed to mediate the orthography–phonology mapping were highly distributed. Individual hidden units contributed to the processing of words with both regular (e.g., LOCK) and exceptional (e.g., YACHT) orthography–phonology mappings. Similar results can be found in many studies of networks with learned internal representations.

Although these studies suggest that highly distributed *acquired* representations can be an integral part of connectionist computation, they are not appropriate guides for an analysis that considers prespecified cognitive representations. For this task, we consider a framework designed to precisely realize cognitive representations in a distributed manner in connectionist networks: tensor product representations (Smolensky, 1990, 2006a, 2006b). In this framework, structural positions are associated with particular vectors (or patterns of activation) rather than particular units. The binding of representational elements to structural positions is performed by calculating the outer (or tensor) product of the structural position vectors with the vectors representing each element.

For the purposes of this discussion, it is critical that tensor products can be used to realize cognitive representations in a fully distributed manner. Returning to the phonological representations discussed above, consider the onset and coda positions (/k/ and /t/ in CAT). In a localist representational framework, the onset position was associated with one set of units, while coda was associated with another set. In tensor product representations, the structural positions are associated with activation vectors rather than particular units. For example, suppose onset corresponds to $(-1, 1)$ and coda $(1, 1)$. If /k/ is represented by the vector $(.5, 1)$, the tensor product representation binding /k/ to onset would be $(.5, 1) \otimes (-1, 1) = (-.5, .5, -1, 1)$;

/k/ in coda would be $(.5, 1) \otimes (1, 1) = (.5, .5, 1, 1)$. Rather than completely independent units realizing each structural position, all units now participate in the representation of both positions.

For the purposes of this analysis, we therefore consider fully distributed representations as defined below.

(D7) *Fully distributed tensor product representations.* A cognitive representation is realized by a fully distributed tensor product representation if:

- *Tensor product realization* (Smolensky, 1990, 2006a, 2006b). The structural positions and representational elements of cognitive representations are associated to linearly independent activation vectors. Elements are bound to positions using the tensor product, and the sum of these bindings realizes a cognitive representation:

$$t = \sum_j e_j^t \otimes r_j$$

where r_j denotes the vector associated with jth structural position, and e_j^t denotes the vector associated to the element bound to the jth structural position in representation t.

- *Distributed representations of structural positions.* There is at least one element where distinct structural position vectors both take on nonzero values.

As discussed in greater length by Smolensky (1990, 2006a, 2006b), tensor products are sufficient for performing a wide variety of symbolic computations in connectionist networks. Furthermore, Smolensky and Tesar (2006) show how many other connectionist representational frameworks as well as empirically documented neurobiological representations can be understood as specific instantiations of the general tensor product formalism. For example, one prominent proposal for representing symbolic structure in connectionist networks makes use of binding-by-timing, where representational elements are bound to particular structural positions by virtue of temporally synchronous activation of the element and structural position (e.g., Hummel & Holyoak, 2003). Although this may appear to be quite distinct from the tensorial representational scheme discussed above, it is in fact closely related. In binding-by-timing, the structural position vectors are not a static pattern distributed over representational units but a dynamic pattern that is distributed across both representational units and time. To return to the example above, suppose the structural position vectors are distributed over time such that onset corresponds to (-1) at Time 0 and (1) at Time 1; coda is (1) at Time 0 and (1) at Time 1. If /k/ is represented by the vector $(.5, 1)$, the (temporally distributed) tensor product representation binding /k/ to onset would be $(-.5, -1)$ at Time 0 and $(.5, 1)$ at Time 1. In contrast, the representation of /k/ in coda would be $(.5, 1)$ at Time 0 and $(.5, 1)$ at Time 1. Tensor products are therefore sufficiently general as to provide a vocabulary for describing both static, atemporal activation patterns as well as binding-by-timing mechanisms (see Smolensky & Tesar, 2006, for further discussion). The wide applicability of this formalism to a variety of connectionist mechanisms for representing symbolic structure suggests that it is an appropriate starting point for analyses of the consequences of distributed network representations.

Note (C2)'s caveat that the distributed representations must be appropriately structured. This is discussed in more detail below. For the remainder of the terms in (C2) we rely on the definitions from the previous section.

Substitution errors and representational overlap

As discussed above, for localist network representations the amount of warping required to produce a substitution error monotonically increases as representational overlap decreases. Since each representational element is realized by a distinct set of network units, the greater the number of representational elements that are nonoverlapping the greater the number of units that must be affected by damage. If the target is "cat," producing the substitution error "bad" will require warping the activation of network units representing both the onset and coda; producing the error "bat" will require warping only of those units representing the coda.

As shown in more detail in Appendix B, the same relationship can hold for distributed representations—but it is not necessarily true. Since each network unit can realize representational elements in multiple structural positions, decreasing representational overlap may in fact decrease the amount of warping required to produce a substitution. For example, suppose producing the substitution error "cat" → "bat" requires changing the activation of network unit A from 0.5 to 0.7 to reflect the change from onset /k/ to onset /b/. If unit A is also involved in the representation of elements in coda position, it is possible that producing the substitution error "cat" → "bad" may require changing the activation of unit A from 0.5 to 0.4 (reflecting the simultaneous change of onset /k/ → /b/ and coda /t/ → /d/). This activation value of this particular unit—which reflects elements in two distinct structural positions—is actually *closer* to the target value than that associated with a change in only a single structural position. Interactions such as these may therefore serve to reduce rather than amplify the distinction between the target and representations with lower degrees of overlap.

To concretely illustrate such an interaction, consider three simple cognitive representations consisting of the features [±nasal] [±coronal] associated with two distinct structural positions, "manner" and "place". Briefly, manner features specify the way in which a consonant is articulated. A +nasal consonant is one in which the velum is lowered, allowing air to escape through the nose (e.g., /m/, /n/); in a −nasal consonant the velum is raised, and air can only escape through the oral cavity. Place features specify where a consonant is articulated. A +coronal consonant is articulated with the tongue tip (e.g., /t/, /s/, /n/); a −coronal consonant uses some other articulator (e.g., the body of the tongue; /k/, /g/). Assume that the target is /n/ (+nasal, +coronal), the closer representation c is /t/ (−nasal, +coronal), and the representation further in distance f is /k/ (−nasal, −coronal). Table 1 summarizes one tensor product realization of these cognitive representations where errors will not reflect representational overlap.

Consider the first element of the tensor product. To produce an /n/ → /t/ substitution, the first element of the diagonal of the damage matrix must be equal to −3 (e.g., −.75/.25). In contrast, for an /n/ → /k/ substitution, the first element must be −1 (e.g., −.25/.25). The damage value for /k/ is therefore closer to the undamaged value of 1 than is /t/: /k/ distance, $(-1 - 1)^2 = 4$; /t/ distance, $(-3 - 1)^2 = 16$. With respect to this element, then, substituting the more similar /t/ representation requires greater damage—more warping of the target vector—than does the less similar /k/ representation.[3]

This effect arises because of interactions between elements in different structural positions. Consider first the component of the tensor product vector that corresponds to the elements where both /t/ and /k/ differ from the target /n/. The binding of [−nasal] to manner yields −.5 (−1 × .5); the binding of [+nasal] yields .5. The difference between the values for the substitution errors and the target is therefore −1. In contrast, for those features where only /k/ differs from the target, the difference in the tensor product vectors is positive; for the target, [+coronal] bound to place yields −.25, while the substitution's [−coronal] yields .25 [.25 − (−.25) = .5]. One component of the tensor product pushes the activation value lower, but the other pushes it higher. The end result of the interaction of representational elements across

---

[3] Note that for the fourth and fifth elements of the tensor product the more similar representation requires less damage (the damage value is −1/3 for /t/, −1 for /k/). However, this does not serve to cancel out the asymmetry on the first two elements.

Table 1. *Inappropriately structured distributed representations*

Segment	Manner feature value	Place feature value	Tensor product representation
/n/	+nasal (1, −1,1)	+coronal (.5,−.5,.5)	(.25, −.25, .25, .75,−.75, .75)
/t/	−nasal (−1,1,1)	+coronal (.5,−.5,.5)	(−.75, .75, .25,−.25, .25, .75)
/k/	−nasal (−1,1,1)	−coronal (−.5,.5,.5)	(−.25, .25, .25,−.75, .75, 75)

Note: The vectors realizing each representational element are shown in parentheses under the element. The structural position vectors are manner = (.5, .5); place = (−.5, .5). Italics highlight tensor product elements where interactions in the realization of distinct structural positions serve to reduce rather than amplify distinctions with the target vector.

structural positions causes the activation with less versus more overlap to be closer to that of the target.

Output unit damage

The preceding analyses can be easily extended to damage to output units. Damage to these units can be viewed as linear transformations of output vectors (cf. Equation 4):

$$oD = tW \qquad (8)$$

where D is an $M \times M$ diagonal matrix. The conditions for substitutions are similar—namely, that the target output vector be warped onto the substitution's (cf. Equation 5):

$$o^s = o^t D^s \qquad (9)$$

The form of the analysis therefore corresponds to that for input vectors above. The results above therefore generalize to errors over both input and output representations.

Discussion: Damage to network units and representational overlap

Many cognitive psychological studies have assumed that error probabilities reflect the degree to which cognitive representations overlap. The analyses have shown that this assumption is valid when the relationship between cognitive and network representations meets certain conditions. For localist or appropriately structured distributed representations, distances between vectors at the network level corresponds to the degree of overlap of cognitive representations. The probability distribution of network errors therefore reflects cognitive representational structure.

However, in distributed representations interactions across different structural positions can serve to distort the relationship between error probability and representational overlap. The representational vector components corresponding to distinct structural positions can differ from the target in different directions. If this occurs, it will cause the distance between network representations to not reflect cognitive overlap. Relative to a representation with a smaller degree of overlap, the network activation values associated with a representation with a greater degree of overlap may be more rather than less distant from the target. Clearly, the nature of the relationship between cognitive and neural structures exerts an important influence on the relationship between behavioural patterns and cognitive structure.

DAMAGE TO CONNECTION WEIGHTS

This section considers another common means of simulating neurobiological damage in connectionist networks: disruption to weights connecting processing units. For example, in Plaut's (1995) study of semantically mediated reading (reviewed above), damage was simulated by removing a set of randomly selected weights in particular portions of the network. (Removing is equivalent to setting the connection strength to 0.) In other simulation studies (e.g., Hinton & Shallice, 1991) connections between units have not been completely ablated, but weights have been distorted by the addition of random noise.

Weight damage as a series of linear transformations

Similar to damage to processing units, weight damage alters the activation that input units send to output units. This can be represented in the output unit activation equation (Equation 1) by multiplying each weight by a "damage value" d_{ji}. In the case of damage by ablating connections, this will be equal to 0 for weights that have been lesioned and 1 for weights that are intact (cf. Equation 3):

$$o_i = \sum_j t_j w_{ji} d_{ji} \qquad (10)$$

Similar to unit damage, allowing weights to be distorted by noise proportional to the strength of the weight can be represented by allowing d_{ji} to take on values other than 0 or 1. For example, to represent damage that reduces the strength of particular weights by 50%, d_{ji} would be set to .5.

Like damage to processing units, weight lesions can also be viewed as linear transformations. Two equivalent methods are available. First, network processing can be recast in terms of vector multiplication that yields the activation of individual output units:

$$o_i = t w_{xi} \qquad (11)$$

where (as above) t is a N-dimensional vector specifying the input; o_i specifies the activation of a particular output unit i; and w_{xi} specifies the weights from all input units to the ith output unit. Let $\mathbf{D}_{xi}$ be an N × N diagonal matrix whose diagonal elements $d_{jD_{xi}}$ are equal to d_{ji} in Equation 10. Since multiplication by diagonal matrices is commutative, the activation of output units following damage can then be written as:

$$o_i = t \mathbf{D}_{xi} w_{xi} \qquad (12)$$

From this perspective, then, weight damage corresponds to input unit damage; it is a linear transformation of the input vector. Unlike input unit damage, however, this transformation is specific to each output unit i.

Alternatively, network processing can be recast in terms of the contribution of individual inputs to the output activation vector:

$$\underset{j}{o} = t_j w_{jx}$$
$$o = \sum_j \underset{j}{o} \qquad (13)$$

where (as above) o is an M-dimensional vector specifying the output; t_j is the activation of input unit j; w_{jx} specifies the weights from this input unit to all output units; and $\underset{j}{o}$ represents the contribution of input unit j to the output activation vector. Let $\mathbf{D}_{jx}$ be an M × M diagonal matrix whose diagonal elements $d_{jD_{xi}}$ are equal to d_{ji} in Equation 10. The output of the damaged network can then be written as:

$$o = \sum_j \underset{j}{o} \mathbf{D}_{jx} \qquad (14)$$

From this perspective, then, weight damage is similar to damage to output units. However, the critical difference is that with weight damage the transformation of output vectors is specific to each input unit j.

Weight damage: Errors over localist representations and cognitive representational structure

Preliminary definitions
This section uses the weight damage formalism to examine how cognitive representational overlap is (or is not) reflected in the probability of errors on localist network representations.

(C3) *Error probabilities following weight damage with localist representations reflect the degree of overlap of cognitive representations.* Suppose at two levels of mental representation I and O the cognitive representations of t and c have a higher degree of overlap than t and f (and c and f are otherwise matched). Subsequent to damage to connection weights between the network levels corresponding to I and O, errors arising on localist network representations of target t are more likely to result in c than f.

Unlike the analyses above, in (C3) representational overlap is matched at both levels of representation. As shown in the analysis below, this reflects fact that weight damage is sensitive to both input and output representational structure.

Except for the definition of how damage (and errors) are probabilistically distributed (below), for most terms in (C3) we can follow those under (C1).

(D8) *Probability distribution of network outputs following weight damage.* Let $\mathbf{Z}$ be a vector of $N \times M$ elements indexed by j, i whose elements specify the degree of damage to each weight w_{ji}. Let $\mathbf{Z}$ be a random variable distributed according to some strictly decreasing function of the degree of damage.

$$\Pr(\bar{\mathbf{Z}} = \mathbf{Z}^a) = f(\|\mathbf{Z}^a - \mathbf{1}^{n \times m}\|)$$

(where $\mathbf{1}^{n \times m}$ is an $N \times M$ vector of 1s).

Let S be the set of all $\mathbf{Z}^a$ meeting the conditions specified in the sections below for producing a substitution error $t \to s$.

$$\Pr(\bar{\mathbf{o}} = \mathbf{o}^s) = \sum_{\mathbf{Z}^a \in S} \Pr(\bar{\mathbf{Z}} = \mathbf{Z}^a)$$

Note that the diagonals of $\mathbf{D}^a_{xi}$ (or, equivalently, $\mathbf{D}^a_{jx}$) are equal to the elements of $\mathbf{Z}^a$ (cf. probability distribution of unit damage matrices: Equation D4).

Substitution errors and representational overlap
For weight damage with localist representations, it is convenient to view network processing in terms of individual output units (following Equation 12). Consider those output elements in the set $\mathbf{i}$ where the target and substitution are unequal ($\mathbf{o}^t_i \neq \mathbf{o}^s_i$). As with input unit damage (cf. Equation 5), a substitution will be produced if:

$$\mathbf{i}^s = \mathbf{i}^t \mathbf{D}_{xi} \quad (15)$$

Since $\mathbf{o}^s_i = \mathbf{i}^s \mathbf{w}_{xi}$, if Equation 15 holds, $\mathbf{o}^s_i = \mathbf{i}^t \mathbf{D}_{xi} \mathbf{w}_{xi}$.

Turning to those output elements in the set $\mathbf{k}$ where the target and substitution error outcome overlap, there are two distinct scenarios under which substitution errors arise. We consider the consequences of each possibility in turn.

Scenario 1. No warping along output dimensions where target and error overlap. Since on the network elements $\mathbf{k}$ the target and substitution yield the same output (i.e., $\mathbf{o}^t_k = \mathbf{o}^s_k$), no transformation of the target is required. That is, no damage is required to yield the correct output for the substitution error. As discussed in greater detail in Appendix C, since less damage is always more probable than greater damage, damage on these units is more likely to result in an error with greater than less (output) overlap with the target. For the other output units, all damage matrices must satisfy the conditions in Equation 15. In this case the proof of (C1) in Appendix A generalizes, yielding higher probability for the representation with greater (input) overlap.

Scenario 2. Warping along all output dimensions. Alternatively, as outlined in Appendix C, the conditions in Equation 15 can be met both for units in the set $\mathbf{i}$ and the set $\mathbf{k}$. Following the discussion of (C1) above, by warping the target's input representation onto the substitution, the substitution's output will be produced. Since by hypothesis the closer representation c has a greater degree of input overlap than the more distant representation f, this form of damage will also be more probable (following the proof in Appendix A).

Therefore, for each *single* instance of damage that produces an error with relatively little overlap at both input and output levels of representation, there are *two distinct forms* of weight damage that produce a substitution error resulting in a representation with greater input and output overlap with the target. These two forms of damage are both more probable. As discussed in more detail in Appendix C, this predicts a large asymmetry in the probability of producing an error with greater versus less overlap with the target.

Weight damage: Errors over distributed representations and cognitive representational structure

Preliminary definitions

This section uses the formalism to examine how cognitive representational overlap influences errors on distributed representations under weight damage.

(C4) *Error probabilities following weight damage with appropriately structured distributed representations reflect the degree of overlap of cognitive representations.* Suppose at two levels of mental representation I and O the cognitive representations of t and c have a higher degree of overlap than t and f (and c and f are otherwise matched). Subsequent to damage to connection weights between the network levels corresponding to I and O, errors arising on appropriately structured distributed network representations of target t are more likely to result in c than f.

Following the analysis above, distributed tensor product representations (D7) are considered. The other terms follow that of the preceding section.

Substitution errors and cognitive representational overlap

Appendix D discusses in more detail two scenarios under which substitution errors can be produced with distributed representations. First, following Equation 12, by viewing network processing in terms of each individual output unit we can specify a scenario similar to that outlined in Equation 15. This creates a situation analogous to substitution error that arise following input unit damage. Building on the results of Appendix B, it is therefore possible to show that damage is more likely to result in errors with greater than less (input) overlap in cognitive representations.

A second scenario for producing substitution errors can be specified by considering network processing in terms of the contribution of each input unit (following Equation 13). As discussed in Appendix D, the conditions are quite similar to those above, but expressed in terms of output rather than input network representational structure. This allows the degree of overlap at the output representational level to also exert an influence on the probability of errors.

Under weight damage, then, there are two scenarios that will produce substitution errors over distributed network representations. Under one, the distributed representation of the target's input vector is warped onto the representations of the substitution's input. In the second, the distributed representation of the target's output (more specifically, the contribution each input unit makes to the output) is warped onto the substitution's output. Note that the conditions for substitution errors are identical for representations with greater and less overlap with the target, although the former is more probable. This stands in marked contrast to the situation with localist representations. As noted above, the localist representation of a cognitive structure with a high degree of overlap with the target provides for two distinct forms of damage that result in a substitution error. One of these forms of damage—where components of the network are undamaged while a substitution error is produced—is critically *not* available for localist representations that have less overlap with the target. This analysis therefore predicts that representational overlap should exert a greater influence on error probability for localist than for distributed representations.

Damage to connection weights and representational overlap

There are clear parallels between connection weight and representational unit damage. Both can be viewed as linear transformations of input/output vectors; this accounts for the role that cognitive representational overlap plays in error probabilities. However, there are also clear differences. Connection weight damage is simultaneously sensitive to overlap at both input and output levels of network representation. These can cause errors to be sensitive not only to input and output overlap but also—in the case of localist representations—to the nature of the mapping between the levels of the representation.

In localist representations the realization of each structural position is independent. If two representations share structure, they share an activation pattern on a subset of units. Since a substitution can be produced without altering the network's output on these units, the target's input will yield the desired output without damaging the network. In contrast, due to the interaction between the realization of different structural positions, this option is not available for distributed representations. Because each network element reflects multiple structural positions, producing a substitution error requires warping between input or output representations. As with the previous analysis, it is clear that the effect of cognitive representational overlap is crucially influenced by how representations are realized at the network level.

SIMULATION ANALYSIS

As noted previously the formal analysis above is facilitated by a number of simplifying assumptions. At the grossest level these simplifications are shared by many other connectionist networks. These computational devices are similar to actual neurophysiological mechanisms only at a high degree of abstraction (see, e.g., Smolensky, 1988, for discussion). Within the class of connectionist networks, the analysis has considered only two-layer networks with linear activation functions. These are well known to be limited in their computational capacity; much of recent connectionist work analysing cognitive processes therefore considers multilayer networks with nonlinear activation functions (see, e.g., Plaut et al., 1996, for discussion). Finally, this analysis has considered only two forms of damaging networks; other researchers have utilized other methods (e.g., adjustments to input gain; Kello et al., 2005). Examining the degree to which these results generalize to systems that are more complex/realistic along these dimensions is left for future work. This section instead focuses on the nature of errors and damage to the network. Two specific assumptions are examined.

1. *Errors are exact substitutions.* In the analyses above, a substitution is assumed to be a complete, exact replacement of the target pattern by some other trained pattern. In practice, connectionist simulations usually rely on a classification procedure to interpret the pattern of activation over output units (i.e., mapping the continuous variation in activation patterns to a predefined set of outputs).

The simulations reported in this section violate Assumption 1 by using a nearest neighbour method: The output of the network is interpreted as corresponding to the trained pattern with the smallest Euclidean distance (ties were resolved by random selection).

2. *Damage is always more likely to result in small rather than large disruptions to processing.* Throughout the analyses above, the probability distribution of damage was assumed to be a strictly decreasing function of distance from the intact network. This is clearly violated in many connectionist simulations of neurological damage. For example, if damage corresponds to the removal of a certain percentage of connections (Plaut, 1995), there is some minimum distance that all damaged weight matrices will be from the intact network.

The simulations here violate Assumption 2 by independently damaging each connection weight.

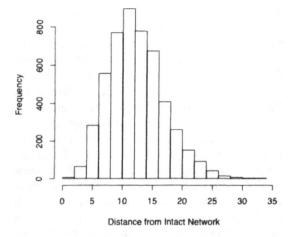

Figure 1. *Distribution of Euclidean distance of damaged weight matrix from intact weight matrix (5,000 damage matrices; 36 connection weights). Probability of damage was independent across each weight (see text for details).*

The damage value d_{ji} for each weight connecting input unit j to output unit i was drawn from the range $[-1, 1]$ sampled at .025 increments (-1.0, $-.975$, $-.95$, etc.). Recall that a damage value of 1 corresponds to no damage. For damage values other than 1, the probability is proportional to $1 / (|d_{ji} - 1|)$. For damage value 1, the probability is proportional to $2 \times$ probability of the damage value .975. Figure 1 illustrates the distribution of distances from the intact network $[\|Z^a - 1^{n \times m}\|$, following (D8)] of 5,000 damage matrices randomly generated following this method. The matrices had 36 weights (corresponding to a feed-forward, fully connected network of 6 input and 6 output units; see below). As the figure shows, for this damage mechanism the probability distribution of damage matrices violates Assumption 2.

Simulations: General methods

These simulations used a simple set of 6 input and output cognitive representations shown in Table 2. For expository purposes these have been associated with phonological features and segments, such that the network computes a mapping from phonological features to segments. To clarify the meaning of these representational elements, recall the section considering input unit damage and distributed representations. There was a brief discussion of the broad dimensions of manner and place, along with a discussion of the specific features [nasal] and [coronal]. With respect to the other manner features utilized here: [fricative] refers to whether air flow is restricted to create turbulence (e.g., /f/ is a fricative); [stop] refers to consonants where air flow is completely obstructed (e.g., /t/). With respect to the other place features: [palatal] refers to an obstruction made on or near the hard palate (e.g., /j/, the initial sound in words like "yes"); [velar] refers to an obstruction occur on or near the velum (e.g., /k/). A more realistic simulation

Table 2. *Cognitive representation of input vectors used in simulations*

	Structural position						
	Manner			Place			
	Components of representational elements						
Input pattern	Nasal	Fricative	Stop	Palatal	Coronal	Velar	Corresponding output representation
1	+	−	−	−	+	−	n
2	−	+	−	−	+	−	s
3	−	−	+	−	+	−	t
4	−	−	+	−	−	+	k
5	−	+	−	−	−	−	f
6	−	−	−	+	−	−	j

Note: Labels are for expository purposes only and are not intended to correspond to any particular theory of phonological structure.

would have of course included many other features (and perhaps different featural characterizations of each segment); this is for illustration purposes only.

The cognitive representations of the output of the network were realized locally by assigning each segment to 1 of 6 output units. Each segment's corresponding network representation therefore consisted of a 1 on this unit and -1 on all other output units.

The cognitive representation of the input was realized in two different representational frameworks. In the localist representational framework, the structural position "manner" was realized over the first three input units with a single unit for each component of the representational element (e.g., nasal corresponded to input unit 1; fricative to input unit 2; etc.) The structural position "place" was realized over the second set of input units. In the distributed representational framework, the two structural positions were associated to two dimensional vectors (these were linearly independent except where otherwise noted). These were chosen such that the network representation of the two structural positions overlapped (following Equation D7). The elements within each position were associated with three dimensional vectors corresponding to the localist representations.

Given that we are utilizing a linear activation function, a two-layer network, and linearly independent input vectors, there is an exact solution for the weight matrix in Equation 2: $\mathbf{W} = \mathbf{I}^{-1}\mathbf{O}$ (where $\mathbf{O}$ is a matrix composed of the 6 output vectors, and $\mathbf{I}^{-1}$ is the inverse of the corresponding matrix of input vectors). Connectionist training algorithms can easily discover this solution (e.g., using the Widrow–Hoff or delta rule; see Kohonen, 1977, for discussion). For ease of simulation this was simply directly estimated using the R function *solve* (R Development Core Team, 2006; this package was used for all elements of the simulations).

This weight matrix was then damaged using the algorithm described above. For each set of training vectors 5,000 damaged matrices were simulated. Following each instance of damage, the first input pattern (features of /n/) was presented to the network as a target, and the network's output was classified as corresponding to the output vector with the smallest Euclidean distance. The dependent measure of interest was the rate at which the network produced errors corresponded to a similar representation (/t/, sharing place, differing in manner) versus a matched, less similar representation (/k/, differing in both place and manner).

The simulations below involve comparison of results across different networks. In each simulation reported in the main text damage was probabilistically distributed as described above. However, due to the differences in representational structure this had differential effects on overall accuracy. The overall error rate is thus not matched across the comparisons. Appendix E reports the results of a parallel set of simulations that matched for overall accuracy; as discussed in more detail there, these reveal the same patterns as those found in the simulations reported in the main text.

Simulation 1: Localist versus distributed representations

The analysis above makes two predictions following weight damage. First, for both localist and distributed representations, errors should be more likely to result in more (/t/) than less (/k/) similar representations. The second prediction is that the magnitude of the effect of representational overlap should be larger for localist than for distributed representations. As discussed above, only the former representational scheme allows multiple types of damage to result in representations with greater degree of overlap.

Method

Recall from above that in both localist and distributed network representations exact substitutions can be produced by warping the input vector of the target onto that of the substitution. The network representations used here were constructed such that the damage matrices required to produce such substitutions were matched in distance from the intact network. These are shown in Table 3.

Table 3. *Network representations used in the first set of simulations*

	Segment	
	/t/	/k/
Network representation: Localist	(−1, −1, .6825 −1, 3.435, −1)	(−1, −1, .6825, −1, −1, 3.435)
Distance of damage matrix	53.33	181.35
Network representation: Distributed	(.25,−.75, .75, −.75, .25,−.25)	(.25, .25,−.25, −.75,−.75, .75)
Tensor product derivation	(−.5,−.5, .5) ⊗ (.5, .5) + (−1, 1, −1) ⊗ (−.5, .5)	(−.5,−.5, .5) ⊗ (.5, .5) + (−1, −1, 1) ⊗ (−.5, .5)
Distance of damage matrix	53.33	181.33

Note: In the localist representations, " + "corresponded to .6825 for manner elements and 3.435 for place. The " − " components of both elements were assigned to −1. In the distributed representations, the structure position vectors were manner: (.5, .5); place: (−.5, .5). For manner, elements were associated with ±.5; place ±1.0.

Results

The number of /t/ and /k/ errors over 5,000 simulated instances of damage for each representational type are shown in Table 4. The results confirm the predictions of the analysis. Within each representational type, there are significantly more errors resulting in /t/ than /k/ (exact binomial test; localist: $p < .0001$; distributed: $p < .0001$). The asymmetry in errors is significantly stronger for localist than for distributed representations: $\chi^2(1, N = 937) = 25.2, p < .0001$.

Simulation 2: Inappropriately structured distributed representations

The analysis above predicts that with distributed representations certain conditions must be met in order for errors to respect cognitive representational overlap. By making a minimal modification to the network representations used in Simulation 1, these conditions can be violated. Specifically, the activation values for manner and place elements can be switched, such that manner is associated with ±1.0 and place with ±.5. (Note: for these simulations, the association of particular structural positions with vectors of particular magnitudes is arbitrary.) The resulting vectors are shown in Table 5.

As shown in the second row, the third element of /t/'s network representation is more distant from the target than is the corresponding element of /k/'s representation. This is because the conditions outlined above (see also Appendix B) are violated. For this network element, the difference between the target and the vector components corresponding to the pooled set of constituents shared by /t/ and /k/ is positive $[1 \times .5 - (-1 \times .5)]$. In contrast, the difference for the disjoint set of constituents (where only /k/ differs from the target) is negative $[(.5 \times -.5) - (-.5 \times -.5)]$.

The results show that errors are more likely to result in representations with a lower degree of overlap. For this simulation, 137 errors resulted in /t/, compared to 352 for /k/. This is a significant bias (exact binomial test, $p < .0001$) in the direction *opposite* to that predicted by representational overlap at the cognitive level. A chi-square test across simulations confirmed that the patterns across distributed representation types were reliably distinct: $\chi^2(1, N = 1088) = 312.5, p < .0001$. Although the cognitive representations

Table 4. *Number of errors over 5,000 instances of damage with localist versus distributed representations*

Representational framework	No. errors		% errors resulting in /t/
	/n/ → /t/	/n/ → /k/	
Localist	316	22	93.5
Distributed	487	112	81.3

Note: Distance of required damage matrices from their respective intact networks is matched across representation types.

Table 5. *Network representations used in the second set of simulations*

	Segment		
	/n/	/t/	/k/
Distributed representation	(.75, −.75, −.25, .25, −.25, −.75)	(.25, −.75, .75, −.75, .25, −.25)	(.25, .25, −.25, −.75, −.75, .75)
Tensor product derivation	(1, −1, −1) ⊗ (.5, .5) + (−.5, .5, −.5) ⊗ (−.5, .5)	(−1, −1, 1) ⊗ (.5, .5) + (−.5, .5, −.5) ⊗ (−.5, .5)	(−1, −1, 1) ⊗ (.5, .5) + (−.5, −.5, .5) ⊗ (−.5, .5)
Distance of damage matrix	−	35.56	30.22

Note: See text for details.

of the networks in Simulations 1 and 2 are identical, the manner in which these representations are realized at the network level has a significant effect on error probabilities.

Simulation 3: Variation in distance of network representations

Although the discussion above has emphasized categorical distinctions between different representational frameworks (i.e., localist vs. distributed; satisfying vs. violating representational conditions), the analysis also predicts that graded distinctions will influence error patterns. In all cases, the asymmetry in error probabilities of representations with higher versus smaller degrees of overlap is a function of the asymmetry in the distance of their corresponding damaging matrices from the intact network. The greater this asymmetry in distances, the greater the effect of cognitive representational overlap.

Method

The vectors realizing cognitive elements that were utilized in Simulation 1 were associated with two new sets of vectors corresponding to the two structural positions. As shown in Table 6, the resulting tensor products differed in the degree of asymmetry between the corresponding damage matrices. For the smaller asymmetry simulation the ratio of the distance of /t/'s damage matrix to /k/'s is .77; for the larger asymmetry simulation, the ratio is .43.

Table 6. *Network representations used in the third set of simulations*

	Segment	
	/t/	/k/
Distributed representation: small asymmetry	(−.729, −1.271, 1.271, −1.653, −.347, .347)	(−.729, −.729, .729, −1.653, −1.653, 1.653)
Tensor product derivation	(−1, −1, 1) ⊗ (.5, .5) + (−1, 1, −1) ⊗ (−.271, .653)	(−1, −1, 1) ⊗ (.5, .5) + (−1, −1, 1) ⊗ (−.271, .653)
Distance of damage matrix from intact network	268.12	348.26
Distributed representation: larger asymmetry	(−.771, −.229, .229, −1.153, .153, −.153)	(−.771, −.771, .771, −1.153, −1.153, 1.153)
Tensor product derivation	(−1, −1, 1) ⊗ (.5, .5) + (−1, 1, −1) ⊗ (.271, .653)	(−1, −1, 1) ⊗ (.5, .5) + (−1, −1, 1) ⊗ (.271, .653)
Distance of damage matrix from intact network	385.33	889.51

Note: The structure position vector for manner was (.5, .5) in both simulations. Place was associated with (−.271, .653) in the small asymmetry simulation and (.271, .653) in the larger asymmetry simulation. Note that these vectors are not linearly independent. Representational elements in both positions were associated with ± 1.0.

Table 7. *Number of errors over 5,000 instances of damage with representations varying in distance of required damage matrices from their respective intact networks*

Asymmetry in distance of damage matrices	No. errors		% errors resulting in /t/
	/n/ → /t/	/n/ → /k/	
Small	513	355	59.1
Large	1,025	506	66.9

Results

The number of /t/ and /k/ errors over 5,000 simulated instances of damage for each representational type are shown in Table 7. The results confirm the predictions. The effect of similarity on errors is significantly stronger for representations with a larger asymmetry in the distance of the damage matrices: $\chi^2(1, N = 2399) = 14.5, p < .0002$.

Discussion: Simulation analyses

These simulations have confirmed the predictions of the formal analyses and have shown that they are relatively stable over minor violations of the assumptions of the analysis. Errors do not have to be limited to exact substitutions; the probability of damage need not be strictly decreasing over all possible damage matrices. Although these findings suggest that the results may generalize beyond the specific assumptions utilized here, more work is clearly required to examine the degree to which these findings hold in more complex connectionist networks.

GENERAL DISCUSSION

These analyses reveal how the relationship between cognitive and neurobiological structures can exert an important influence on behavioural data. Many cognitive psychological studies have assumed that error probabilities reflect the degree to which cognitive representations overlap (such that more representations with greater overlap are more likely to interact in errors). These analyses show that this assumption is clearly valid for localist representations. When specific network elements correspond to specific cognitive structures, error probabilities will always reflect the overlap of cognitive representations. In contrast, when cognitive representations are distributed across overlapping sets of network elements, error probabilities reflect the degree of cognitive representational overlap only if certain conditions are met. Namely, at the level of individual network units interactions in the realization of elements across structural positions must serve to enhance, not decrease, differences from the target. Furthermore, even when such conditions are met, these analyses show that following weight damage networks with localist representations will show greater sensitivity to overlap at the cognitive level.

Implications of cognitive theories for neurobiological representations

These results suggest that cognitive theories may provide strong constraints on the neural organization of representations. In many domains—particularly in the case of language—empirical studies have documented strong links between error probabilities and cognitive theories of representational structure. What the results show here is that it is not the case that any arbitrary neural representational framework can account for these data. In particular, neurobiological representations must be organized such that the distance between distinct representations reflects the degree of cognitive overlap.

Such a constraint has been satisfied by many connectionist representational frameworks. For example, most localist connectionist models have associated different structural positions with different sets of units (e.g., Dell, 1986, associates onset position with one set of units, coda with another). Similarly, in most of the binding-by-timing frameworks discussed above (e.g., Hummel & Holyoak, 2003), representational elements that are bound to different structural positions are *strictly* temporally separated. In these representational frameworks, there is no interaction between the neurobiological realization of elements in different structural positions. They are therefore appropriately structured in the sense that decreasing cognitive representational overlap will necessarily increase the distinction in neurobiological representations.

A more interesting challenge is to understand the implications of these results for frameworks in which representations are not prespecified but learned. As noted above, such representations are often highly distributed (e.g., Plaut et al., 1996). Do the distributed representations that emerge from statistical patterns in the training data respect or violate the conditions imposed by this analysis? Although these analyses have shown that it is *possible* for errors on distributed representations to not reflect cognitive representational overlap, it has not demonstrated that such an outcome is *probable*. Future research should explore the extent to which connectionist learning algorithms converge on representations that do or do not respect the conditions outlined above.

Issues in using error patterns to induce representational structure

If distributed neurobiological representations are structured such that representations with a high degree of overlap at the cognitive level are, at the network level, the same distance or even further away from the target than representations with a low degree of overlap, this analysis predicts that error probabilities will not reflect cognitive representational structure. This may present an issue in interpreting studies that use patterns of interactions in errors to induce representational structure (e.g., van den Broecke & Goldstein, 1980). Since a specific relationship between error probability and representational overlap is not guaranteed, these studies may lead to incorrect conclusions regarding the cognitive representations underlying the production of errors. However, this is not to say that such analyses are destined to fail—it suggests only that they are not destined to succeed. Consequently, it is important for speech error researchers to follow the general strategy of seeking converging evidence from multiple methodologies. If error patterns suggest a different cognitive representational structure from other methodologies, it may reflect the influence of the distributed structure of neurobiological representations.

The role of formal analysis in connectionist research

Building on the formal analysis of Smolensky (1986), the work has shown how two common forms of simulating neurological damage in linear, feed-forward connectionist networks can be viewed as linear transformations of input and/or output vectors. This reveals three properties of error generation in connectionist networks.

First, this analysis characterizes the production of a substitution error as transforming or warping the representation of the input onto that of the error. This allows us to transparently see how degree of overlap of network level representations can influence error probabilities. Since network representations with higher degrees of overlap require less warping, they require less damage to produce. The analysis reveals why (if particular conditions are met) error probabilities must reflect cognitive representational overlap. In comparison, although we may make predictions about the behaviour of simulated systems it is not until the actual simulations are completed that we are certain of how the system behaves. For example, we might make the prediction that error probabilities are correlated with cognitive representational overlap. When utilizing simulations, this remains a conjecture until we actually observe many simulated instances of disruption to network processing; only then are we certain that such a relationship holds. This is not to deny the advantages of simulations—they are essential in understanding systems that are not amenable to closed-form methods. But analyses such as these reveal that additional insight can be gained from close formal analysis of such systems.

The immediately preceding section provides two such examples. First, there are conditions under which errors on distributed representations will not be more likely to result in representations with higher than with lower overlap on the cognitive level. This reveals that degree of cognitive representational overlap is not necessarily reflected in error probabilities. Second, following damage to connection weights the strength of the effect of cognitive representational overlap is modulated by the specific relationship between cognitive and network representations (i.e., it is stronger for localist than for distributed representations). Although these insights may have been observed in the course of a simulation study (perhaps in the course of exploring the effect of various simulation parameters) it would be considerably more difficult to determine the cause of such effects. By forcing careful consideration of the properties of the network, formal analysis has produced two unexpected predictions for network behaviour—predictions that are based on a careful understanding of network processing mechanisms.

CONCLUSIONS

A full understanding of cognition requires not just acknowledging that the mind and brain are related but specifying the nature of that relationship. Articulating the correspondence between cognitive and neural structures and then understanding its consequences holds important implications for using behavioural data to inform both neural and cognitive computational theories of the mind/brain.

Manuscript received 5 December 2006
Revised manuscript received 16 March 2007
Revised manuscript accepted 19 March 2007
First published online 4 March 2008

REFERENCES

Caramazza, A. (1984). The logic of neuropsychological research and the problem of patient classification in aphasia. *Brain and Language, 21*, 9–20.

Caramazza, A. (1986). On drawing inferences about the structural of normal cognitive systems from the analysis of patterns of impaired performance: The case for single-patient studies. *Brain and Cognition, 5*, 41–66.

Dell, G. S. (1986). A spreading activation theory of retrieval in sentence production. *Psychological Review, 93*, 283–321.

Dell, G. S., Schwartz, M. F., Martin, N., Saffran, E. M., & Gagnon, D. A. (1997). Lexical access in aphasic and nonaphasic speakers. *Psychological Review, 104*, 801–838.

Dunn, J. C., & Kirsner, K. (2003). What can we infer from double dissociations? *Cortex, 39*, 1–7.

Garrett, M. F. (1976). Syntactic processes in sentence production. In R. J. Wales & E. Walker (Eds.), *New approaches to language mechanisms* (pp. 231–255). Amsterdam: North Holland.

Garrett, M. F. (1980). Levels of processing in sentence production. In B. Butterworth (Ed.), *Language production: Vol. 1. Speech and talk* (pp. 177–220). New York: Academic Press.

Hinton, G. E., McClelland, J. L., & Rumelhart, D. E. (1986). Distributed representations. In D. E. Rumelhart, J. L. McClelland, & the PDP Research Group (Eds.), *Parallel distributed processing: Explorations in the microstructure of cognition* (Vol. 1, pp. 77–109). Cambridge, MA: MIT Press.

Hinton, G. E., & Shallice, T. (1991). Lesioning an attractor network: Investigations of acquired dyslexia. *Psychological Review, 98*, 74–95.

Hubel, D. H., & Wiesel, T. N. (1962). Receptive fields, binocular interaction and functional architecture in the cat's visual cortex. *Journal of Physiology, 160*, 106–154.

Hummel, J. E., & Holyoak, K. J. (2003). A symbolic-connectionist theory of relational inference and generalization. *Psychological Review, 110*, 220–264.

Joanisse, M. F., & Seidenberg, M. S. (1999). Impairments in verb morphology following brain injury: A connectionist model. *Proceedings of the National Academy of Sciences of the United States of America, 96*, 7592–7597.

Kello, C. T., Sibley, D. E., & Plaut, D. C. (2005). Dissociations in performance on novel versus irregular items: Single-route demonstrations with input gain in localist and distributed models. *Cognitive Science, 29*, 627–654.

Kohonen, T. (1977). *Associative memory: A system-theoretical approach*. Berlin: Springer-Verlag.

McCloskey, M. (1993). Theory and evidence in cognitive neuropsychology: A "radical" response to Robertson, Knight, Rafal, and Shimamura (1993). *Journal of Experimental Psychology: Learning, Memory, and Cognition, 19*, 718–734.

McCloskey, M. (2001). Future directions in cognitive neuropsychology. In B. Rapp (Ed.), *What deficits reveal about the human mind/brain: A handbook of cognitive neuropsychology* (pp. 593–610). Philadelphia: Psychology Press.

McCloskey, M. (2003). Beyond task dissociation logic: A richer conception of cognitive neuropsychology. *Cortex, 39*, 196–202.

Medin, D. L., Goldstone, R. L., & Gentner, D. (1993). Respects for similarity. *Psychological Review, 100*, 254–278.

Mesulam, M.-M. (1990). Large-scale neurocognitive networks and distributed processing for attention, language, and memory. *Annals of Neurology, 28*, 597–613.

Page, M. (2000). Connectionist modeling in psychology: A localist manifesto. *Behavioral and Brain Sciences, 23*, 443–512.

Pinker, S., & Ulman, M. T. (2002). The past and future of the past tense. *Trends in Cognitive Sciences, 11*, 456–463.

Plaut, D. C. (1995). Double dissociation without modularity: Evidence from connectionist neuropsychology. *Journal of Clinical and Experimental Neuropsychology, 17*, 291–321.

Plaut, D. C. (1997). Structure and function in the lexical system: Insights from distributed models of word reading and lexical decision. *Language and Cognitive Processes, 12*, 765–805.

Plaut, D. C., McClelland, J. L., Seidenberg, M. S., & Patterson, K. (1996). Understanding normal and impaired word reading: Computational principles in quasi-regular domains. *Psychological Review, 103*, 56–115.

Plunkett, K., & Bandelow, S. (2006). Stochastic approaches to understanding dissociations in inflectional morphology. *Brain and Language, 98*, 194–209.

R Development Core Team. (2006). *R: A language and environment for statistical computing* [Computer software]. Vienna, Austria: R Foundation for Statistical Computing. Retrieved October 5, 2005, from http://www.R-project.org

Rapp, B., & Caramazza, A. (1997). From graphemes to abstract letter shapes: Levels of representation in written spelling. *Journal of Experimental Psychology: Human Perception and Performance, 23*, 1130–1152.

Rapp, B., & Goldrick, M. (2000). Discreteness and interactivity in spoken word production. *Psychological Review, 107*, 460–499.

Smolensky, P. (1986). Neural and conceptual interpretations of parallel distributed processing models. In J. L. McClelland, D. E. Rumelhart, & the PDP Research Group (Eds.), *Parallel distributed processing: Explorations in the microstructure of cognition* (Vol. 2, pp. 390–431). Cambridge, MA: MIT Press.

Smolensky, P. (1988). On the proper treatment of connectionism. *Behavioral and Brain Sciences, 11*, 1–74.

Smolensky, P. (1990). Tensor product variable binding and the representation of symbolic structures in connectionist networks. *Artificial Intelligence, 46*, 159–216

Smolensky, P. (2006a). Formalizing the principles: I. Representation and processing in the mind/brain. In P. Smolensky & G. Legendre (Eds.), *The harmonic mind: From neural computation to optimality-theoretic grammar: Vol. 1. Cognitive architecture* (pp. 147–206). Cambridge, MA: MIT Press.

Smolensky, P. (2006b). Tensor product representations: Formal foundations. In P. Smolensky & G. Legendre (Eds.), *The harmonic mind: From neural computation to optimality-theoretic grammar: Vol. 1. Cognitive architecture* (pp. 271–344). Cambridge, MA: MIT Press.

Smolensky, P. (2006c). Computational levels and integrated connectionist/symbolic explanation. In P. Smolensky & G. Legendre (Eds.), *The harmonic mind: From neural computation to optimality-theoretic grammar: Vol. 2. Linguistic and philosophical implications* (pp. 503–592). Cambridge, MA: MIT Press.

Smolensky, P., & Tesar, B. (2006). Symbolic computation with activation patterns. In P. Smolensky & G. Legendre (Eds.), *The harmonic mind: From neural computation to optimality-theoretic grammar: Vol. 1. Cognitive architecture* (pp. 207–234). Cambridge, MA: MIT Press.

Stone, G. O. (1986). An analysis of the delta rule and the learning of statistical associations. In J. L. McClelland, D. E. Rumelhart, & the PDP Research Group (Eds.), *Parallel distributed processing: Explorations in the microstructure of cognition* (Vol. 1, pp. 444–459). Cambridge, MA: MIT Press.

Van den Broecke, M. P. R., & Goldstein, L. (1980). Consonant features in speech errors. In V. A. Fromkin (Ed.), *Errors in linguistic performance: Slips of the tongue, ear, pen, and hand* (pp. 47–65). New York: Academic Press.

APPENDIX A

Proof of (C1): Representational overlap and localist network representations

Given the conditions for substitution errors in Equation 7, we need to demonstrate that D^c is more probable than D^f. Following (D4), this is true if D^c is less distant from the intact network matrix than is D^f. Specifically, we must demonstrate that the following inequality is true:

$$\|diag(D^c) - 1^n\| < \|diag(D^f) - 1^n\| \quad (A1)$$

Rewriting Equation A1 in terms of diagonal elements of the damage matrices yields the following inequality:

$$\sum_i (d_i^c - 1)^2 < \sum_i (d_i^f - 1)^2 \quad (A2)$$

Assuming that no vector elements are equal to 0 (see Footnote 2), these diagonal elements are given by:

$$d_i^c = \frac{c_i}{t_i} \quad d_i^f = \frac{f_i}{t_i} \quad (A3)$$

Given the definition of matched cognitive representations that vary in similarity to the target (D2) and the definition of localist network representations (D3), there must be at least one unit a in the set A where $t_a = c_a \neq f_a$. For all such elements $d_a^c = 1$ and $d_a^f \neq 1$. For all other units, $d_k^c = d_k^f$ (either $t_k = c_k = f_k$ or $t_k \neq c_k = f_k$). Rewriting (A2), eliminating common elements from both sides, yields

$$\sum_{a \in A} (d_a^c - 1)^2 < \sum_{a \in A} (d_a^f - 1)^2 \quad (A4)$$

Substituting in the known values for these elements yields

$$\sum_{a \in A} (1 - 1) < \sum_{a \in A} (d_a^f - 1)^2$$
$$0 < \sum_{a \in A} (d_a^f - 1)^2 \quad (A5)$$

This must be true, since the square of any nonzero real number is positive. Because less damage is required to map the target input vector onto a similar nontarget vector, errors on localist representations are more likely to result in representations with a higher than a lower degree of overlap at the cognitive level.

APPENDIX B

Proof of (C2): Representational overlap and appropriately structured distributed network representations

In the context of tensor product representations, the diagonal elements of the damage matrix are: (cf. Equation A3; note following above this assumes vectors do not have 0 elements)

$$d_i^c = \frac{c_i}{t_i} = \frac{\left(\sum_j e_j^c \otimes r_j\right)_i}{\left(\sum_j e_j^t \otimes r_j\right)_i} \quad d_i^f = \frac{c_i}{t_i} = \frac{\left(\sum_j e_j^f \otimes r_j\right)_i}{\left(\sum_j e_j^t \otimes r_j\right)_i} \quad (A6)$$

where $\left(\sum_j e_j^t \otimes r_j\right)_i$ denotes the ith element[4] of the tensor product representation of target representation t.

Recall from Appendix A that to demonstrate that similar representations are more probable error outcomes than more dissimilar representations we must prove the inequality given in Equation A1. Substituting the elements of Equation A6 in this yields:

$$\sum_i \left[\frac{\left(\sum_j e_j^c \otimes r_j\right)_i}{\left(\sum_j e_j^t \otimes r_j\right)_i} - 1\right]^2 < \sum_i \left[\frac{\left(\sum_j e_j^f \otimes r_j\right)_i}{\left(\sum_j e_j^t \otimes r_j\right)_i} - 1\right]^2 \quad (A7)$$

Given the definition of matched cognitive representations that vary in degree of overlap with the target (D3) and the definition of distributed tensor product representations (D7), there must be at least one constituent a in the set A where $e_a^t = e_a^c \neq e_a^f$. For all other constituents j not in this set, $e_j^t = e_j^f$. Note that for constituents a in A, for the inequality of representational elements to hold it need only be the case that there is at least one vector element i of the tensor product representation where $(\sum_a e_a^t \otimes r_a)_i \neq (\sum_a e_a^f \otimes r_a)_i$.

For the other vector elements x, $(\sum_a e_a^t \otimes r_a)_x = (\sum_a e_a^c \otimes r_a)_x = (\sum_a e_a^f \otimes r_a)_x$; thus, for these elements the two sides of the inequality in Equation A7 are equal. We can

---

[4] Note that the tensor will have a rank of at least 2 (perhaps higher; see Smolensky, 2006b, for further discussion). To highlight the parallels to the localist analysis, assume the elements of the n-rank tensor have been ordered and mapped onto an equivalent 1-rank tensor.

therefore restrict our attention to those vector elements like i. Rewriting Equation A7 for one such unit yields:

$$\left[\frac{\left(\sum_{j \in A} e_j^c \otimes r_j + \sum_{j \notin A} e_j^c \otimes r_j\right)_i}{\left(\sum_{j \in A} e_j^t \otimes r_j + \sum_{j \notin A} e_j^t \otimes r_j\right)_i} - 1\right]^2 \\ < \left[\frac{\left(\sum_{j \in A} e_j^f \otimes r_j + \sum_{j \notin A} e_j^f \otimes r_j\right)_i}{\left(\sum_{j \in A} e_j^t \otimes r_j + \sum_{j \notin A} e_j^t \otimes r_j\right)_i} - 1\right]^2 \quad (A8)$$

Combining the differences on each side into a single ratio and eliminating common terms yields

$$\left[\left(\sum_{j \in A} e_j^c \otimes r_j + \sum_{j \notin A} e_j^c \otimes r_j\right)_i \\ - \left(\sum_{j \in A} e_j^t \otimes r_j + \sum_{j \notin A} e_j^t \otimes r_j\right)_i\right]^2 \\ < \left[\left(\sum_{j \in A} e_j^f \otimes r_j + \sum_{j \notin A} e_j^f \otimes r_j\right)_i \\ - \left(\sum_{j \in A} e_j^t \otimes r_j + \sum_{j \notin A} e_j^t \otimes r_r\right)_i\right]^2 \quad (A9)$$

For elements in the set A, $e_a^t = e_a^c$, so

$$\sum_{j \in A} e_j^c \otimes r_j - \sum_{j \in A} e_j^t \otimes r_j = 0.$$

Eliminating these terms, let

$$p_i = \left(\sum_{j \notin A} e_j^c \otimes r_j - \sum_{j \notin A} e_j^t \otimes r_j\right)_i \\ = \left(\sum_{j \notin A} e_j^f \otimes r_j - \sum_{j \notin A} e_j^t \otimes r_j\right)_i$$

Rewriting yields:

$$[p_i]^2 < \left[p_i + \left(\sum_{j \in A} e_j^f \otimes r_j - \sum_{j \in A} e_j^t \otimes r_j\right)_i\right]^2 \quad (A10)$$

This is true if p_i and

$$\left(\sum_{j \in A} e_j^f \otimes r_j - \sum_{j \in A} e_j^t \otimes r_j\right)_i$$

are of the same sign and the latter term is nonzero. If this condition holds for all appropriate units i, for all terms of the sums in Equation A7 either the two sides of the inequality are equal or the left-hand side is less than the right-hand side. Since, for such appropriately structured representations, there must be at least one term in the sum where the two sides are inequal, the damage matrix for the more similar representation is more probable than the matrix for the less similar representation.

To provide a more intuitive understanding of the inequality in Equation A10, note that it has two basic terms. The first, p_i, refers to the difference between the target and the *pooled* set of vector elements realizing constituents where c and f are equal. The other refers to the difference between the target and the *disjoint* set of vector elements where c but not f overlaps with t. The inequality holds if these two differences are in the same direction: that is, if they serve to emphasize or amplify one another. For example, if the difference in the pooled set is negative, the difference in the disjoint set must push the representation to be more negative—further away from the target vector. If it does not, the elements in the disjoint set will actually decrease the distance of f's vector from the target. The potential for such interference across different structural positions is a natural consequence of the use of distributed representations in which different structural positions are realized on the same network unit(s).

APPENDIX C

Proof of (C3): Representational overlap and localist weight damage

Consider damage vector Z^f whose corresponding damage matrices produce a substitution error on target t resulting in the output appropriate to f. This section demonstrates that for any such damage vector there are *two* more probable Z^c (whose damage matrices produce the output c for target t) that can be constructed. To demonstrate this, it must be shown that:

$$\|Z^c - 1^{n \times m}\| < \|Z^f - 1^{n \times m}\|. \quad (A11)$$

This is done by decomposing the Z^c and Z^f into the separate damage matrices D_{xi}^c and D_{xi}^f for all output units i.

Scenario 1. Given the definition of matched representations of varying degrees of similarity (D2), there must be at least one output unit a in the set A where $o_a^t = o_a^c \neq o_a^f$; for all other units k not in the set A, $D^c_{xk}=D^f_{xk}$ (as $o^c_k=o^f_k$). For such units a, D^f_{xa} must satisfy the conditions in Equation 15. In contrast, D^c_{xa} can be equal to the Kronecker Delta; undamaged, the network will produce the output appropriate to c. Since $\|diag(\text{KroneckerDelta}) - 1^n\|=0$:

$$\|diag(D^c_{xa}) - 1^n\| < \|diag(D^f_{xa}) - 1^n\| \quad (A12)$$

Returning to the inequality in Equation A11, we can express each term as the sum of damage matrices. For the elements of this sum, either the damage matrices for c and f are equal (for units not in A), or (following Equation A12) the matrix for c is closer (for units in A). Thus, a higher probability form of Z^c can be generated for Z^f; substitution errors resulting in c are therefore more probable than those resulting in f.

Scenario 2. In addition to the Z^c described above, there is an additional higher probability form of Z^c that can be generated. For those output elements in the set A, D^c_{xa} is not required to be equal to the Kronecker Delta. As outlined above, for these elements the exact same output will be produced if D^c_{xa} satisfies the conditions in Equation 15: that is, warping the input representation of the target onto that corresponding to c will yield the desired output. As noted above, Equation 15 is analogous to the conditions for input unit damage; therefore, following the proof of (C1) in Appendix A:

$$\|diag(D^c_{xa}) - 1^n\| < \|diag(D^f_{xa}) - 1^n\| \quad (A13)$$

This has the same form as Equation A1, showing that this additional damage matrix is also higher in probability than Z^f. Note that there is no such second damage matrix available for f. This further increases the asymmetry in probability between substitution errors resulting in representations with higher versus lower degrees of overlap at the cognitive level.

APPENDIX D

Proof of (C4): Representational overlap and weight damage over distributed representation

Consider damage vector Z^f whose corresponding damage matrices produce a substitution error on target t resulting in the output appropriate to f. This section demonstrates that for any such damage vector a single more probable Z^c (whose damage matrices produce the output c for target t) can be constructed.

Case 1: A substitution error t → s will be produced if the diagonals of the damage matrix for each output unit are equal to:

$$d_{jD_{xi}} = \frac{\left(\sum_p e^s_p \otimes r_p\right)_j}{\left(\sum_p e^t_p \otimes r_p\right)_j} \quad (A14)$$

where e^t_p denotes the network vector corresponding to the element bound to the pth structural position in the input representation of target t, and r_p denotes the vector corresponding to the pth structural position in the input. Following Appendix B, $\left(\sum_p e^t_p \otimes r_p\right)_j$ denotes the jth component of the tensor product input representation of t.

Suppose Z^f is specified by the conditions in Equation A14. Let Z^c be specified by the corresponding conditions for c and t's inputs. Following the proof of (C3), we can represent the terms of the inequality in Equation A11 as the sum of the component damage matrices for each output unit i. Following the proof of (C2), we know that for appropriately structured distributed representations

$$\sum_j (d^c_{jD_{xi}} - 1)^2 < \sum_j (d^f_{jD_{xi}} - 1)^2$$

for at least one i. Since the inequality holds for each element of the sum,

$$\|Z^c - 1^{n \times m}\| < \|Z^f - 1^{n \times m}\|.$$

Case 2: Alternatively, a substitution t → s will be produced if for each input unit j the diagonals of the damage matrix are equal to:

$$d_{iD_{jx}} = \frac{\left(\sum_p f^s_p \otimes q_p\right)_{j\ i}}{\left(\sum_p f^t_p \otimes q_p\right)_{j\ i}} \quad (A15)$$

where f^t_p denotes the network vector corresponding to the element bound to the pth structural position in the output representation of target t, and q_p denotes the vector corresponding to the pth structural position in the output. Following Equation 13,

$$\left(\sum_p f^t_p \otimes q_p\right)_j$$

denotes the contribution that the jth input unit makes to the output representation of target t.

Suppose $\mathbf{Z}^f$ is specified according to the conditions in Equation A15. Let $\mathbf{Z}^c$ be specified by the corresponding conditions for c and t's outputs. Following the proof of (C3), we can represent the terms of the inequality in Equation A11 as the sum of the component damage matrices. Following the proof of (C2), we know that for appropriately structured distributed representations

$$\sum_i (d^c_{iD_{\cdot j}} - 1)^2 < \sum_i (d^f_{iD_{\cdot j}} - 1)^2$$

for all j. Since the inequality holds for each element of the sum,

$$\|\mathbf{Z}^c - \mathbf{1}^{n \times m}\| < \|\mathbf{Z}^f - \mathbf{1}^{n \times m}\|.$$

Thus, regardless of the form of $\mathbf{Z}^f$, a single higher probability form of $\mathbf{Z}^c$ can be generated; for appropriately structured distributed representations, weight-damage-induced substitution errors resulting in c are therefore more probable than those resulting in f.

APPENDIX E

Simulations matching for overall error rates

Note that the overall number was not matched across simulations. To determine whether this difference accounts for the differential distribution of errors, a second set of simulations was conducted in which overall accuracy was matched as closely as possible.

Simulation 1: Localist versus distributed representations. Two changes were made to the baseline simulations. Rather than using the full set of 6 trained patterns to interpret network responses, nearest-neighbour matching was performed over a restricted subset (/n/, /t/, /k/). In addition, the simulation using distributed representations was damaged to a slightly smaller degree; the probability of damage values was proportional to $1/(|d_{ji} - 1|)^{1.5}$. Under these circumstances, overall accuracy was 91.7% for the simulation with localist representations and 92.2% under distributed representations. The same asymmetry in error patterns was found. For the localist network, 87% of errors on /n/ ($n = 414$) resulted in /t/. In contrast, when using distributed representations, only 73% of the errors ($n = 388$) resulted in /t/, $\chi^2(1, N = 802) = 23.0, p < .0001$.

Simulation 2: Inappropriately structured distributed representations. Similar methods were utilized to match for overall accuracy here, except that for the appropriately structured distributed representation damage values were distributed proportional to $1/(|d_{ji} - 1|)^{1.25}$ (the damage values for the inappropriately structured representation were distributed according to the formula used for all other simulations). Similar results were found. The overall accuracy rate was 86.94% for the appropriately structure representations and 86.88% for the inappropriately structured representations. The proportion of errors resulting in /t/ was 69.5% for the appropriately structured ($n = 653$) versus 26.1% for the inappropriately structured distributed representations ($n = 656$); $\chi^2(1, N = 1309) = 247.7, p < .0001$.

Simulation 3: Variation in distance of network representations. To match for overall accuracy here, the damage values for distributed representations with a small asymmetry in the distance of network representations were distributed proportional to $1/(|d_{ji} - 1|)^{1.1}$; damage for the network with representations possessing a large asymmetry were distributed proportional to $1/(|d_{ji} - 1|)^{1.5}$. Similar results were found. The overall accuracy rate was 77.3% for the representations with a small asymmetry and 76.1% for those with a large asymmetry. The proportion of errors resulting in /t/ was 54.4% for the representations with a small asymmetry in network representational distances ($n = 1,135$) versus 65.0% for the large asymmetry simulations ($n = 1,193$); $\chi^2(1, N = 2328) = 27.2, p < .0001$.

SUBJECT INDEX

activation functions
    interactive/recurrent flow 132, 143–155, 218, 256, 257, 280
    linear transformations 291–292, 298, 301
    nonlinear 132, 136, 165, 200, 218
anomia, phonological dyslexia 180–182
aphasia
    phonological dyslexia 176–179, 182–184
    Wernicke–Lichtheim model 131, 134
    word production, frequency effects 134, 256, 260, 261, 263–267, 270, 277–283
attention, visuospatial planning 198, 212

behavioural distinctions, representational structure 288, 306
bottom-up influences, travelling salesperson problem (TSP) 194, 198, 199, 200, 209, 210

chaining theories, spelling 218–255
cognitive representations 287, 292–297, 300, 302–308
competitive learning algorithm 201–202, 204, 209, 211, 212, 216–217
competitive queueing networks 225–226, 238–239, 250
compound chaining theory, spelling 133–134, 218–255
computational modelling
    background 131–132
    nested incremental modelling approach 134, 198–210, 212–213
    performance prediction 133, 136
    phonological dyslexia 165–193
    representational structure and errors 133, 134, 287–313
    serial order mechanism, spelling 133–134, 218–255
    simple recurrent network (SRN) 133–134, 218–219, 226–255
    simplicity 134–135
    single-system account 136–164
    supported by data 132–133, 136, 165, 194
    using mean data 133
    visuospatial planning 194–217
    word production, frequency effects 256–286
conceptual knowledge, semantic dementia 136–164
connectionist approach 132
    binding-by-timing 295, 296, 306
    cognitive–neural correspondences 289–290, 301
    connection weight damage 297–301, 302, 308, 311–312
    input unit damage 291–297
    lexical frequency effects 257
    output unit damage 297
    representational structure and errors 134, 287–313
    semantic and lexical deficits 136–164
    simulated damage 291–301, 302–303, 307–308, 311–312
    tensor products 295, 296–297, 305
    visuospatial planning 194–217
cueing system, spelling 221–225, 237

dementia, single-system account 136–164
distributed representations 132, 136, 218, 287–313
double dissociations 287–288, 289
dual-route cascade (DRC) model, phonological dyslexia 132, 165–193
dysarthria 278
dysgraphia
    competitive queing networks 225–226, 238–239, 250
    serial-order mechanism deficits 218–255
dyslexia
    neurophysiological differences 141
    phonological, DRC model 132, 165–193

error probabilities 287–313

frequency effects, word production 134, 256–286
frontal lobe, transcranial magnetic stimulation 194, 197–198, 207, 210, 211, 213

Gabor filters 199–200, 201, 204, 211, 216
graphemic buffer, serial-order mechanism deficits 218–255

heuristic switching 194–217

individual differences, semantic dementia 136, 139–140, 150, 156–157

learning
    adaptive weight change 132
    competitive learning algorithm 201–202, 204, 209, 211, 212, 216–217
    incremental 134
lexical deficits, single-system account 132, 136–164
lexical representations
    error probabilities 287
    frequency effects 134, 256–286
    jolting mechanism 280–281
    simulation experiments 234, 246
localist representations 132, 165, 256, 257–258, 287–313

metacomputational cognitive psychology 134, 287

neural data
    nested incremental modelling approach 134, 198–210, 212–213
    region-specific atrophy 134, 141–142, 146–147, 156–157
nonpolynomial combinatorial optimization 195, 205, 209
nonwords
    lexical frequency effect 256, 260, 265–267, 273–283
    phonological dyslexia 165–193

orthographic lexicon 219–220

parallel distributed processing (PDP) model, semantic/lexical processing 138, 139–140

perceptual grouping, visuospatial planning 199–200, 210, 213
phonological dyslexia, dual-route cascade (DRC) model 132, 165–193
phonological representations
    frequency effects 134, 256–286
    spelling system 219
    word production model 258, 268
picture naming
    semantic/lexical deficits 136–164
    word production 134, 256–286
planning
    constant replanning model 201–209, 210
    mismatch detection mechanism 201–206, 210
    visuospatial 194–217
prefrontal cortex, transcranial magnetic stimulation 194, 197–198, 207, 210, 211, 213
pseudohomophones, phonological dyslexia 165–193

reading
    connectionist theory 294
    CPD+ model 167, 189
    dual-route cascade (DRC) model 132, 165–193
    semantic/lexical deficits 136–164
    triangle model 167–168, 189
representational structure, errors relationship 134, 287–313

saliency maps 202, 204
search model, lexical frequency effects 257, 282
segmental stage, word production 258, 268, 270, 278, 280
semantic deficits
    frequency effects 134, 256–286
    single-system account 132, 136–164
serial-order mechanisms, spelling 133, 218–255
simple chaining theory 222–223
simple recurrent network (SRN), spelling 133, 218–219, 226–255
single-system account, semantic/lexical deficits 136–164
speech production
    error patterns 288, 307
    lexical frequency effects 134, 256–286
spelling

SUBJECT INDEX

serial-order mechanism
   compound chaining theory 133–134, 218–255
   computer simulations 225–228, 247–248
   cueing system 221–225, 237
   positional theories 221–222, 225, 247
statistics, inferential 133, 165, 233
substitution errors 293–294, 295–297, 299–300, 301, 307

top-down influences, travelling salesperson problem (TSP) 194, 198–201, 203–205, 207, 210–211
Tower of Hanoi (ToH) 195

transcranial magnetic stimulation, planning 132, 194, 197–198, 210–211, 213
travelling salesperson problem (TSP) 13, 194–217

visuospatial planning, travelling salesperson problem 194–217

Wernicke–Lichtheim model 131, 134
word length, spelling accuracy 218, 229–233, 242, 244–250
word production, frequency effects 134, 256–286